W9-DCC-220

Trade of the Tricks

Trade of the Tricks

INSIDE THE MAGICIAN'S CRAFT

GRAHAM M. JONES

UNIVERSITY OF CALIFORNIA PRESS

Berkeley   Los Angeles   London

University of California Press, one of the most distinguished
university presses in the United States, enriches lives around the world
by advancing scholarship in the humanities, social sciences, and
natural sciences. Its activities are supported by the UC Press Foundation and by philanthropic contributions from individuals and
institutions. For more information, visit www.ucpress.edu.

University of California Press
Berkeley and Los Angeles, California

University of California Press, Ltd.
London, England

© 2011 by The Regents of the University of California

Library of Congress Cataloging-in-Publication Data

Jones, Graham M.
 Trade of the tricks : inside the magician's craft / Graham M. Jones.
  p. cm.
 Includes bibliographical references and index.
 ISBN 978-0-520-27046-6 (cloth : alk. paper)
 ISBN 978-0-520-27047-3 (pbk. : alk. paper)
 1. Magic tricks. I. Title.
 GV1547.J57 2011
 793.8—dc22

                                          2011011165

20 19 18 17 16 15 14 13 12 11
10 9 8 7 6 5 4 3 2 1

To Mom and Dad
Presto!

Contents

Videos of some of the magicians described in this book
are available at www.ucpress.edu/go/tricks.

Illustrations

Preface and Acknowledgments

I recently saw a great documentary that reminded me why I wrote this book. The 2008 film *Man on Wire* chronicles a truly stupefying feat performed by French magician, juggler, tightrope walker, and all-around trickster figure Philippe Petit.[1] On August 6, 1974, after six years of covert training and undercover reconnaissance, Petit and a team of co-conspirators snuck into the nearly complete World Trade Center complex in lower Manhattan. During the night, they laboriously bridged the 140-foot gap between the Twin Towers with a cable weighing 450 pounds. Early the next morning, Petit consummated what he later called "the artistic crime of the century," stepping out onto that wire for a forty-five-minute tightrope walk a quarter of a mile above the street.

People on their way to work craned their necks to see him, while police watched helplessly from the rooftops. In a news conference following Petit's arrest, a responding officer told reporters, "I observed the tightrope 'dancer'—because you couldn't call him a 'walker'—approximately halfway between the two towers. And upon seeing us he started to smile and laugh and he started going into a dancing routine on the high wire. . . . Unbelievable really. . . . Everybody was spellbound in the watching of it."

Perhaps the most extraordinary thing about the film is what it leaves unsaid. As every viewer must know, twenty-five years later another group of conspirators would perpetrate a far more sinister crime involving the World Trade Center. While *Man on Wire* never mentions the attacks of September 11, that monumental act of violence is the inescapable counterpoint to Petit's monumental act of play. This implicit contrast struck a personal chord. Having recently moved to New York to study anthropology, I watched the events of September 11 unfold at close range. Like everyone else, I spent the following months in a state of shock, not sure how to process recent horrors or adapt to grim new realities. It was at that point that I discovered magic.

That semester, for a final project in a graduate seminar on apprenticeship, a partner and I filmed a brief lesson at a local magic shop. Close analysis revealed a sophisticated form of expertise hidden behind the seemingly simple trick the novice magician learned that day. This revelation raised more questions. *Where did such expertise originate? Is it codified? How is it perpetuated? How is it shielded from prying eyes?* Our professor encouraged us to explore these questions further, and before long they gave rise to the project that ultimately became this book. Magic not only fascinated me; in the wake of September 11, it reassured me that imaginative play was still a vital dimension of human experience. I let my curiosity guide me, without fully realizing that magic would engross me for most of the next decade, thanks largely to the extraordinary magicians I came to work with in France. They never cease to amaze me—with their skillful tricks, of course, but also with their intelligence, passion, creativity, and humor. Words cannot suffice to thank them for the wisdom they shared and the kindness they showed, but here goes.

A number of people were particularly generous and influential guides to the French magic scene: Abdul Alafrez, Zakary Belamy, Peter Din, Christian Girard, Pierre Guédin, Jean Hladik, Jan Madd, Mimosa, Georges Proust, Daniel Rhod, and David Stone. I owe a unique debt of gratitude to my magic teachers Stefan Alzaris and Jérôme Cadéac, and to Frank

Debouck, who organized introductory courses through the Fédération Française des Artistes Prestidigitateurs (FFAP). Nemo was an especially important teacher and a cherished friend. I thank him, along with Philippe Day, Hugo. (so good his name includes the period), Loïc Marquet, Jérôme Mollier, Isabelle Moya, Bruno Peugnet, and Philippe Thalhouedec, for the pivotal role they played in this project, and for consistently reminding me of life outside magic.

For tolerating my presence and indulging my curiosity, I heartily thank members of the following magic clubs: Amis de la Magie, Cercle Français de l'Illusion, Cercle Magique de Paris, Club des Magiciens Collectionneurs, Club Magique de Paris, Illegal Magic Club, Pizza Magicos, Magie Bourgogne of Dijon, and Cercle Robert-Houdin of Angers. Among the Paris magic institutions that opened their doors to me, I am grateful to the Musée de la Magie, the Double Fond, and the Théâtre Metamorphosis. Guy Lore and his staff kindly let me while away many afternoons at the now sadly closed shop Paris Magic. Céline Noulin, Didier Marquet, Arnaud Delaine, and all their colleagues at the Maison de la Magie Robert-Houdin gave me a warm reception in Blois, as did Jean-Claude Eude and the organizers at the Centre International de la Prestidigitation et de l'Illusion. Finally, I thank Henri Broch and the Laboratoire de Zététique at the University of Nice for hosting me for a magic-filled evening.

In addition, I want to recognize the generosity and support of the following magicians (with apologies in advance to anyone I fail to mention): Abacus, Gwen Aduh, Alex, Elisabeth Amato, Eric Antoine, Gilles Arthur, Gérard Backner, Sébastien Bazou, Bébel, Ben & Alex, Jean-Luc Bertrand, Gaëtan Bloom, Pierre Brahma, Ian Buckland, Sébastien Clergue, Cocodenoix, Eric Constant, Jean-Pierre Crispon, Clément Debailleul, Alexandra and Dominique Duvivier, Pierre Edernac, Filaos, Jean-Marc Gaheri, Stéphane Gali, Gary, Michel Herbelin, James Hodges, Xavier Hodges, James, Guilhem Julia, Ludovic Julliot, Guy Lamelot, Laurent and Marie-Odile Langloÿs, Ivan Laplaud, Lefty, Maeva, Gérard Majax, Henri Mayol, Jean Merlin, Sébastien Mossière, Georges Naudet, Raphaël Navarro, Claude Nops and Musidora, Nourdine, Pallas, Alain Poussard, Professor Wonderfool, Prompto and Béa, Didier Puech, Ratcékou, Patrick Rivet, Romaric,

Lully Sakaguchi, Maurice Saltano, Frédéric Tabet, Thomas, Thomas Thiébaut, Arthur Tivoli, Jacques Voignier, Woody, and Julien Zazzi.

I would like to honor the memory of Jack Alban, Pierre Jacques, Bob Read, and Serge Schouhmacher—all extraordinary characters who enriched this project and enlivened my research. I particularly regret that Jacques Delord did not live to see this book in print. Gaëtan Bloom told me that Jacques considered magic first and foremost a vehicle of spiritual elevation—which made him something of an anomaly among magicians. Yet magicians in France widely recognized his dedication and artistry: shortly before his unexpected death in 2006, the FFAP honored him with the Médaille Robert-Houdin for lifetime achievement. Jacques expressed the hope that my research would enrich the art of magic, and that the art of magic would, in turn, enrich my life. The benefits to me have been inestimable; I hope that the many magicians and magic lovers who have helped me will find that this book contributes in some humble way to the wider understanding and appreciation of their art.

It would be glib for me to thank Bambi Schieffelin for believing in magic, though without her faith, this improbable project would have never been possible. It was in her electrifying course, "Acquisition of Cultural Practices," that I first developed an interest in magic. Her early encouragement and subsequent support as my dissertation advisor both stimulated and sustained me. Bambi's influence permeates this book. Over the years, she has offered nuanced comments on countless permutations of its various parts and pieces. More importantly, her irrepressible, infectious curiosity has inspired me as a scholar and as a human being. I cherish her friendship deeply.

Through his influence as a teacher and guidance as an advisor, Fred Myers had a tremendous impact on the shape of this project. It often took me years to assimilate his suggestions, and I'm grateful for both his perspicacity and his patience. Susan Carol Rogers initiated me to the field of anthropology, and helped me position myself within the anthropology of Europe. Emily Martin offered careful commentary on my dissertation and moral support through the writing process.

Among the scholars and colleagues who have helped me in innumerable ways, I would particularly like to thank Tom Abercrombie, Tom Beidelman,

Ed Berenson, Dave Bergan, Don Brenneis, Jillian Cavanaugh, Herrick Chapman, Francesca Coppa, Alessandro Duranti, Michel de Fornel, Andrew Gardner, Stéphane Gerson, Faye Ginsburg, Zeev Gourarier, Emmanuel Grimaud, Larry Hass, Jean-Pierre Hassoun, Antoine Hennion, Caroline Hodak, David Hoffman, Sophie Houdart, Michael Houseman, Elizabeth Keating, Don Kulick, Tanya Luhrmann, Marika Moisseeff, Elinor Ochs, James Peck, Christophe Prochasson, Rayna Rapp, Anne Raulin, Joel Robbins, Emmanuelle Saada, David Samuels, Michel Savy, Shalini Shankar, Roberta Shapiro, Fred Siegel, Pierre-Emmanuel Sorignet, Nicole Stahlmann, Victor Stoichita, Randall Styers, Anne-Marie Thiesse, Denis Vidal, and Florence Weber. I am grateful to members of the anthropology departments at the University of Virginia, the Massachusetts Institute of Technology, the University of California–Los Angeles, and Temple University for giving me the chance to present parts of this project and offering critical feedback.

Over the years, friends inside and outside the academy have played a pivotal role in my research. I wish to thank Lauren Shweder Biel, with whom I conducted that fateful first project on magic, and the many other anthropology graduate students who made New York University such an exhilarating place, particularly my dear friends Shanti Avirgan and Aaron Glass. In Paris, Laure Carbonnel and Julien Gavelle provided invaluable assistance, challenged me to think in new ways about anthropology, and shared the trials and tribulations of fieldwork. I owe an inestimable debt to the Fisseau and Sadras families for making me feel so at home in France over the years. I am also grateful to Séverine Coupaye, Sylvain Courrech du Pont, Sabine Gagnier, Kim Romero, Allison Sheedy, and Vla Tuffa.

This book is based on fieldwork conducted with generous funding from a Social Science Research Council International Dissertation Research Fellowship and a Fulbright Student Fellowship. The Department of Social Sciences at the École Normale Supérieure gave me a warm reception in Paris, both as a visiting student in 2003 and during the course of my fieldwork from 2004 to 2005. The Centre National de Recherche Scientifique (CNRS) funded a return trip in the summer of 2006. I am deeply grateful for a Dissertation Diversity Fellowship from the Ford Foundation and a Dean's Dissertation Fellowship from New York University's Graduate School of Arts and Sciences, which allowed me to write up my results.

Princeton University provided me an ideal setting in which to complete this book. As a postdoctoral member of the Society of Fellows, I relished sustained dialogue with warm and engaging colleagues. As a dissertation reader, faculty mentor, and friend, Rena Lederman has helped me in countless ways. I benefited immensely from the opportunity to present my research at the Anthropology Department, and from the generous feedback of my colleagues there. Among the many Princeton scholars who influenced and inspired me, I would like to thank the following people, who directly helped me with this book in ways they might not even know: Leonard Barkan, João Biehl, James Boon, John Borneman, Daphne Brooks, Maggie Browning, Scott Burnham, Margot Canaday, Isabelle Clark-Decès, Paul DiMaggio, Carol Greenhouse, Abdellah Hammoudi, Pete Kurie, Mendi Obadike, Larry Rosen, Sarah Ross, Carolyn Rouse, Gayle Salamon, Saul Schwartz, P. Adams Sitney, and Susan Stewart. While at Princeton, grants from the David A. Gardner '69 Magic Project and the University Committee on Research in the Humanities and Social Sciences enabled me to make return trips to France in 2008 and 2009.

A number of people have helped me by reading and commenting on various parts of this manuscript. Jim Clark was a steadfast ally to a callow scholar trying to navigate the thickets of academic publishing. I am immensely grateful to him, along with Mary Harper and Carol Rigolot, for invaluable commentary on drafts, and to Lucia Allais for her help with transcripts. Gabriella Coleman and Ricardo Montez gave me particularly useful feedback on individual chapters. Throughout every stage of this project, Howard Becker has been a generous mentor, and I thank him for his comments and encouragement. For their stimulating feedback on drafts of this book, I'm also deeply grateful to Richard Bauman and Peter Nardi.

Working with Reed Malcolm at the University of California Press has been a joy, even as (or especially because) he challenged me to develop this manuscript in ways I otherwise wouldn't have thought possible. I appreciate the work of everyone who has made the publication process run smoothly, particularly Stacy Eisenstark, Barbara Goodhouse, Kalicia Pivirotto, and Kate Warne. I count my blessing for the gorgeous original cover art by the inimitable Giuseppe Sartorio; this book would feel incomplete without it. I thank my cherished colleagues in the Anthropology Program at the Massachusetts Institute of Technology for their words of wisdom and reassurance during the production process, and for helping me feel so quickly at home in a new institution.

Chapters 1 and 3 include material from my essay "Laboring under Illusionism," in Andrew Gardner and David M. Hoffman, eds., *Dispatches from the Field: Neophyte Ethnographers in a Changing World* (Long Grove, IL: Waveland Press, 2006), 167–178. Chapter 5 includes material from my essay "The Family Romance of Modern Magic: Contesting Robert-Houdin's Cultural Legacy in Contemporary France," in Francesca Coppa, Lawrence Hass, and James Peck, eds., *Performing Magic on the Western Stage from the Eighteenth Century to the Present* (New York: Palgrave Macmillan, 2008), 33–60. I thank the original publishers for granting permission to use this material.

I was lucky to have the support of a loving family on this intellectual odyssey. My parents, Carol and Richard Jones, have always encouraged creative thinking and forgiven creative excess. While this book has a scholarly genealogy, it also represents a culmination of lessons they have taught me over the course of a lifetime. I also wish to express love and thanks to my sisters, Shauna and Lindsey, to Allan, Lisa, and Christopher Wang, and to my entire extended family for their continuing interest in and encouragement of my work. Finally, the person who hocus-pocused my heart deserves a special mention. My wife, Val Wang, has been an unwavering source of strength, inspiration, critical feedback, and—at crucial moments—levity. Finishing this book is all the sweeter because we can celebrate together.

INTRODUCTION Men of a Thousand Hands

Stroll down the Boulevard St. Germain in the chic sixth arrondissement of Paris on a summer evening, and you're liable to encounter an extraordinary character of the crossroads. Amid the polyglot throng of barhopping students, lovers hand in hand, and tourists enjoying gelato, he sits at a card table under a streetlight's glow, wearing a bowler hat and a puckish smile. "Come closer," he coaxes in a creaky voice. "You can see better *here* than *there*!" As you join a circle of passersby cautiously edging in, he holds up three acorn-sized white balls and, with the wave of a magic wand, makes them disappear from his fingertips one by one. He taps three empty brass cups with the wand, making them resonate like bells, and tips them over to reveal the balls, rematerialized. Onlookers glance at each other in disbelief, laughing. *Oh-là-là*, someone interjects.

For the next several minutes, time seems to stop under the magician's spell. In the supple choreography of his hands, the balls dance on the threshold of reality—vanishing instantaneously from one place, reappearing somewhere else, doubling or tripling under a single cup. "Where is it? *Ouketi, ouketi*? Here or here?" he asks in an auctioneer's staccato, indicating two of the cups. Inevitably, spectators guess wrong. "Don't ever play this game," the magician wryly cautions. "You can't win!" Two snickering young men slip behind him, hoping to catch a glimpse of concealed maneuvers. They screw up their eyes, crouching and craning—*it's impossible*, they shrug. *He's too good*! When the magician stacks the cups, a ball placed on the top passes through three layers of solid metal, landing on the table underneath the bottom cup. In a final salvo, he places one ball under each cup. When he turns them over, the little white balls have transformed into red balls the size of ripe plums—so big a hand couldn't conceal them. By now thirty people have encircled him. They applaud warmly and toss coins into a platter, then cede room to a new crowd. "You can see better *here* than *there*!" the magician beckons.

This is a typical day at the office for the magician Bébel. For those lucky enough to catch him in his usual spot by the Métro Mabillon, his mind-boggling performances are a delightful part of the mosaic of urban life in a modern metropolis like Paris. But his artistry also transforms an everyday street corner into the theater for a timeless drama. At least since classical antiquity, performers like him have drawn crowds of eager onlookers in European marketplaces and squares with the Cups and Balls illusion—magic's "oldest deception."[1] Some time around the second century AD, the Greek sophist Alciphron vividly described the trick in the fictional letter of a historical country farmer writing home from Athens: "One thing I saw made me almost speechless with astonishment. A man came forward, and, setting down a three-legged table, placed three little cups on it. Then under these cups he hid some little round white pebbles. . . . At one moment he would hide them one under each cup; and at another moment (I don't know how) he would show them all under a single cup; and then again he would make them entirely disappear from under the cups and exhibit them between his lips."[2] A fifteenth-century painting by Flemish artist Hieronymus Bosch depicts a magician performing the same trick for a crowd of gaping market-goers; one distracted spectator has her purse pilfered by someone who may well be the magician's accomplice, prompting critics to interpret this scene as an allegory for the danger of credulity.[3] With few differences, Bébel's performances closely parallel the scenes of entertainment evoked by the ancient writer and the medieval painter.

Why does a trick this old continue to amaze? Marveling at the longevity of the Cups and Balls illusion, magician Paul Curry writes that the survival of this "little trick" even as "whole countries and civilizations have risen, flourished, and faded away" is "proof that, while all else may change, man's curiosity is constant."[4] So too is our capacity to be deceived. In the late nineteenth century, pioneering French psychologist Alfred Binet recognized that, through generations of cumulative experience, magicians had developed an elaborate working understanding of the mainsprings of perception along with a corresponding repertoire of sleight-of-hand techniques calibrated to induce perceptual error. Seeking to illuminate the mental processes of perception, Binet—who later developed the first IQ test—employed stop-motion photography to dissect magicians' sleight-of-hand performances. These experiments led him to conclude that magic is an art governed by laws as precise and immutable as those of the psychology on which it depends.[5] Binet wrote that magicians' sleight-of-hand repertoire resembles "pieces of classical theater, embedded in a tradition that dictates every action in minute detail . . . and whose methods are so powerful that hardly anyone can resist them."[6]

Bébel and his contemporaries are the living heirs of this tradition. This book explores their secretive subculture, examining how they perpetuate their mystifying art today in France, the country where many believe modern magic originated. The transmission of a tradition is a puzzling affair in an activity like magic: *how do people learn a practice in which expert knowledge is secret by definition?* Hoping to answer this question, I immersed myself in the Paris magic scene as a participant observer and apprentice magician in different settings where magicians practice their craft: magic clubs, classes, shops, and performance venues. Over the course of nearly two years, I learned about the art of illusion from people who devote themselves, by vocation and avocation, to the production, circulation, and display of secret skills. As I acquired the rudiments of magicianship, I discovered how magicians strive to make magic meaningful to themselves, to each other, and to their public, plying the overwhelmingly artisanal craft of face-to-face illusionary performance in a world dominated by high-tech entertainment industries and computer-generated special effects.

Traditions are deceptive, especially when magicians are involved. Far from static, they are "dynamic and always situated at the confluence of continuity and change."[7] While Bébel's performance may appear timeless, it is profoundly contemporary. As I will ultimately argue, the excitement of watching a magician exhibit embodied skills in face-to-face contact with spectators may take on special meaning for precisely those audiences most accustomed to consuming entertainments from mass-mediated sources, just as artisan-made foods and crafts have taken on renewed significance in an era of globalized industrial capitalism,[8] particularly in contemporary France.[9] Furthermore, while the street corner audiences who watch him in amazement probably don't know it, among cognoscenti, Bébel is widely regarded as one of the world's top sleight-of-hand artists, and he actively participates in exclusive international networks that traffic in cutting-edge trade secrets. His every movement, while emerging from an ancient tradition, also represents the state of the art in embodied conjuring skill.

Magicians have known for generations what social scientific research has only recently demonstrated: that the taken-for-granted reality of everyday life is produced and maintained through sedimentary habits of thought and highly conventionalized patterns of interaction.[10] In order to create illusion, they engineer situations in which reliance on these habits and conventions leads spectators to experience things that they know to be impossible, in ways that are surprising and fun.[11] For this to work, magicians must cultivate the ability to anticipate what spectators will think and do in particular situations. They must also retain an advantage of secrecy, maintaining and renewing a stock of secret procedures and techniques that spectators do not know and cannot imagine. This imperative, along with magicians' innate curiosity, pro-pels the refinement of expert knowledge in the continuing manufacture of secrets.

SECRECY AND RISK

This is a book about secrets. A magician's artistry of deception hinges on secret procedures, concealed maneuvers, and veiled intentions. In a practice shrouded in mystery and brimming with passion, secrets are often the source of conflict; they can be suppressed, stolen, and even intentionally destroyed. Yet the dynamism of magic depends on robust social networks and the sharing of intellectual resources. The magic scene, as I encountered it in Paris, takes shape through perpetually unfolding exchanges of knowledge and skill, in which an expert like Bébel might offer to explain secrets of the Cups and Balls to a fellow magician during the weekly meeting of a local magic club (Figure 1). For a newcomer to magic like myself, wading into the confusing give-and-take of secrets raised a number of questions: how does one master the protocols for concealing and revealing secrets, and how are those protocols enforced? How have recent mediating technologies like video and the Internet transformed the delicate ecology of knowledge exchange among magicians? How does immersion in a practice structured by secrecy change magicians as people? How would it change me?

Few people cherish secrets as much as entertainment magicians, and secreted knowledge is a primary social tender among them. Social life in the magic world flows from the giving and withholding of secrets. Revealed and exchanged among insiders, and widely available to sufficiently curious outsiders in the form of books, videos, online content, and commoditized tricks, these secrets are surprisingly promiscuous. Still, any magician will tell you that knowing how a trick is done and knowing how to perform it are altogether different matters. Virtually anyone can be made to understand the secret behind a trick, but the ability to apply that knowledge to the creation of illusion is reserved for those who, through practice and training, have acquired the requisite performance skills.

Figure 1.   Bébel (*right*) teaches Otto Wessely (*left*) the Cups and Balls. Photo by the author.

Magicians do not merely *know* secrets; they embody secrets as *know-how*. In other words, magicians' secrets aren't just memorized instructions for performing tricks; they are skills and procedures that magicians imprint on their bodies through never-ending training, conditioning, and experimentation, both alone and in the company of other magicians. Magicians spend as much time as possible with materials in their hands, manipulating cards while watching television or holding stacks of coins in their palms while riding the subway. Manipulations must become second nature before they can be used in performance, both because the procedures must be as close to fail-safe as possible to avoid embarrassing errors, and because performers cannot afford to think about technique in front of an audience. The magician has to be able to tell spectators one thing while thinking—and doing—something entirely different.

Magicians' bodies are repositories of secret skill, trained to execute complicated feats of manipulation without attracting the least attention.

This training develops chiseled tone in muscles that most of us don't even know we have, such as the hand's small *adductor pollicis*, essential for holding objects hidden in the palm. Some magicians boast fingers so sensitive that they can immediately determine the number of cards in each half of a randomly cut deck. World champion illusionist Pierre Brahma told me he sands his fingertips to keep them as sensitive as possible for manipulating coins and balls. As I will demonstrate, this training not only changes magicians' bodies but also affects the way they think, as they grow ever more alert to the opportunities for surprise lurking just beneath the surface of everyday life.

Of course, professionals of many kinds jealously guard trade secrets for competitive advantage and social distinction.[12] Insofar as magicians' skills are subject to imperatives of trade secrecy, this book will be useful for anyone interested in the way professions take shape through the regulation of knowledge flows. But while the technical knowledge that skilled artisans and craftspeople monopolize is always a means for the manufacture of material goods or the provision of skilled services, in the art of magic, exhibiting secrets in the form of tricks is an end in itself. Other professions may have tricks of the trade, but magic is, quite literally, the trade of the tricks.

These tricks entail skills similar to those used in any number of serious activities involving strategic deception—spying, diplomacy, and warfare, to name just a few.[13] Thus, in the 1950s, the CIA contracted famed American magician John Mulholland to pen manuals of trickery and deception for its agents.[14] I found that the only North American research institution to own a copy of *The Magic Way*, magician Juan Tamariz's brilliant book on deception, was the CIA Library (and when I attempted to request it a second time through interlibrary loan, the volume had mysteriously vanished).[15] In contrast to the field of espionage, magic makes deception a form of play and, at times, elevates it to the status of a fine art.

Magic responds to what the pioneering German sociologist Georg Simmel calls "the fascination of secrecy," that is to say, "the attractions and values of the secret beyond its significance as a mere means." [16] This fascination is twofold, alluring those both in and out of "the know." Simmel explains that, for insiders, having secret knowledge confers a "strong feeling of possession" and "a position of exception." For outsiders excluded from the secret, awareness of concealment provokes intense curiosity. "Before the unknown," Simmel writes, "man's natural impulse to idealize and his natural fearfulness cooperate toward the same goal: to intensify the unknown through imagination."[17] In esoteric religions or initiatory societies of revelatory knowledge, secrecy functions to protect the uninitiated from dangerous knowledge, and to amplify the aura of power emanating from concealed realities.[18] Modern magicians may make us doubt our grasp on reality, but their performances do not point to a concealed ontology. In performing, magicians mobilize secret knowledge and skill to create mysterious situations or effects that spectators intensify with their own imaginative abilities. With cunning artistry, they lead us to wonder at the reality we inhabit and construct for ourselves.

Because this is a book about secrets, it is also a book about risk. Whatever is concealed can also be revealed, and whenever magicians perform, they imperil the secrets they subject to an audience's scrutiny. As Simmel writes, "the secret . . . is full of the consciousness that it *can* be betrayed."[19] The electrifying prospect of disclosure is present every time a magician performs: should a trick fail or a performer fumble, audiences could discern the hidden mechanisms of deception. Further, if spectators believe, rightly or wrongly, that they can intuit how a trick is performed, the magical illusion disintegrates. The associated element of risk is part of the titillation of magic for spectators and magicians alike.

Performing magic entails both crafting deception and presenting oneself as a craftsperson of deception before a public. The magician's identity as a competent deceiver hinges on the ability to display secrets effectively, to manifest the efficacy of those secrets in mystifying illusions without revealing them to outsiders. The possession of these secrets confers charisma on magicians, endowing them with uncanny abilities. In face-to-face encounters, spectators inevitably pepper them with the same questions: *How did you do that? How do you learn magic? And How much do you have to practice?* Short of offering explanations, magicians are only too happy to indulge or even provoke audiences' curiosity about their art. Because of the element of risk, performing magic rewards courage—sometimes even audacity—with a special kind of prestige. Magicians in this book explain that the kind of interactional prestige that comes from performing magic can be intensely gratifying for individual performers, but that it can also create serious impediments to successful performance: spectators react with hostility to a magician who seems to be asserting power or status through the exhibition of secret skill.

Although magic may be a particularly risky genre, risk is not particular to magic. It is intrinsic to all performance. Charles Briggs and Richard Bauman write that performance carries with it the "assumption of accountability to an audience for a display of virtuosity, subject to evaluation for the skill and effectiveness with which the display is accomplished."[20] While most performers take "performance precautions"[21] to reduce risk through preparation, some genres seem to *require* risk as a precondition for satisfactory performance. Thus, Webb Keane describes Indonesian rituals that seek not just "to control risk but also to *instigate* it."[22] These rituals imply that "if action is real, it must be subject to failure. If it is valuable and powerful, it must display itself as overcoming failure."[23] Magic appears to be precisely this kind of performance: magicians establish conditions that make their feats seem difficult if not impossible—for instance, by having their deck of cards thoroughly shuffled or their straitjacket fastened by volunteers from the audience—and then defy spectators to understand how they nevertheless thwart failure by finding the selected card or liberating themselves from restraint. Of course, the parameters of risk in any genre aren't the same for everyone: for instance, as we shall see in regard to magic, women performing in a genre traditionally associated with men and male prerogatives take added risks because audiences scrutinize their performances more closely—but their outsider status may also confer some advantages.[24]

BEING MAGICAL

The mysterious skills that magicians master have made them enduring objects of curiosity, positioned prominently in the Western imagination.

As culture heroes, they appear in countless works of art, film, and literature under various guises: sinister, liminal, daring, romantic, depraved, and ridiculous. Sometimes they appear as trickster figures, "the mythic embodiment of ambiguity and ambivalence, doubleness and duplicity, contradiction and paradox."[25] At others, they personify the fantastic, as in a 1953 poem by surrealist author, filmmaker, and magic lover Jean Cocteau:

> Men of a thousand hands, I salute you.
> Do you not represent the time and space
> that combine to deceive us
> and defy us with innumerable walls?
>
> Men of a thousand hands, what you make us believe
> is more real than the reality we dream. For in this game,
> you have the role of fate and mystery.
> Your lies amaze us more than our humble truth.
>
> Men of a thousand hands, I pray that
> your Art endures, because it speaks
> to the best thing that the world still holds:
> childhood.[26]

Writing to commemorate the fiftieth anniversary of France's largest magicians' association, Cocteau offered a touching prayer for the perpetuation of an art whose illusions are "more real than the reality we dream," more marvelous "than our humble truth." His image of "men of a thousand hands" is an extraordinary evocation of the special kind of dexterity associated with magicians—recognizably human, but mystifyingly prodigious.

Sleight of hand. Legerdemain. Jugglery. Prestidigitation. Whatever we call it, the practice of dexterously manipulating small objects so that they either appear to be where they are not or appear not to be where they are is the cornerstone of the magician's craft. In magicians' parlance, the basic maneuvers of this kind of magic are called *sleights*; they constitute the hidden *method* through which the performer produces an *effect*—the illusion an audience experiences.[27] Methods might also involve *gimmicks*, generally hidden pieces of technical apparatus that facilitate or even automate an effect. Most magicians especially esteem tricks like the Cups and Balls that rely on pure sleight-of-hand skill rather than gimmicked apparatus. Sleights are an embodied form of knowledge that depends on the miniaturist virtuosity of small gestures imperceptible to the untrained eye. With colorful names, often richly detailed proveniences recorded in the published literature and oral lore of conjuring, and sometimes numerous variants in circulation, they are, along with gimmicks, basic units of intellectual property among sleight-of-hand magicians.

A set of cups and balls, like other tools of the trade—cards, coins, silk handkerchiefs, and ropes—provides a versatile medium in which magicians have elaborated, over many centuries, a panoply of sleights that can be combined, according to grammar-like rules, to produce a variety of effects. When a magician like Bébel performs his Cups and Balls routine, he employs sequences of sleights to surprise spectators with the appearance and disappearance of material objects contrary to everyday expectations. But this is only part of the story. To produce a convincing and engrossing illusion, he must meld dexterous sleight of hand with rhythm, timing, coordinated body language, calculated facial expressions, carefully managed sight lines, verbal patter that guides spectators' attention, and a unifying sense of dramatic structure and logical coherence. Every part of the magician's body and every aspect of comportment can contribute to (or detract from) what magic theorists Peter Lamont and Richard Wiseman term *misdirection*: "that which directs the audience towards the effect and away from the method" of a trick.[28] As sociologist Peter Nardi puts it in his pathbreaking microsociological analysis of magic performance, for an effect to successfully amaze, "spectators must be kept from developing a simple explanation for it, even if it is an incorrect one."[29] To accomplish this, he explains, magicians use misdirection "to control attention away from the real sequence [of actions] through the construction of apparent causal sequences and by the development of events not expected within [a] logical framework."

The methods magicians use are examples of what Alfred Gell calls *techniques of enchantment*, expert expressive practices cultivated for the sake of arousing fascination and awe.[30] Like all techniques of enchantment, they can captivate attention in a variety of settings, serving a variety of ends.

Until now, anthropology has focused on the role of such illusionary practices almost exclusively in the domain of ritual. Shamans the world over employ legerdemain to give the impression of extracting disease objects from the bodies of sick patients during the course of healing rituals.[31] While Western observers have often dismissed such performances as charlatanism, anthropologists have argued that, in many cultural settings, healers' "tricks" are not fraudulent cures, but rather simulations of intended cures that structure and orient the healing process.[32] On similar grounds, anthropologists have also challenged allegations of charlatanism directed at circumpolar and Native North American mediums who, bound hand and foot during clairvoyant séances, produce eerie spirit manifestations using a combination of legerdemain, ventriloquism, and other theatrics.[33]

In the modern West, illusionary techniques of enchantment have reached their fullest development in the form of secular entertainment variously known as *conjuring, illusionism,* or most often simply *magic* (I employ these terms more or less interchangeably, along with the related agentive nouns *conjurer, illusionist,* and *magician*). Tanya Luhrmann explains that, for anthropologists, the term *magic* customarily "describes supernatural actions done to achieve instrumental ends, such as acquiring love or money, punishing an enemy, or protecting a friend. It seems to rely on causal connections that a rational observer would describe as irrational."[34] In contrast to this kind of instrumental, ritual magic, she defines entertainment magic as "the deliberate attempt to fool an audience that knows that it is being fooled,"[35] highlighting the importance of the background knowledge and expectations that spectators bring to such performances.[36] Among the few anthropologists to discuss this latter form of magic at length, Alexander Goldenweiser links its appeal to the contradiction between what an audience *knows* to be impossible and what it nevertheless *sees* the magician do: "our reactions to the emergence of a rabbit out of a silk hat or to the levitation of a magician's female companion until she hangs suspended in mid-air are visual experiences which for the time being are accepted as facts, not tricks. It is to this that our amazement is due."[37]

Why do audiences derive consistent pleasure from this kind of deceptive illusion and seek it out as entertainment? Magicians respond to this question in a variety of ways, patterning their performances accordingly. However, some notion of wonder or surprise invariably emerges from any attempt to explain magic's attraction. American conjurer Jamy Ian Swiss identifies the thrill of the mysterious as the key to audiences' enjoyment. By creating "the experience of mystery, we have the chance to bring our audience face to face with both their wishes and their fears," he writes.[38] "When you put the truly impossible in front of someone . . . people react. Things happen. And it can be very interesting to be part of it when they do." Laughter is among the most common reactions to magic tricks, suggesting strong parallels with jokes: "A large portion of the comic effect of humor involves the audience's taking a set interpretive frame for granted and then being surprised when the [performer] shows their assumptions to be unwarranted at the point of dénouement. . . . In this way the work of comedians and the work of . . . magicians is similar." [39]

Spectators' reactions to tricks are often immediate and visceral. Roger Caillois accordingly classifies magic performances among the forms of play—from ecstatic dance to amusement park thrill rides—directed at inducing what he terms *vertigo* or *voluptuous panic*: "a surrendering to a kind of spasm, seizure, or shock which destroys reality with a sovereign brusqueness."[40] By "destroying" reality, magic can also elevate awareness of the experience of perception, performing the function of *defamiliarization* or *making strange* that literary theorist Victor Shklovsky characterizes as the essence of all art.[41] Stefan Alzaris accordingly describes the magician as "an artisan of the construction of perception who invites us to reconsider our habitual experience of reality."[42]

Magicians may be variety artists, performing primarily in settings of light entertainment, but the ability to challenge people's grasp on reality is no small matter. Many of the several dozen magicians I interviewed approach their work with considerable care and seriousness of purpose—none more so than Bébel. In a world of large egos and ostentatious self-promoters, he stood out to me for his quiet charisma of meticulous magicianship. For our one and only interview, I met the forty-five-year-old son of Algerian immigrants at his Pigalle apartment late on a gray summer afternoon in 2005. Nocturnal by profession, he was just beginning his day, preparing for a twilight performance by the Métro Mabillon.

Although he performs professionally for lavish corporate events and fancy private parties, "doing the street" remains a labor of love. Every surface in his small living room was covered with magic paraphernalia—hundreds, maybe thousands, of decks of playing cards, and shelves weighted down with reams of conjuring literature in a variety of languages. We set off for a nearby café. Wheeling his magic setup with one hand, Bébel, a survivor of childhood polio, used a cane with the other. As we discussed his approach to magic over coffee, I was initially surprised to find one of the world's most accomplished sleight-of-hand artists—an artist who performed for a stretch in France's most prestigious theater, the Comédie Française—reserved, even self-effacing. His measured words conveyed unmistakable dedication.[43]

"A problem with magicians," he said, "is that they've done magic so long that they cease to be amazed by it, and they assume that it's the same for everyone else. That's a mistake. Magic requires mystery. People crave mystery from us. To convey it, we have to believe in it ourselves." For Bébel, magicians must not only believe in mystery but also embody it. "You have to *be* magical. Every gesture and every utterance has to emanate magic." He explained how he sought to accomplish this by developing what he called a "language of modern magic," a system of gesture in which every movement is studied, codified, and legible. "When I want a spectator's chosen card to move to the top of the deck, I do this," he said, rotating his palms upward and wiggling his fingers in a rhythmical, rising motion—a signature pantomime I immediately recognized from watching him perform. "Spectators intuit what's happening. I don't need to tell them. Plus it gives the effect credibility. *Why did the card rise? Because he wiggled his fingers!* I cause the magic to happen. The magic is in me, not in the materials."

Like any successful magician, Bébel grapples with questions of how to stage his effects and style his persona. These are matters of what magicians call *presentation*, the manner of performing effects or framing them as somehow significant.[44] In everyday parlance, they distinguish it from *technique*, the skillful execution of a trick. Presentation concerns the layers of theatrical embellishment necessary to make a technically proficient trick become a compelling and entertaining illusion rather than just an intellectual puzzle.[45] While good technique is indispensable, many magicians consider decisions about presentation to be the essence of their creative process—the key to self-expression through magic. Bébel had summed up his approach to presenting magic in the succinct prescription: "you have to *be* magical." This outlook aligns him with the most influential school of thought about magic presentation in recent history—the school of Robert-Houdin.

In a short professional career lasting from 1845 to 1852, Parisian illusionist Jean-Eugène Robert-Houdin codified the conventions of presenting magic as we know it today. As I describe in Chapter 5, his reputation as what Jim Steinmeyer calls "the model magician"[46] depends on his widely imitated style of presenting magic in the persona of an urbane gentleman in elegant evening wear and ingeniously showcasing his knowledge, skill, and inventiveness. Down to the present, this style has defined "modern magic" as a genre. In homage to these achievements, American magician Ehrich Weiss took the stage name "Houdini," and magicians everywhere still refer to Robert-Houdin as the "Father of Modern Magic." In his native France, magicians continue to view Robert-Houdin as the foundational figure in a distinctive national tradition; from this perspective, modern magic is none other than French magic.

In a primer on conjuring, Robert-Houdin summed up his approach to presentation in a formula that has since become magic's most oft-cited dictum: "the illusionist is not a juggler, but an actor playing the role of a real magician."[47] Characteristic of a performer who sought to elevate the status of magic as an art form, Robert-Houdin's formulation calls attention to the theatrical, rather than purely mechanical, dimensions of magic performance. Furthermore, it implies a difference between magicians who deceive for entertainment's sake in the secure space of the theater and their "dangerous doubles":[48] charlatans and criminals who mingle among an unsuspecting public, preying upon victims with insidious deceptions. Achieving a safe distance from disreputable deceivers was an important step in the emergence of modern magicians as professional entertainers. Of course, when Bébel performs in the street, without a theatrical setting to immediately guarantee his legitimacy, passersby can still mistake him for one of the three-card-monte hustlers who con tourists on busy corners. Some steer clear, perhaps wary of becoming a victim like the spectator in Bosch's painting. I've heard some who stay nevertheless quip, "Watch your wallet!" or "I wouldn't play cards with him!" as if to exorcise a lingering doubt.[49] To put the audience at ease, Bébel must establish his identity as a modern magician through aspects of performative self-presentation: costume, accoutrements, patter, body language, and interaction with the public.

The most important feature of Robert-Houdin's formula and the key commonality with Bébel concerns the significance it prescribes for tricks: rather than a demonstration of "jugglery" (that is, technical skill), each trick should be a special effect authenticating the onstage persona of a "real magician." Marcel Mauss famously describes the "real" magician as, more than simply someone with paranormal abilities, "the object of strong social feelings" due to "their abnormal character" and "a social status which may be defined as abnormal."[50] Indeed, modern magicians generally adopt personae that are socially distinctive. Some, following Robert-Houdin, cultivate the style of dashing socialites; others go to an opposite extreme of comic buffoonery. Many portray extravagant or unusual figures with stage names that evoke mystery, glamour, or the exotic and flamboyant or showy outfits that place them outside everyday convention. They may affect an air of grim mystery and associate themselves with imagery of the esoteric and occult; or, as is more often the case, assume an exaggeratedly gregarious demeanor, cracking jokes, ostentatiously flirting, and defying social boundaries and taboos.

Robert-Houdin remains the "model magician" for another reason: he made magic respectable by embodying contemporary ideals of middle-class, heterosexual, European masculinity.[51] To this day, in both France and the United States, magic remains largely a province of white men, although women and people of color are increasingly asserting their creativity within the art. Any exploration of how magicians choose to present magic leads inevitably to questions about how they operate creatively within aesthetic conventions that can empower and constrain them as culture makers. How do aspects of individual identity affect the opportunities and challenges one faces as a magician? Is the role easier for some to assume than others? How do contemporary performers thematize gender and ethnicity, explicitly addressing stereotypes associated with the figure of the modern magician? What do performers seek to express through magic, and what kinds of resources does magic provide them for self-expression? Is Robert-Houdin's imposing model a timeless standard, or has it hampered the development of new forms of magic better suited to contemporary taste?

MAGIC AS A CULTURE OF EXPERTISE

The magic performances most people see—at parties, in theaters, or on television—constitute merely the front stage of a vast world of backstage activity intentionally hidden from nonmagicians. Magicians cultivate their craft alongside friends, colleagues, and rivals in networks that extend locally, nationally, and internationally. Magic clubs constitute the principal node of organized and sustained social interaction within these networks. In addition to providing a regular gathering place, they organize performances, host lectures by visiting magicians, and sponsor formal competitions. As practitioners seek to share their secretive practice with other knowledgeable insiders, a club of some sort will likely form in any town with more than a half-dozen dabblers. In Paris, where there are hundreds of amateur and professional magicians, there is a correspondingly vibrant club scene. During the course of my research, I regularly attended meetings of seven different clubs—one weekly, one biweekly, and the rest monthly—ranging in size from a few dozen to over a hundred regular participants. I describe these clubs in greater detail in Chapter 1; here, I want to make a few general observations about magic as a broadly defined "culture of expertise" [52] and about the role of "enactments of expertise" [53] in relationships among magicians.

United by bonds of secrecy, magicians share with each other knowledge scrupulously hidden from outsiders, whom they refer to (sometimes with a hint of condescension) as "laymen" in the United States and *profanes* in France.[54] The division between insider-magicians and outsider-laymen is the principal social fact of magic. Magicians are a community of connoisseurs. Laymen necessarily lack the aptitude for connoisseurship;

the true nature of magicians' skill is always concealed from them. If magicians generally hide their dexterity from audiences, however, they display it unabashedly to each other (except when doing so would lead to the revelation of a prized secret) and tirelessly discuss the technical nuances of sleights, gimmicks, tricks, and effects.

Magicians and laymen approach magic performance with radically divergent criteria. Magic theorist Henning Nelms explains that "conjurers are fascinated by subtle devices and difficult sleight of hand," but "laymen are incapable of appreciating either the subtlety or difficulty. In fact, if the performance succeeds, the layman cannot even guess what methods have been used."[55] This dichotomy creates a potentially frustrating situation for magicians, whose principal clientele is often unable to accurately assess a performer's skill. Of course, this situation arises for a variety of professionals in service settings, leading to "the problem of dramatizing one's work" in order to make it apparent that one is "performing well."[56]

The fellowship of other insiders gives magicians opportunities to display their skill and rank themselves according to expert criteria. A small elite of virtuosi enjoys especial prestige, and other magicians solicit them for mentorship or simply for demonstrations of technical prowess. Among French magicians, for instance, Bébel has earned this status. Other magicians make pilgrimages to the Métro Mabillon to see him perform, and eagerly await his arrival at the club meetings he frequents. Years of experience performing on the street have given him the ability to improvise prodigiously with a simple deck of cards, building on audience reactions to string together dizzying sequences of effects.

At one magic meeting, I watched in awe as Sébastien Clergue, a brilliant young innovator working as a consultant for David Copperfield, challenged Bébel to accomplish a series of increasingly outlandish effects. Placing four aces at random places in a shuffled deck, Clergue began by asking Bébel to produce them magically. Bébel picked up the cards and, after a few manipulations, ejected the aces one by one onto the table—followed in rapid succession by the four kings and the four queens.[57] "Now do it with one hand while singing the Marseillaise,"

Clergue deadpanned. A starstruck amateur standing beside me whispered, "Bébel doesn't have hands—he has tentacles!"

When magicians watch each other perform, their trained eyes peer through the skein of illusion to the underlying succession of illusionary techniques. One complained to me, "I was at a magic meeting the other day. Bébel performed a beautiful trick. At one point, he did such a fantastic *secret* sleight that everyone applauded. To me, that's a perversion! A roomful of magicians applauding not for the product of a trick, but for its process, which a spectator should never see!" Depending on their level of expertise, magicians are effectively impervious to the sleights and gimmicks that mystify laymen. Still, magicians are drawn together by the hope of fooling each other, and by the hope of being fooled. Fooling a knowledgeable magician is a challenging proposition, requiring substantially more skill and ingenuity than it takes to impress an intelligent nonmagician. Stories about magicians managing to fool an acknowledged master become the legendary basis for the reputations of individuals and their inventions—tricks, gimmicks, or sleights. Those who perform what's known as "magic for magicians" design effects that apparently cannot be accomplished through the methods familiar to insiders, challenging experts to "find the solution." Such tricks are literally *about* the method, not the effect.

Insofar as the pursuit of technical mastery engenders a community of technical aficionados, amateur and professional, the magic world represents a typical "geek" subculture, like HAM radio operators and computer hackers.[58] One author defines a *geek* as "one who becomes an expert on a topic by will and determination. Thus, geeks can be found in specific groups and spaces that . . . have been stereotyped as sites for community among intelligent experts. . . . These groups might identify themselves as computer geeks, anime geeks, trivia geeks, gamers, hackers, and a number of other specific identifiers. Regardless of classification, these geeks share the experience of being experts."[59] In calling magic a domain of "geek" expertise, I mean to evoke both the positive and negative connotations of the term (which, as of 2010, the *Robert* and *Larousse* dictionaries have accepted as part of the French language). On the one hand, magic is an activity in which self-motivated individuals cultivate an extremely demanding kind of specialized technical knowledge upon which they rightfully pride themselves. On the other, it is a practice that outsiders sometimes construe as trivial or stigmatize as socially marginal—negative attitudes that magicians may have to confront when performing for an audience.

Another way of thinking about the magic subculture is as a *scene*. This metaphor is familiar enough to employ uncritically, but it is worth pausing to reflect on the resemblance it posits between theater and social life. In dramaturgy, a scene is the setting for a performance or the basic unit of action in a piece of theater. Similarly, in sociological terms, a scene is an arena of social activity focusing on a common theme or interest, whose members actively display their competence to each other and evaluate each other's performances. Members of a scene embrace insider criteria, distinguishing themselves into categories and classes based on nuances of competence irrelevant to outsiders. Of course, it is possible to be a magician without participating actively in the magic scene. As we shall see, some may reclusively avoid it, but the scene inevitably remains "where the action is," [60] that is, the setting in which technical innovations enter into circulation and individual reputations are established through more or less agonic displays of skill. In the scene, magic can at times resemble a competitive form of play in which, to borrow from Caillois, "there is an element of rivalry" and "possessors of the same toys congregate in an accustomed or convenient place where they test their skill." [61]

Magicians classify themselves according to the scale on which they perform. Most of the magicians I worked with specialize, like Bébel, in a genre of magic known, in both French and English, as *close-up*. As the name implies, close-up magicians perform under conditions of maximized proximity. Unlike the genres of *salon* and *stage* magic, adapted to incrementally larger venues and bigger audiences, it is best suited to groups of spectators numbering in the single digits who, situated in face-to-face contact with the magician, participate actively in the performance. While small-scale tricks have always been part of the magical repertoire, it was not until the 1950s and 1960s that North American magicians brought recognition to close-up as an independent genre. With a distinctive toolkit of methods, repertoire of effects, and dynamic, international subculture all its own, close-up retains a modish, youthful cachet in the French magic scene.

Salon and stage magic involve many of the iconic elements the public at large associates with magic: glittery props, colorful boxes, live animals, and human assistants. By contrast, close-up magicians use everyday objects, including things like banknotes and jewelry borrowed from spectators themselves, to create illusions under conditions of intense scrutiny that seem to neutralize the magician's advantage. Close-up magicians generally specialize in sleight of hand, and the microscopic conditions under which they perform highlight their skill and cunning. These conditions also give them opportunities to display charm and humor in interacting directly with individual spectators. At the same time, these conditions maximize interactional risks for the performer. While stage or salon magicians have a theatrical setting that guarantees their legitimacy and ensures some buffer between themselves and the audience, close-up magicians must rely on their skill to establish authenticity and their wit to deflect challenges from potentially recalcitrant spectators.

For a variety of reasons, close-up magic is by far the most widely practiced form of magic today. First, amateurs are much more likely to specialize in close-up than stage magic: whereas the former is inexpensive, portable, and versatile, the latter is expensive, cumbersome, and limited in the performance opportunities it affords. Second, in the changing political economy of the magic business, venues for performing live salon and stage magic have dwindled, while opportunities for close-up magicians have burgeoned. Professionals who specialize in close-up magic mostly perform what they call *table-à-table* (table-hopping), circulating among tables at a bar, restaurant, or banquet. The type of engagement they call *cocktail* (walk-around or strolling) similarly involves performing for small groups of standing spectators at a cocktail party or reception. As the professional form that close-up magic usually takes today, table-hopping and walk-around magic are the primary genres that the magicians in this book are most frequently employed to perform.

I speculate that reasons beyond sheer practicality account for the current popularity of close-up magic. The style and ethos of close-up magic are particularly well suited to the present cultural climate, privileging embodied skills and human contact in an era when entertainment is so often associated with high-tech production and mediation. Spectators, mainly accustomed to seeing magic on television specials, often remark how much more gratifying it is to have a magician performing in close proximity. Likewise, a majority of the close-up magicians I have interviewed cite "contact with the public" as the thing they love most about their work. Mimosa, an outrageous comedy magician with a mind like a steel trap, even identifies social interaction as the real purpose of table-hopping, magic being but a means to that end (see Figure 2). "At the dawn of this new century," he writes, "when people suffer from loneliness, I try to get them to communicate with the people sitting around them, to amuse myself at the same time as them, to turn life into simple merriment for a few minutes. With what? Some balloons, whatever I find on the table, not much magic, really." [62]

Close-up magicians may further specialize in working with a particular medium: cards, coins, sponge balls (foam rubber implements made especially for magicians), and, most recently, scrunchies (the brightly colored hair ties popular among preadolescent girls). Specialists of card tricks are by far the most common; in France, they are known as *cartomanes* (cardicians). Card magic is the lingua franca of the magic world, and cardicians its dominant demographic. A neophyte can learn a simple card trick in minutes, and a skilled magician can entertain for hours with an everyday deck of playing cards. The possibilities for magic making with cards could not be exhausted in many lifetimes.

Although members of the lay public probably think of stage magic as synonymous with "grand illusions," large-scale tricks featuring elaborate apparatus and people appearing, disappearing, levitating, or otherwise defying the laws of nature, it also comprises other subfields. Escapes are the province of *escapology* (Harry Houdini's department), mental marvels (e.g., predictions, telekinesis, and telepathy) belong to the field of *mentalism*, practitioners of *pickpocketry* demonstrate the ability to steal belongings from under a volunteer's nose, and *dove magic* involves productions of live birds from out of thin air. Many French magicians also practice a range of variety arts they refer to as *arts annexes* (ancillary arts) such as ventriloquism, shadowgraphy, and juggling. For any magician

Figure 2.   Mimosa clowns around with a deck of cards. Photo by Zakary Belamy.

who works with children, balloon sculptures are de rigueur; those who specialize in balloon acts call themselves *twisters.*

The boundaries between close-up, salon, and stage magic are more permeable than they may seem at first glance. Many close-up magicians have entire stage shows, which they perform whenever the opportunity arises. Likewise, stage magicians can incorporate close-up effects into their theatrical repertoire, for instance by inviting volunteers onstage to participate in a card trick as representatives of the audience as a whole. Notwithstanding, dichotomizing discourses that emphasize differences rather than similarities are not uncommon in this factious world. Priding themselves on the technical skill it takes to produce dazzling effects just inches from an audience , close-up magicians may characterize stage magicians as glorified actors who rely on self-working props and gimmicks. For their part, stage magicians reproach close-up magicians for emphasizing digital dexterity at the expense of theatricality and showmanship.

The modern magic scene operates on an international scale, with commercial gimmicks, props, and instructional books or videos circulating the globe as commodities, and magicians traveling abroad to perform, lecture, and compete. In this sense, local scenes around the world exhibit remarkable similarities. In a monograph describing the development and intersection of amateur and professional careers in the Canadian magic scene of the late 1970s, sociologist Robert Stebbins argues that his strictly Canadian sample reflects the "international, multilingual, vocational-avocational subculture of magic" whose members "are alike in the values, attitudes, beliefs, and behavior patterns related to its distinctive scope" and that "survives and grows, in part, through [their] shared experiences." [63] I agree that similar social patterns seem to emerge wherever magicians congregate, in part because of magic's long-standing international connections, and in part because the kinds of skills magicians cultivate and the secrecy they embrace seem to attract similar people and impose similar social psychological dynamics. Still, as I describe in the chapters to come with particular reference to the French magic scene, these broad patterns of cross-cultural convergence belie surprising cultural inflections in different national contexts.

One of the most striking features of the global magic scene continues to be its extreme gender segregation—another feature it shares with subcultures of geek expertise.[64] What Peter Nardi wrote of American magic clubs twenty years ago could equally apply to the magic clubs I encountered more recently in France: "The organization of the world of magic resembles a male social club. . . . Although magic clubs are open to women, the message conveyed by the brochures, books, magazines, and magic kits is that this is really an activity for males." [65] In seeking to explain this striking gender disparity, Nardi points to the congruence between the dynamics of magic performance and stereotypically masculine interactional styles: "Magic is an aggressive, competitive form involving challenges and winning at the expense of others. . . . It is creating an illusion that involves putting something over [on] someone, to establish who is in control, and to make the other (the audience) appear fooled." [66] This type of aggressive role in an agonic interaction might not only be especially appealing to males but also be socially difficult for females to play. Nardi explains that, because of the co-constructed nature of magic performance, "audience members . . . must allow themselves to be tricked, to be one-upped. They must relinquish control to the performer. . . . Perhaps audiences are not likely to do this with someone of perceived lower status" or, for that matter, with anyone for whom such a socially dominant position seems interactionally inappropriate.[67]

In the chapters to come, I explore how the structure of the magic scene affects the production of magic as a genre of entertainment and its reproduction as a social activity. What kinds of social relationships do magicians maintain with one another, and how does this affect the circulation of knowledge and the development of styles? How do various categories of magicians (amateurs and professionals, beginners and experts, etc.) relate in terms of social networks, prestige, and lineages of learning? How are technical and aesthetic innovations developed and diffused in the magic scene? What factors affect who becomes a magician, and why does magic remain a male-dominated subculture despite the prominence of women in other performing arts? How do magicians mediate between an expert appreciation of their artistry and the value laymen (who cannot comprehend their skill) attach to magic as a form of expertise?

STAGING TALK

I approach the Parisian magic scene as what Lave and Wenger call a "community of practice," a social group shaped by mutual orientation toward a shared activity, and in which expertise develops through the "apprenticeship" or "legitimate peripheral participation" of "newcomers" alongside "old-timers."[68] Such a community is "a set of relations among persons, activity, and world" and "an intrinsic condition for the existence of knowledge" that "provides the interpretive support for making sense of its heritage."[69] From this perspective, magic endures because magicians remain members of a community that fosters the cultivation of illusionary skills and deceptive abilities, even as recent mediating technologies—especially the Internet—radically impact the established patterns of knowledge transmission within that community.

Lave and Wenger signal that learning to talk in locally appropriate, relevant ways is "key to legitimate peripheral participation."[70] Like every community of practice, the magic world is also a "speech community"[71] with distinctive, socially significant ways of talking. Magicians talk about magic wherever they meet: backstage, club meetings, conventions, parties, magic classes, or magic shops. When in the company of laymen, they disguise messages about magic in coded phrases, and use acronyms to refer to particular sleights or gimmicks. Taking part in their ongoing conversations about magic entails mastering jargon and argot, assimilating cultural references, and recognizing the implicit—and sometimes counterintuitive—conventions of the speech genres associated with activities from swapping secrets to swapping stories.[72] The particularistic ways French magicians talk about their expert activity verbally mark their place in the world, differentiating them from nonmagicians. Joining magicians' community of practice goes hand-in-hand with learning to participate in their conversations.

As part of his "dramaturgical" approach to social life, Erving Goffman uses the term "staging talk" to denote private conversations among social actors about the activity of performing.[73] In staging talk, Goffman explains, "Questions are raised about the condition of sign-equipment; stands, lines, and positions are tentatively brought forth and 'cleared' by the assembled membership; the merits and demerits of available front regions are analyzed; the size and character of possible audiences . . . are considered; past performance disruptions and likely disruptions are talked about; news about . . . one's colleagues is transmitted; the reception given one's last performance is mulled over in what are sometimes called 'post mortems'; wounds are licked and morale is strengthened for the next performance."[74] While Goffman considers it to encompass the "gossip" and "shop talk" of any trade, the notion of "staging talk" has the advantage of calling attention to concerns central in magicians' conversations: verbally strategizing, reviewing, and planning performance. Furthermore, it signals that often magicians talk together quite simply to entertain with verbal artistry.[75] While staging talk concerns performance, it is itself also a performance: magicians *stage talk* for each other just as they stage illusions for laymen. Weaving between creativity and convention, they craft staging talk to convey expertise as well as showcase it.

In some ways magic resembles boxing, "an ultraindividual sport whose apprenticeship is quintessentially collective":[76] magicians' staging talk reflects the extent to which they depend on each others' input, feedback, and emotional support in readying themselves for what are almost invariably solitary performances. Of necessity, magicians themselves are acutely attuned to spectators' reactions, which they discuss and analyze in minute detail. In the staging talk I consider in this book, magicians are largely concerned with successfully managing the dimension of performance known as "co-construction," which is "the fundamentally interactional basis of the human construction of meaning, context, activity, and identity."[77] This may seem obvious, but magical illusions have no objective existence. Magicians provide only evidence of illusory realities; the actual illusions exist subjectively in spectators' minds. Magical illusions are therefore co-constructed accomplishments. So too is the magical performance as a situated event in which magician and audience both play complementary roles. Successfully managing co-construction entails not only leading spectators to experience a sensory illusion, but also persuading them to endorse one's self-presentation as a magician.

As I illustrate in the chapters to come, magicians' staging talk focuses attention on the dynamics of co-construction in performance. It is therefore a central feature of practicing the trade of the tricks, and I examine it in a variety of manifestations, from face-to-face talk to wider-ranging arenas of interaction such as print, video, and computer-mediated communication. Many of the examples of staging talk I analyze involve what Deborah Tannen calls "constructed dialogues," in which the speaker performs the speaking roles of one or more parties in an interaction. According to Tannen, "constructed dialogue in conversation . . . is a means by which experience surpasses story to become drama. Moreover, the creation of drama from personal experience and hearsay is made possible by and simultaneously creates interpersonal involvement among speaker . . . and audience."[78] The way magicians build the views and voices of real and hypothetical others into their staging talk thus signals both their awareness of the profoundly co-constructed nature of magic and their creative and interpersonal investment in the activity of staging talk for one another.

Throughout this book, I approach magicians' staging talk as an "expert register"[79] of language that both manifests expertise and constitutes it, and therefore as evidence of the larger world of backstage activity that goes into preparing oneself—technically, artistically, and psychologically—to perform in front of an audience. I draw heavily on the theories and methods of linguistic anthropology to disclose structures of knowledge and feeling immanent in and emergent through magicians' talk.[80] The close analysis of recorded and transcribed talk is a pivotal part of my argument. Transcriptions are never written replicas of talk; they are selective representations prepared for expository purposes.[81] By adopting transcription conventions that closely parallel the standard punctuation of written English, I have endeavored to make the transcripts accessible to the widest possible range of readers.[82]

ALL THE TRICKS IN THE BOOK (AN OVERVIEW)

Precisely because it is a community of practice constituted through informal exchanges of knowledge between people of varying skill levels, the magic world afforded me a natural role to assume as an initially ignorant researcher: an apprentice. Positioning myself as a novice magician, I carried out over eighteen months of archival and participant observation fieldwork between 2003 and 2005 (with multiple return visits between 2006 and 2011), primarily in Paris-area magic clubs, classes, heritage sites, and performance contexts. During this time, I conducted open-ended interviews, usually ranging from one to four hours, with several dozen amateur and professional magicians, and engaged in informal exchanges with countless others. To complement oral history, I spent many days in the Bibliothèque Nationale Française combing through over a century's worth of Francophone magic periodicals. My apprenticeship culminated in June 2005 with my induction—upon passing an examination before a panel of expert judges—into the Fédération Française des Artistes Prestidigitateurs (FFAP), the French Federation of Prestidigitatory Artists.

Walter Benjamin famously called Paris the "capital of the nineteenth century."[83] By objective measures, its global stature may have declined, but Parisians don't seem to have noticed. The cumulative force of their swaggering cosmopolitanism makes this pale city of monumental boulevards and narrow ruelles feel like it is still every bit the center of the world. With one-fifth of the national population concentrated in the metropolitan area, it is France's hub of political, economic, cultural, and intellectual life. The same goes for magic, and magicians are no more immune to the bewitching vanity of Paris than anyone else.

I took full advantage of the ample opportunities Paris offers to see live magic performed. Ranging from seedy to swank, Paris's world-famous cabarets almost always feature at least one magician among an afternoon's or evening's entertainment. Jan Madd performed daily stage shows aboard his sumptuous riverboat theater, the Metamorphosis, anchored along the Quai de la Seine. Several blocks north in the medieval Marais, magicians performed salon shows every hour, several days a week, in the Musée de la Magie, a charming private museum devoted to the history of magic. At the nearby Place Sainte Cathérine, audiences could see several close-up performances every evening at a magic-themed bar, Le Double Fond, owned and operated by magician Dominique Duvivier. Aside from these high-profile institutions, I followed magicians into other venues for periodic performances: theaters, circuses, close-up engagements in bars or restaurants, and street-corner busking. Most of the time, the magicians I worked with were not "entertainment attractions" working in theatrical settings, but rather "service entertainers"[84] hired to perform at private events: weddings, children's birthdays, bar and bat mitzvahs, holiday parties, and corporate functions. Though access was rarely feasible, I attended these events whenever possible.

In Chapter 1, I describe my fieldwork in greater detail, recounting my journey from absolute novice to certified member of France's largest magic organization. In the process, I sketch the contours of the Parisian magic world as a secretive community of practice. Focusing on the learning process itself, I explore some of the intellectual aptitudes that novice magicians develop as they acquire experience and expertise as performers. In Chapter 2, I consider how magicians produce and circulate secrets as a kind of property perpetually menaced by dispersal—particularly in the Information Age, when online sources make magicians' secrets more freely available than ever. Turning to the moment of performance in Chapter 3, I examine the kinds of prestige and authority that magical abilities can confer, with particular attention to the dimensions of gender and power that attach to the performative display of secrets.

If the first part of this book largely concerns the social psychology of learning and performing magic, the final two chapters investigate the status of magic as an expressive form in contemporary France from the perspective of the anthropology and sociology of art. Chapter 4 addresses magicians' career trajectories, looking at the relationships between amateur and professional magicians, and examining the kinds of employment prospects available to magicians today. Magicians I spoke with in France often complained of magic's low cultural status as an entertainment service industry generally excluded from spheres of high cultural prestige. Chapter 5 explores the horizons of cultural possibility for magic as a vehicle of creative expression, considering the efforts of several French magicians to assimilate magic to the realm of high culture, and particularly to the status of Art with a capital A. In recent years, these efforts have coalesced around a fledgling "new magic" movement, which defines itself as a genre distinct from the modern magic of Robert-Houdin, and introduces a novel set of discursive practices to magicians' staging talk.

Drawing on oral recollections and archival records, this book has a strong historical dimension, but not a synoptic historical chapter. Instead, I incorporate relevant elements of history into the thematic arc of individual chapters, blending cultural historiography with contemporary ethnography. Taken together, the scattered historical passages do add up to an account of the major trends that have shaped magic today, with an emphasis on the cultural mediation of historical transformations making continuities over time particularly apparent. For instance, while the types of concerns about divulging secrets I describe in Chapter 2 remain a historical constant from the late nineteenth century to the present, they intensify episodically with the advent of new forms of knowledge dissemination that threaten to disrupt established patterns of transmission. Similarly, in Chapter 4, I show that relatively benign tensions between amateur and professional magicians are a recurring motif throughout the twentieth century, but that changing conditions of work and competition have brought them pointedly to the fore in recent years. Finally, Chapter 5 addresses the cultural mediation of history itself, comparing ways French magicians invoke the notion of tradition as a source of prestige or as an inertial impediment to desirable aesthetic change.

I conclude this introduction with a few general remarks. It should be clear by now that I draw on many technical and theoretical texts written by and for magicians. A large number of these sources are in English, but that does not mean they are removed from the practice of conjuring in France. Indeed, during the course of my fieldwork, most of these works were introduced to me by French consultants who knew them intimately. Magic is, like science, a discipline whose technical procedures transcend the local preoccupations of any particular community of practitioners. As in the sciences, English is currently the lingua franca in the international magic world, and magicians around the globe rely on texts, videos, and other materials produced in that language, principally in the United States. The specialist literature on magic is vast, and I make no effort to review or synthesize it, but rather draw selectively on published works of magic theory to supplement my own interviews and direct observations.[85]

Over the course of centuries, magicians have developed a complex jargon to describe their craft. As in scientific and technical domains, many specialized terms (mostly in French and English) have been adopted internationally; others remain specific to particular countries or languages. While my research was conducted entirely in French, in this book I use American English equivalents for terms of French magic jargon, which are often close cognates (as with method/*méthode*, effect/*effet*, and presentation/*présentation*). In some cases, French magicians displayed consistent preferences for English loan words over equivalents in their own language; thus, instead of *détournement de l'attention*, they generally say *misdirection*, and instead of *brisure* (a sleight used in card tricks), *break*. Rarely, I use the argot of Anglophone magicians to describe things of importance for which French magicians do not have a specially designated term (such as "tipping" for giving a secret, or "sessioning" for the collaborative exchange of ideas). In the rare instances that I have not been able to determine a satisfactory translation for a French expression or piece of magicians' cant, I employ the French term, indicating an English gloss. I have translated spoken quotations into colloquial English, with explicit commentary on the utterance form only where relevant to the analysis. Unless otherwise indicated, all quotations from French textual sources are likewise my own translations.

All transcripts are from audio or video recordings. Quotations within the text are from field notes and/or recordings. I have done my best to ensure factual accuracy in providing a written account of my observations, and take sole responsibility for any misrepresentations.

Magicians may disagree with some of the decisions I made in writing this book. Over the years, magicians in France and the United States have contended that places like Las Vegas, a city virtually synonymous with magic, or Madrid, the current global capital for close-up innovation, would be more exciting places to study magic than Paris. Others have complained that my research does not accord enough prominence to magic's international elites. These criticisms depend on the insider criteria of connoisseurs, which necessarily differ from the comparative analytical criteria of a social scientist. As an anthropologist, my principal interest is how everyday life unfolds within the subculture of magic, among a community of magicians at a specific place and time. In this sense, Paris is a microcosm of magic as a whole; but it is also home to some extraordinary magicians who approach magic in ways that strongly reflect French culture. Appearances aside, this isn't *really* a book about magic anyway; it is a book about the social organization and valuation of expert knowledge that just happens to focus on magic.

Finally, a caveat to nonmagicians. I said this was a book about secrets, but it is not a book *of* secrets. In order to become a member of the FFAP, I took the following oath: "I swear on my honor neither to divulge any secrets that are part of illusionists' cultural patrimony, nor to describe them in written or audiovisual materials intended for laymen. I swear on my honor to be loyal to my fellow magicians, to respect their artistic property, and to practice the art of conjuring with befitting dignity. I swear to do my utmost to elevate the art of magic to the highest level of prestige." Obviously, this oath has clear implications for what I can and cannot discuss in the pages to come. Although acquiring secret knowledge, both discursive and embodied, was a pivotal component of my research meth-odology, I am bound to dissimulate much of that knowledge in writing this book, as I would in an actual magic performance. Moreover, I've be-come convinced that any secrets I could reveal would distract readers' attention from something more magnificent still: the world of passion, intelligence, and cunning that brings those secrets to life and endows them with meaning.

ONE An Apprenticeship in Cunning

In French, it's called le trac. Every magician gets it, but it always remains an intensely personal experience. French close-up superstar David Stone describes its symptoms as "an elevated heart-rate, a dry mouth, nervous shaking . . . clammy palms . . . weak knees, stomach cramps, cold-sweats, shortness of breath (even hyperventilation), stuttering, blurry vision . . . maybe even hives on your face. . . . It can also bring on . . . irritability, difficulty concentrating, and memory loss. When it's a frequent occurrence, you may begin to suffer from nagging fatigue, a lack of motivation . . . a lack of muscle coordination . . . depression, phobias, and anxiety disorders." [1] *I've seen its debilitating effects on seasoned professionals and first-time performers alike. Sometimes le trac pounces like a crouching predator just minutes before a performance. Or it may slowly creep up over the course of weeks. "The moment I book a gig," a magician in his late fifties told me, "I get it so bad that I immediately begin wishing they'd call back and cancel. The more experience I have, the worse it gets. The more I know what can go wrong."*

Stage-fright surged upon me suddenly, like a tidal swell of adrenaline. I paced the wings of the large theater that would shortly fill with over a hundred spectators eager to be amazed. It was May 2005, and I was preparing for a performance at the Les Halles community center in the heart of Paris, where I had been taking a magic class since the fall. While the class began with seven students, besides me there were only three left: Denis, a soft-spoken Franco-Vietnamese marketing specialist at a telecommunications firm; Antoine, a junior high student who had shot up several inches since the beginning of the year; and Jean-Jacques, an affable, middle-aged employee of the national rail system. Having never practiced in the theater, we anxiously went over the music and lights with the techie. Backstage, Denis and I worked with Antoine on his technique for producing a bottle of Scotch from thin air, adjusting for what magicians call "angles"—spectator sight lines. We executed small rituals of protection and transformation, arraying our props in neat little piles behind the curtain, changing into our stage attire, awkwardly applying makeup, testing our gimmicks, and exchanging reassurances.

In front of our friends, families, and colleagues, we were about to exhibit skills we had spent a year mastering. Would our artistry impress? Would our illusions astonish? With the expectant gaze of "real" spectators fixed upon us, would we be able to successfully embody those qualities synonymous with magicianship—mystery, dexterity, craftiness, and cunning? The sense of risk was both terrifying and exhilarating. We looked within ourselves, and we waited for the audience to arrive.

PROFILES IN CUNNING

There are many ways to describe how magicians are made. One would be to trace the acquisition of embodied skills, the meticulous "techniques of the body"[2] that allow innocent-looking gestures to dissemble covert manipulations. While magicians strive to make their body language naturalistic, their every move is codified according to tradition, methodically adapted to suit individual needs, rehearsed thousands of times (often in front of a mirror or video camera), and fine-tuned over the course of a career. But while many spectators believe that hand-is-quicker-than-the-eye dexterity accounts for the magicians' deceptive abilities, in fact, an enormous amount of mental strategizing underlies every illusion. As illusionist Pierre Brahma explains, "We deceive through speech, gesture, the most imperceptible mimicry, silence. . . . We deceive through what we do and what we do not do. Behind every good magic trick there lies hidden (and must always remain hidden) a veritable science that applies understanding of the mainsprings of the human mind and heart, and of psychological ploys that can, at times, reach a level of astonishing subtlety."[3] A trick, he continues, "is based on manual dexterity of course, but also on a mastery, a perfect grasp, on the reactions and the reasoning of spectators who believe themselves free, but whose mind and senses are always secretly under our control."

This chapter approaches apprenticeship in terms of not magicians' acquisition of embodied skills like sleights, but rather the cunning intelligence that inhabits their limbs and digits. How do magicians assimilate artifice, learning the crafty style of thinking essential to their art? After introducing some of the settings where they pursue projects of enskillment, I explore how cunning develops in tandem with a refined intersubjective awareness that enables magicians imaginatively to see the world through the eyes of the spectators who co-construct illusion.

A skilled practitioner of the trade of the tricks must be able to outwit and outmaneuver spectators alert to impending deceptions, and to perceive opportunities for surprise in the interstices of everyday life. British conjurer Bob Read, in Paris for a gig, told me over a morning pint, "I don't ever walk into a room without being aware of the possibilities for holding up my end of the situation. Once you get into that state of mind, you want to know the shape of the glasses, the shape of the lights, what people are wearing, the place where that guy put down his newspaper." Read paused to take a sip. I heard the loud concussion of his teeth against the glass, and he doubled over in pain. I leapt to my feet. Laughing, he opened his hand to reveal, not a tooth, but the coin he had snapped against the side of the glass to create the auditory illusion of a painful accident. As Read demonstrated, sufficient cunning makes the possibilities for trickery endless.

Becoming a magician transforms the way one sees the world. Everyday material objects—rubber bands, paper clips, sandwich bags, and even breath-freshening strips—disclose properties that could make them amenable to use in tricks. Indeed, magicians often come to rely on properties of commercial goods to which most consumers attach no significance: for instance, one of my friends despaired that hair curlers no longer contain the metal springs he once extracted to construct a prized gimmick. When Lucky Strikes introduced a new kind of cigarette box featuring a large front chamber and smaller second chamber, I joined a group of magicians who spent nearly an hour discussing how to repurpose it for a magic effect. Practicing magic also suggests new ways of thinking about everyday social situations as potential occasions for performance. "Say you tell your girlfriend, 'Watch me produce a hamburger. . . . Presto!' She might be impressed," magician Sébastien Mossière once told me. "But if you bide your time, waiting for her to say, 'I'm hungry,' and *then* produce a hamburger, you can accomplish a miracle."

Gaëtan Bloom, one of France's most inventive magicians, spoke with me at length about the nature of magician's intelligence. I met him between shows at a café across the street from the Crazy Horse cabaret, where he has been a regular performer for decades. With his wire-rim glasses, a white scarf around his neck, and a newspaper in his lap, Bloom looked more like a scholar than a magician. But just minutes before, I had seen him onstage, sandwiched between two striptease acts ("the beast among the beauties," as he put it). Speaking a mishmash of a half-dozen languages (a little something for everyone in the international crowd), he performed an outrageous cut-and-restored rope trick with his microphone cord— apparently getting electrocuted in the process (see Figure 8). Bloom brought a video camera to the café and showed me some footage of a new trick he had recently shot in his home workshop. On the small screen, I watched him saunter up to a banquet table sagging with food. He picked up a heaping bowl of spaghetti and poured it instantly down his throat, followed by an enormous salad, a platter of fries, a plate of meatballs, a basket of fruit, and so forth until, within a matter of seconds, the "human vacuum cleaner" as he called it had apparently ingurgitated enough to sate an entire rugby squad.

Bloom told me that there is a simple, but fundamental, difference between the way magicians and laymen think. "A layman will come up to you and say, 'I've always wanted to know how you guys do that trick where the magician gets tied up in a sack, locked inside a trunk, and then instantly changes places with his assistant.'[4] Then you ask if he's ever thought about it. 'No, not really.' That's the difference. A magician would say to himself, 'Well, you could start by cutting a hole in the sack, and putting a trapdoor in the box. . . . But there must be something more cunning still!'" The word Bloom used—*malin*—can mean cunning, clever, crafty, or tricky. It's an irresistible urge to find *something more cunning still* that has made him one of the most prolific innovators, French or otherwise, in contemporary magic ("I can't resist inventing; it's a sickness, a disease"), but cunning intelligence is something all magicians share. Not surprisingly, many have backgrounds in fields related to science and technology, where similar kinds of intellectual work and manual tinkering are also valued.

Malin is the French adjective that best evokes the peculiar quality of a magician's intelligence, and magicians use it all the time to praise each other and their inventions. They also express unqualified admiration for deceptive performances and performers with words like *astucieux* (shrewd), *vicieux* (devious), and *vicelard* (shady). While they clearly enjoy the moral ambivalence language such as this connotes, these tricksters nevertheless operate within a culturally condoned sphere of essentially benign deception, fooling audiences who expect (and preferably pay) to be deceived. But they also link magical cunning with more practical kinds of intelligence like street smarts. Illusionist Laurent Langloÿs recounted that once, after performing in a Pigalle cabaret, he was held up by several thugs. "Just let me show you something first," he told them, making a coin appear out of thin air and then vanish. After several minutes of magic, the would-be muggers expressed their thanks and escorted him to his car. "They called me *Monsieur* and everything."

Expert performers in a variety of domains consider cunning an essential element of style and skill—from capoeira and improvisational music to computer hacking.[5] Associated the world over with trickster figures and artisans, it also can be a culturally prized quality of persons more generally.[6] Known as *metis*, it was "at the heart of the [ancient]

Greek mental world," emphasized in "large sectors of their social and spiritual life,"[7] and embodied in culture heroes like Odysseus, "the man of twists and turns."[8] Historian Robert Darnton similarly identifies cunning as a "master theme of French culture in general, at its most sophisticated as well as its most popular."[9] Darnton calls the particularly French kind of wily intelligence *Cartesian cunning*, the knack for outwitting powerful adversaries and flamboyantly dispatching intellectual challenges. Indeed, contemporary Frenchmen widely perceive themselves in precisely these terms; in a recent book, a prominent historian of philosophy documents the prevalent belief in France that "Cartesian" intelligence somehow defines the national character.[10]

If French magicians partake of an ideal of Cartesian cunning, they ironically deplore it in their audiences. For them, it is a truism that French spectators are "too Cartesian" to enjoy the pleasures of being deceived. They often complained to me that the French are "ashamed to not understand something." I heard—not without mild pique—a number of French magicians praise Americans as "big children" who "just want to be entertained" and who are "always willing to play along." "In the United States," one magician told me, "people don't have a problem accepting things they don't understand. It's like, 'Oh whatever, no big deal.'" The stereotypical go-with-the-flow American stood as a kind of idealized Other for the hyperrational Frenchman who always wants to understand the "trick" behind the magic effect or, worse still, who pretends to understand in order to "save face." (One French magician told me that, by contrast, Italian spectators are too credulous: "if you show them a card trick, they'll ask you to heal their sick child.")

Given the widespread belief that French audiences are especially resistant to being deceived, it is all the more important that French magicians hone their craftiness. In this chapter, I describe the world of activity in which they cultivate cunning and give their wily imaginations free rein. In particular, I focus on magic clubs as sites of informal apprenticeship and magic classes as sites for formal instruction, taking my own experience as a novice alongside other novices to exemplify the process of acquiring a magician's cunning more generally. In doing this, I focus closely on language to show how magicians' ability to deceive relates to the expert ways they describe, analyze, and prepare for performance through talk. In particular, I show that the ability to evoke the viewpoint of hypothetical or generic spectators is a verbal skill central to their staging of deception.

JOINING THE TRIBE

In Paris, magic as a social activity is primarily organized into clubs, whose regular meetings set the rhythm of life in the magic subculture. While some shun the club scene altogether, most magicians attend meetings, if not regularly, at least selectively. The social boundaries of the magic community are nearly coterminous with the orbit of magic clubs, which therefore became the principal sites of my field research. The membership of the two biggest magic clubs in Paris largely overlaps. The Cercle Magique de Paris (CMP) is the local branch of the national magic federation (the FFAP); during my research, it held biweekly meetings in the large theater of a community center on the outskirts of the city, and workshops in the FFAP's one-room national headquarters downtown. The Cercle Français de l'Illusion (CFI), which also has several affiliated branches in the provinces, met monthly in a conference room inside an international student dormitory. While both clubs attract members young and old, regulars are overwhelmingly adults, a large percentage of whom are elderly retirees. These regulars are also overwhelmingly amateurs, though professionals drop in from time to time.

As a default, club meetings of the CMP and CFI primarily comprise performances of tricks or routines by club members, usually followed by an explanation. Some people spend a month or more preparing a routine just for their club, using the opportunity to perform as an impetus for their training and creativity. Others only come to watch, never performing. Both clubs occasionally hire professionals to lecture at meetings. Afterward, the lecturers sell gimmicks, books, videos, and lecture notes—often turning a tidy profit.

As supportive as magicians generally are of one another, the standards for behavior at magic meetings sometimes made the former junior

high school teacher in me cringe. A portion of the audience entirely ig-
nores what's happening onstage, engrossed in manipulating cards or
coins. Back-row kibitzers maintain a whispered commentary on the performances. Inevitably members of the audience hurl taunts (*lancer des
vannes*, they say) at the performers and at each other. The steady stream
of sometimes lewd raillery can constitute a performance in its own right.
For instance, one evening at the CFI, the magician onstage asked the
audience to volunteer a number for a mathematical effect. "67," the man
next to me offered. "Is that your age?" another shouted. "No, it's the size
of my penis," the first responded. "The length?" asked a third. "No, the
diameter." Meanwhile, the performer onstage simply waited for things
to settle down. Another evening at the CMP, a magician demonstrated a
trick for children, making a lollipop mysteriously stand on end in his
outstretched palm. "I just got a text message from your wife," a wisen-
heimer shouted from the back of the auditorium. "She'd like you to employ that technique with another object."

This kind of repartee reflects the locker-room mentality that sometimes prevails in the overwhelmingly male magic world, in terms of
both off-color content as well as an interactional style marked by often
aggressive joking and teasing. It is not surprising that magicians gravitate to verbal dueling, which offers another occasion for showcasing the
kind of quick-wittedness and guile that they value in conjuring performance. But it may also constitute a barrier for women's participation in
the magic world. For, other than male magicians' wives or girlfriends—
who are often also their assistants—there are hardly any regular female
attendees at these meetings.

I received a reliable estimate on the number of female magicians in
France from Mimosa, then president of the CFI and former treasurer of
the CMP (who also happened to be a brilliant computer programmer
trained at France's top engineering school). While the clubs were diverse
according to some measures—in education, profession, and income—
the gender imbalance was glaring. In 2004, Mimosa calculated that there
were 3,500 magicians in all of France—including both professionals and
serious amateurs—and that only 2 percent of them were female. According to that estimate, there were around 60 female magicians in France

during my research, or about one for every million people in the country. My anecdotal observations over the course of several years suggest that, if anything, this was a generous estimate.

The most unusual meeting in Paris was called (in English) the Illegal Magic Club. Regulars (there were no "members") referred to it as the "Illegal" or simply *le club*. A decadent walpurgisnacht inaugurated by comedy magician Otto Wessely, the Illegal was a weekly get-together for professional magicians after an evening's gigs, convened in a pillbox Latin Quarter pub that was sweltering in the summer and always filled with smoke (at least before the 2008 smoking ban). While some gravitate to the air of debauchery, many younger magicians are drawn to the Illegal by the generally high level of talent and the tantalizing prospect of rubbing elbows with international magic luminaries passing through Paris. The Illegal is a grueling proving ground, where magicians came to show off their material, and engage each other in playfully competitive "cutting contests"—often sparked by the presence of women (cabaret magicians sometimes showed up with exotic dancers in tow). Evenings often unfolded like a battle scene from the *Iliad*: from out of the close-packed tumult, attention would suddenly concentrate on an individual magician, with dozens edging in to see a trick. Many of these Homeric aristeia focused on Bébel, always able to improvise staggering arpeggios of illusion. Personally, I liked the opportunities the club afforded for unpredictable conversations that could last until well after sunrise.

Far from the pitch of the Illegal, a kind of Olympian detachment reigned at meetings of the Club des Magiciens Collectionneurs. Only a small fraction of the attendees were, or had been, professional magicians. Many were amateurs who had abandoned the practice of magic to pursue other career interests (the president, for example, was a recently retired nuclear physicist), but later turned to collecting as an alternative outlet for their continuing interest in the art. The club, which constitutes a sort of collective memory of the magic world, devotes each of its monthly meetings to an esoteric theme—the obscure origins of particular effects, the biographies of little-known performers, the proper use of forgotten pieces of apparatus. The collectors reminded me of the Melanesian kula ring traders of Malinowski's *Argonauts*.[11] Like kula valuables, magic collectibles often circulate with an oral record of provenance. Collectors remain keenly aware of the whereabouts of desirable objects in each other's collections, and are capable of strategizing for decades to broker an exchange or sale. As they displayed their treasures—an old magician's poster or handbill, or an historical automaton—I loved to hear them recount their triumphal treasure hunting at garage sales, flea markets, antique shops, and bouquinists.[12]

Magic conventions are the peaks of "collective effervescence"[13] in the life of French magic. The annual national convention hosted by one of the FFAP's forty-seven regional chapters can attract close to a thousand participants and lasts for five days (I attended in 2004 and 2009). There are a number of smaller annual festivals and conventions, including daylong events sponsored by the CMP and CFI in Paris. Virtually every convention features juried competitions (in categories such as close-up, stage, and comedy magic, for instance), gala shows, lectures or workshops by celebrity experts, and a dealer exhibition. The latter often induces orgies of binge buying; participants joke about jamming their suitcases full of effects they will probably never use. Attendees generally agree that the most gratifying part of any convention takes place after hours, during the late-night sessions in hotel bars or lobbies.

A variety of media extend the face-to-face interactions of the magic scene in both space and time. Two prominent magic magazines, L'Illusionniste and La Revue de la Prestidigitation, official publications of the CFI and FFAP respectively, first appeared at the dawn of the twentieth century. Initially, they primarily chronicled the scuttlebutt, quarrels, and frequent festivities of the clubs themselves. "If, in say a hundred years, a collection of this publication falls into the hands of a scholar," one early article read, "he will certainly . . . take us for gourmands, each issue bringing, as it does, either the proposition for or the report of some magic banquet."[14] As their circulation grew, these periodicals increasingly provided sustained contact between magicians in different parts of the country and different social spheres, allowing French magicians to imagine themselves as a community or constitute themselves as a public in new ways.[15] As the years passed, both journals came to accord an increasing amount of space to instructions for tricks.[16]

Another periodical, *Magicus*, occupies a curious spot in the French magic subculture. Edited by firebrand Didier Puech in Toulouse, it combines thoughtful reportage, trenchant satire, historical features, and belletristic essays into a singular publication of record. The subtitle *Magazine of Presti-Agitators* accurately reflects Puech's commitment to stirring sometimes uncomfortable debates. For instance, his 2005 cover story on minorities in magic asked, "Is the Magic World Misogynistic, Bigoted, and Racist?"[17] (Short answer: kind of.) In recent years, *Magicus* has devoted special issues to topics like women in magic, the politics of magic, and magic as a form of therapy for people with mental and physical disabilities.[18] Puech admits that many magicians aren't inclined to think in such expansive—and critical—terms about magic. "I do this for everyone else!" he told me.

In recent years, the Internet has created new opportunities for magicians to engage in staging talk and knowledge exchange. One site in particular, VirtualMagie.com, or "VM" for short, has emerged as the nervous system of French and Francophone magic at the dawn of the twenty-first century. Founded in 1998 by amateur magician Thomas Thiébaut, by 2005 the website had well over 4,000 registered users, and logged between 50,000 and 60,000 visits per month. In addition to announcements, classified ads, and reviews of books, gimmicks, DVDs, and magic shows, the major draw of VM is the forums: asynchronous message boards where users—known as VMistes—can start or contribute to discussions about any topic related to magic. Only magicians with a confirmed level of expertise can access the forums devoted to technical topics, but the nontechnical forums, open to virtually anyone who registers as a user, constitute a relatively democratic space for debate.[19] The discussions that flourish online often spill over into face-to-face conversations, and vice versa. In a close-knit world where many of the participants maintain online and offline relationships, few VMistes participate in the forums anonymously, and vocal participation has catapulted relative unknowns into the national spotlight of the French magic world. When I asked him to describe the purpose of VM, Thiébaut said, "One word: exchange."

Between meetings of the CFI, the CMP, the Illegal, the Collectionneurs, and several other Paris clubs, I averaged two to three magic meetings a

week.[20] As I became a more familiar presence at magic events, participants' requests to see me demonstrate my conjuring skills steadily increased. At first I assumed this was a way of policing access to what is an
undeniably secret world and of asserting hierarchies of expertise within
it. The pressures of secrecy make it difficult to be a passive observer in a
world where the lines are clearly drawn between magicians and laymen.
By putting me on the spot to display skills I had little mastered, experts
were also sending me the message that novices are welcome to participate
in club activities provided they manifest serious commitment to magic. In
this way, they were tacitly telling me something essential about the nature
of the social relationships between magicians.

A secret art, magic can also be a solitary one, requiring long hours
of monkish study and practice. Further, unlike other performing artists, magicians generally work alone. In magic clubs, they can delight in a
mutual appreciation for skills necessarily hidden from outsiders and re-
gale each other with stories about the triumphs and tribulations of their
vocation. Sharing an impassioned interest in illusionary techniques and
the rich human stories in which they are embedded draws magicians
together for purely social reasons. In the context of these meetings, being recognized as an engaged, engaging person hinges on participating
in interactions that quickly shuttle between talk and performance. Because magicians discuss magic while and by doing it, practicing along
with them proved necessary for me to enter into their ongoing dialog.

When magicians meet for the first time, they establish their credentials by performing tricks for each other. "You have to show what level
you place yourself on," one explained to me. A self-appointed gatekeeper
might ask a new arrival to demonstrate a particular technique; it is not
uncommon to hear requests like "Show me your Elmsley" (a fundamental technique in close-up card magic, but not a trick in itself). In a conversation about how easy it is to size up other magicians, one old-timer
said, "I can tell by their Double Lift" (another sleight). "I can tell by the
way they hold their deck [of cards]," a second offered. "I can tell by the
way they take their cards out of the box," said a third. (Removing cards
from the box and holding the deck are embodied skills magicians indeed practice and discuss in detail.) Techniques or even gestures come

to function as shibboleths determining the level of access a new arrival will be granted, or as what Simmel terms "signs of recognition through which the individual legitimates himself as a member" of a secret society.[21]

Despite hierarchies of skill, magicians maintain a strong sense of fraternal solidarity, evinced in the very way they communicate. In every sector of French life, alternation between formal and informal terms of address—between the polite *vous* (you) and the familiar *tu* (thee)—marks relative social distance or proximity.[22] In stark contrast to other settings, French magicians—even total strangers—almost categorically use the solidary *tu* in addressing each other, regardless of differences in age, class, gender, race, or skill level. In so doing, they verbally signal shared membership in a corporate social group.[23]

While they may identify as "magicians," "illusionists," "prestidigitators," or "sleight-of-hand artists" (*escamoteurs*) to laymen, French magicians refer to themselves and each other as *magicos* (both singular and plural). This label is formed by modifying the noun *magicien* with the diminutive suffix -*os*, which serves in French argot to make quaint or familiar variants of preexisting words.[24] To be a magicos is to be a member of a group with a strong sense of corporate egalitarianism—despite the presence of perpetually renegotiated internal hierarchies.[25] One magician explained to me that the term *magicos* can have "a positive or negative connotation depending on who says it." Used pejoratively, he said, it can mean a small-timer or a hack. But among insiders, it serves as a badge of solidarity and familiarity. He continued, "In essence, it means that the guy who uses it is in the tribe. You call someone a magicos because you're a magicos yourself."

Far from seeking to exclude me, by pressuring me to perform even as (or especially because) they recognized my limited ability, experts were making an inclusionary gesture of incorporating me into the tribe of magicos. Placing me in the position of a novice, they constituted me as a potential beneficiary of the expert instruction that only they could offer. Perhaps most importantly, they thereby gave me an opportunity to study magic by taking part in one of the forms of social activity— apprenticeship—that keeps it a flourishing popular tradition in France and around the world. Yet mine was a precarious apprenticeship, for as one magicos told me, "If you were a magician, you could never do the kind of research you're doing: everyone would be too afraid you were going to steal their secrets." Another warned, "Be careful not to let magic take over your life. You'll never finish your book!"

Of course, it is not uncommon for fieldworkers to adopt the lifeways of the communities they study, and many recent ethnographies employ formal apprenticeship as a field method,[26] particularly in settings where this is the locally befitting mode of knowledge transmission.[27] A number of ethnographers have even adopted a reflexive stance on apprenticeship, taking their own socialization as the primary object of study.[28] When apprenticeship involves the transmission of secrets—as it often does—fieldworkers face difficult questions about how to write about what they have learned without violating the trust of their teachers. For instance, after an apprenticeship in Mexican wrestling, Heather Levi reports that writing about the sport feels like "an act of betrayal" because she must inevitably "reveal a secret," namely, that "professional wrestling matches are fixed." [29] My own response to this dilemma mirrors the strategy Johnson uses in writing about his apprenticeship in Brazilian Candomblé: describing the circulation of secrets without disclosing their content.[30]

For anyone hoping to learn magic, Paris offers a wide range of instructional opportunities. In addition to securing private lessons, at various points throughout my research I also enrolled in regular classes. These classes provided one of the most useful entrées to magic for a variety of reasons. There is no doubt that, as an academic, I found the structured classroom format congenial—especially compared to the pell-mell club scene. Moreover, being a student allowed me to inhabit the role of a novice fully, alongside other learners at a comparable level. Most importantly, I found that, in teaching magic, experts verbally articulated and objectified knowledge that would have been difficult to elicit in casual conversation or formal interview. Instruction generally followed a predictable pattern, with each session focusing on one or more tricks or techniques. Like many other students, I audiorecorded every class or lesson, took copious notes, and sometimes photographed or filmed strips of activity.

My first class, at the Les Halles community center, was taught by Nemo, a professional magician and one of the best friends I made in the magic world. With naturally arching eyebrows, a carefully groomed goatee, and a fondness for the color black, Nemo looked the part of a magician. We lived on opposite edges of Chinatown in Paris' thirteenth arrondissement, and usually saw each other several times a week for reasons related to magic or just to hang out. When we watched movies together, I was struck by the way Nemo dissected them with a magician's eye for aesthetic and technical minutiae. George Lucas's remastering of the *Star Wars* films was an endless source of aggravation for him: "In the original, when Obi-Wan says, 'These aren't the droids you're looking for,' there was a fraction of a second pause before the Storm Trooper responds, 'These aren't the droids we're looking for.' You could sense the power of the Force working on his mind. In the new version, the response is instantaneous. All the magic is gone—it's an atrocity!" Though I found it hard to empathize with Nemo's disconsolation, his meticulous attention to psychological nuances—and a quixotic perfectionism—gave his approach to performing and teaching magic a special mark (see Figure 3).

Nemo had been steeped in the Paris magic scene since childhood and regaled me with stories about the magicos we encountered. "When I was little," he said, "I had a magic set, and I put on shows for my family. Finally, my mother agreed to take me to a meeting for other magicians [the CMP]. It was a wild scene. Coming up the stairs, we ran into Patrick." The image was clear in my mind: Patrick Rivet, a handicapped comedy magician who pitches in tirelessly for several Parisian clubs, is an irrepressible cutter of capers. "He said he must have a pebble in his shoe and then he took out a rock the size of a cobblestone! Then, when my mom was filling out the paperwork for me, Charles Barbier was standing right behind her." Again, I knew exactly whom Nemo was talking about: Barbier is a specialist in what magicians call lightning calculation—the rapid execution of complex mathematical operations. "He peered over her shoulder, and when she wrote my birthday, he said, 'It was a Tuesday, Madam.' She practically fell over."

Nemo and I were part of a loose circle of young magicos in their late twenties and early thirties we sometimes called "the gang" (*la bande*).

Figure 3. Nemo (*left*) teaches a card effect. Photo by the author.

Isabelle had been frequenting the magic scene for years. Though she had a sharply discerning eye, she remained a relative beginner like myself, and we teased each other about our slow progress. Loïc Marquet was a professional close-up magician who taught magic classes at a community center in an affluent suburb. A dapper Parisian with a mordant wit, he often stirred up trouble on the VM forums with hilariously cantankerous posts (see Chapter 4). "I'm prematurely a bitter old man," he told me. Philippe Day, a kindhearted professional with a fertile imagination, had spent several years developing a comedy magic duo with Bruno, a barrel-chested former army officer with an expansive personality. Along with Nemo, Isabelle, and Loïc, I spent many evenings in the basement theater of a Parisian bistro watching Philippe, in the role of a deranged mentalist, engage in a hilarious duel of wits with Bruno, playing a schmaltzy magician in a mustard yellow blazer with tricks literally spilling from his sleeves.

I had two principal instructors besides Nemo: Stefan Alzaris and Jérôme Cadéac.[31] The former was a semiprofessional magician and a doctoral student in philosophy whom I contacted after reading his excellent mass-market book on magic, *Illusionnisme et magie*.[32] He had formed an association called CÉSAME for teaching magic at a community center in his diverse neighborhood in northeast Paris. He had developed a thoroughgoing pedagogy for teaching magic based on what he called *katas*, the term used in Japanese martial arts for "highly precise practice exercise forms."[33] For each effect we covered, he gave me homemade handouts detailing parallel streams of activity—gesture, patter, and gaze—along with copious stage direction. Breaking down magic into these elementary sequences, which we repeated week after week, Stefan helped me grasp how subtle nuances of performance contribute to an illusionary gestalt. By contrast, Jérôme shoved his students into the prestidigitatory deep end, teaching us demanding card tricks that often entailed combinations of multiple sleights. An established professional who taught and performed at the Musée de la Magie, he was a technical ace with a deep knowledge of close-up esoterica. As I show in the pages to come, Nemo, Stefan, and Jérôme together helped me learn to think like a magician, while also giving me valuable evidence of significant patterns and emphases in magicians' pedagogy.

.   .   .   .   .

Peering from behind the curtain, I watched Denis perform a balletic routine on a darkened stage. Bright little points of light hovered mysteriously around him, like fireflies moving in synch with electronic dance music. As he caught a light in one hand, it flickered out, appearing in his other hand or in his mouth. Having only practiced with him around the table in our classroom, I was amazed by his elegant use of the stage's expanse. As he exited the stage to thunderous applause, I readied myself to go on. I was up next.

"People always ask me why I'm a Francophile," I began, smiling out at a sea of encouraging faces. "France has given the world great literature, film, and art. But what I personally admire the most is the French tradition of magic, and the French tradition of pastry." The audience laughed uncertainly. "It's true!" I reassured them. "It was here in France that both magic and pastry achieved the status of true art forms. And it's strange that people don't make the connection between them more often." I went on to tell them how the most famous French

magician of all time, Jean-Eugène Robert-Houdin, ended his show by wheeling a model bakery on his elegant Second Empire stage. A small mechanical pastry chef emerged from the front door to take orders from the audience, and then went back into the bakery to fetch piping hot miniature pastries. That night, I would perform my own rendition of the same effect with nothing more than a cardboard pastry box and a little wind-up robot.

I showed the box empty and placed the little robot inside. I asked each member of the audience to write the name of a pastry on a slip of paper, and then chose a girl at random to serve as a proxy for the crowd by picking one "order" from the pile. She announced that the billet she selected read 'macaron.' "What's that?" I asked in consternation.

A helpful spectator yelled out, "It's a cookie!"

"It's like a little hamburger with creamy filling!" someone else clarified.

"But that's not a pastry!" I protested.

The audience turned on me in an instant. "Yes it is!" they yelled with gleeful Schadenfreude. I shrugged forlornly and asked the crowd to shout "MACARON" at the count of three. "If he takes a macaron out of that box, I'm dead," I heard someone whisper. When I opened the box, there it was—a miracle—a neatly wrapped Parisian macaron. The little girl took the donut-sized cookie, and the crowd cheered.

The culmination of almost a year of work, this trick reflected the input of dozens of magicians. Once I hit upon the idea of a pastry-themed homage to Robert-Houdin, it would take me months to work out a satisfactory rendering of the effect. I turned to all the available sources—magic books, magic dealers, and other magicians. One friend taught me how to make a gimmick for determining what pastry the volunteer had selected, and another shared plans for constructing the pastry box that would be used to produce it. In the process, I learned that, while magic performance is generally individual, the process of enskillment leading up to it often takes a very social form, with the novice enlisting support, assimilating influences, and internalizing skills made available through interactions with experts.

INTERNALIZING MAGIC

From a technical standpoint, the essence of conjuring is what information architect Edward Tufte and magician Jamy Ian Swiss call "disinformation design," the presentation of visual and verbal cues that lead spectators to make erroneous inferences about the world.[34] Successful disinformation design follows a number of fixed principles to which all conjurers learn to adhere, consciously or unconsciously. Around the French Revolution, amateur magician Henri Descremps promulgated a list of thirteen such principles, upon which intervening centuries have little improved. In an introductory magic course I took through the FFAP, students received a copy of these precepts on the first day of class. Beginning with Descremps's first precept—"Never announce the Trick that you are going to perform lest the spectator, advised of the effect, have the time to guess its cause"—we covered each rule one by one. (The third recapitulates the first: "Never perform the same Trick twice . . . as you will inevitably violate the first precept").[35] When followed faithfully, such principles reliably hamper spectators' ability to explain away a magical effect, leading them headlong into astonishment.

In recent years, cognitive scientists, following in the footsteps of Alfred Binet, have come to recognize the incredible sophistication of magicians' working knowledge of human perception and cognition, identifying an *empirical* dimension of magicianship. A recent article in *Neuroscience* asserts that a "long legacy . . . of informal research by magicians aims to determine what conditions allow for the maximum manipulation of human attention and perception."[36] Likewise, a review article in *Trends in Cognitive Sciences* argues that "any serious magician has a theory about how to deceive his or her audience. If this theory is wrong, the magic trick will fail and the audience will spot the secret."[37] It follows that "each performance can be viewed as an experiment that tests the magician's theory. . . . Years of such testing enables a magician to learn much about human cognition. Moreover much of this knowledge is shared with fellow magicians and is passed on from one generation to the next."

In this section, I suggest that one of the crucial means whereby magicians pass on this knowledge is a style of teaching that leads novices to think like magicians. When students in the classes I took attempted to perform, instructors did not assume the role of passive spectators but rather drew on their own performing experience to engineer challenges that required novices to use cunning to succeed. When novices were stumped, instructors interrupted to indicate possible lines of response to difficulties. This pattern of instruction exemplifies what psychologist Lev Vygotsky terms *internalization,* a series of developmental events that transforms an external activity into an internal one, and an interpersonal process into an intrapersonal one.[38] In the ways that they engineer difficulties, expert magicians allow novices not only to hone skills for coping with the challenges of performing before real audiences, but also to internalize dispositions indispensable to the expert practice of magic.

To get a sense of how this process works, I will provide a relatively straightforward example, drawn from my first lesson with Stefan. He began by teaching me a simple card trick he called "Cirque" (Circus), in which the magician discovers a selected card after a volunteer has placed it on top of a randomly dealt pile of cards and repeatedly cut the deck. A "self-working" trick—that is, one requiring no sleight of hand— "Cirque" hinged on misleading spectators about a simple mathematical principle. It therefore gave me an opportunity to focus on the dynamics of performing without worrying about difficult manipulations. After learning the trick, I performed it several times, with Stefan serving as a spectator. In that role, he seized pivotal junctures to disrupt my performance. During one run-through, I dealt the cards in a pile by packets of five or six, asking Stefan to stop me whenever he wanted. "Stop!" he said.

"Put down your card," I instructed, intending him to place it on top of the cards I had just dealt. Instead, he tossed it haphazardly on the table. I laughed in frustration. "No, no! Here, on the pile!"

"So you see what you have to say?" he asked, breaking the performance frame. "I'm acting as if I were a real—"

"Pain in the ass?"

"No, not even! Just a normal spectator who has never seen a card trick and who does exactly what you say without thinking too hard about it." With Stefan's help, I learned to clarify my instructions and to mime the actions I wanted a volunteer to perform—in this case, indicating the exact spot where I wanted the card to be placed. In feigning reactions ranging from innocent confusion to incorrigibility and downright mischievousness, Stefan drew on his own performance experience as a semiprofessional magician to alert me to weak points in my presentation. At the same time, he inculcated an awareness of the intersubjective nature of performance, calling attention to an allocentric perspective—the way the trick we were studying would appear to spectators.

Skills I acquired in the context of learning one routine infused my performance of other routines, and influenced the way I approached learning new material.[39] As frustrating as these simulations were to me, over the course of the coming months, they would gradually help me to prepare for the range of potential spectator actions and reactions I might go on to encounter. This is a textbook example of what Vygotsky defines as the *zone of proximal development*, "the distance between the actual developmental level as determined by independent problem solving and the level of potential development as determined through problem solving under [expert] guidance or in collaboration with more capable peers."[40] Stefan used his own insight into the intersubjective dimension of magic performance to create a situation in which I too, as a novice, had to look at my own performance from the perspective of an audience. As I show in the next section, internalizing this kind of intersubjective awareness is the *sine qua non* of illusionism.

Partially as a consequence of this interactional mode of knowledge acquisition in which an expert engineers challenges prompting a creative response, knowledge transmission in magic has an inherently emergent quality. Even at the most rudimentary levels, teaching can be the occasion for the reinvention of tradition and the production of new knowledge ("You always learn something new when you have to teach things you already know," said Nemo). Later in the same magic lesson, Stefan asked me to show him another card trick using a principle we had practiced in "Cirque." Although I had ostensibly mastered the principle, I was unprepared to employ it in a new trick. I improvised a routine, having Stefan select a card and return it to the deck. This time, I passed the cards one by one, and ended up in an awkward position: a card face up in the deck told me that the next card was Stefan's selection. Although I had located his card, I didn't have a "magical" way to reveal it. I froze, breaking the performance frame. "How do I get myself out of this?"

Stefan took the cards, picking up where I left off. "Maybe you could do something like this: *All the cards are face down, and this is the only one that's face up? How odd.*" He looked all the way through the bottom of the deck. "And then you could do something, like, *OK, so I haven't found it . . .*" Saying this, he turned the face-up card over, apparently setting the deck aright (the dramatized speech with which Stefan accompanied his manipulation vocalized the *intention* his actions were meant to convey to a lay spectator).

"Yes!" I said, grasping where he was headed.

"I'm just improving here on the basis of your trick. I've never done this before." He began looking through the deck a second time to make sure all the cards were now facing the same way. Again, one was reversed— but this time it was the selection. "*It's funny because the chosen card, the card that you selected, is the only one facing the wrong way! And we just checked, too!*"

"Yeah, that's great!"

"And I just invented that trick on the spot. You gave me the idea, and it's not bad!" It wasn't a finished trick yet, but a barebones idea for an effect that we refined further over the next ten minutes. Strictly speaking, this trick did not entail any new techniques, nor was the effect original (there are infinite variations on the chosen-card-face-up-in-the-deck motif, which is called a "reversed card" effect). But the particular configuration of technique and effect was a novel by-product of a lesson in which Stefan drew on his expertise to transform my beginner's misstep into the basis for a new trick. "In this class," he told me, "we don't do things that are finished. We experiment."

As a result of the emergent quality of knowledge transmission, learning a trick in face-to-face contexts often entails the co-production of new situational knowledge. Magicians' collective repository of knowledge bears the quality that Vygotsky's contemporary Mikhail Bakhtin called *dialogism*:[41] as they are transmitted from magician to magician, tricks retain traces of the co-constructed form they assume in the context of revelation. When magicians compare variations on tricks, they are also comparing legacies of learning and transmission with this relatively diffuse community of practice.

SEEING THROUGH A SPECTATOR'S EYES

As we have seen, magicians must remain constantly aware of how potential spectators will perceive their words and actions. Enacting carefully designed deceptions involves "an expression game,"[42] in which the
deceiver must strategically manage an internally consistent flow of true
and false information, orchestrating a participant framework in light of
an intended illusion, or "fabrication."[43] To pull off such deceptions, one
must not only master shared signifying conventions and regulate external demeanor so as to cloak one's real intentions, but also take up the
perspective of the other on the world. The awareness of "other minds"
develops in all children as part of the normal process of socialization,[44]
and is enhanced through forms of strategic play.[45] Within an arena of
deceptive performances such as magic, however, the capacity for intersubjective awareness is, by necessity, elevated to the level of an expert,
self-reflexive skill.

Magicians are keenly aware that spectator psychology does not exist
outside of time. Their deceptions require that magicians operate beyond a
threshold of spectators' technical knowledge, which changes historically
through the increasing (or, in some cases, decreasing) awareness of particular techniques or technologies. Furthermore, an evolving cultural senso-
rium accustoms audiences to variable patterns of perceptual stimulation.
Thus, a magicos with several decades of experience assured me that
changing trends in cinematography have had a dramatic effect on the
way spectators respond to visual cues. Because films and videos today
have so many rapid jump cuts, he explained, "our eyes are used to pro-
cessing things much more quickly." He has seen a decline in spectators'
ability to follow tricks that require a long attention span, and now strives
to infuse his performances with rapid sequences of so-called flash effects,
like sudden appearances, disappearances, and transformations. He explained that, while these changes make today's spectators harder to fool,
they also allow magicians to use sleights that look unnatural when performed slowly but are unnoticeable when performed quickly.

Magicos interested in the psychology of deception often refer to the
work of Spanish cardician Juan Tamariz, one of today's foremost magi-

cal theoreticians. Tamariz places spectator psychology at the heart of his influential theory of "false solutions." He writes, "We must know what spectators think during and after a trick, gauge the quality of the effect produced in their minds, and determine whether or not they suspect, rightly or wrongly, the methods we have used. We have to make sure that spectators not only don't know how the trick was done, but that they cannot even imagine how it was or how it could have been done. Moreover, spectators must be persuaded that they are utterly incapable of finding the true method, or any other method."[46] To do this, the magician must establish, over the course of performing an effect, that every *possible* way to explain it is in fact a *false* solution. Only then can a spectator be truly amazed.[47]

Some means for falsifying solutions are highly codified. For instance, the magician can allow the spectators to examine the props before, during, or after an effect—or allow examination of his or her person ("Nothing up my sleeves, nothing in my head," the joke goes). As psychologist Harold Kelley writes, "to discourage various relevant hypotheses" about the method, "the magician may tap the dice to show that they are solid, when in fact they are not. Members of the audience are shown or even allowed to inspect the cabinet to show that it is empty and contains no hidden compartments, though in fact neither may be true."[48] In my "Little Baker" routine, for instance, I had to ensure that spectators had the indubitable impression that the choice of the pastry was purely random, and that the pastry box was completely empty at the beginning of the trick.

Falsifying potential solutions requires some degree of conscious reasoning about how spectators think and perceive. One common strategy for imagining spectators' viewpoints in the context of magic instruction and staging talk is to verbalize their thoughts as direct reported speech. As a pervasive feature in everyday talk, reported speech occurs whenever people present the speech of themselves or others as a quoted utterance.[49] Sometimes speakers report speech that they claim actually occurred. At other times, quoted utterances are patently hypothetical demonstrations of what someone might have been thinking or what someone might say or think.[50] In magicos' talk, spoken representation of hypothetical thought has a specialized, if not explicitly theorized, use: to dramatize the viewpoint of spectators as part of planning or preparing to perform. In addition to playing the role of lay spectators for the purposes of practice and instruction, expert magicians voice the perspective of lay spectators in talk using hypothetical inner speech. By examining a number of examples, I show how magicians use talk to cultivate the cunning intelligence necessary to design disinformation.

Understandings of mental phenomena vary across cultures. Some cultures proscribe verbal speculation about the contents of others' minds,[51] although this clearly does not mean that members of these cultures don't have a "theory of mind" in the psychological sense.[52] In other cultures, verbal speculation about the thoughts and feelings of others is permissible, and enabled by relevant linguistic forms such as quotatives—words or phrases that serve to introduce quotations of speech or thought. French magicians draw upon the resources of their language to construct the mental contents of real and imagined spectators. Their systematic use of reported speech implies what we might call a "working theory of mind"—a heuristic model that, in this case, construes mentation as a continuous inner monolog. This construal is calibrated both to the specific dynamics of magic performance as a "situated activity system"[53] and to the exigencies of magic pedagogy. It is also worth noting, in this context, that magicians who work with children have very clear—and field-tested—understandings of what kinds of effects spectators are capable of understanding at different developmental stages.[54] The following examples all concern magic intended for adult audiences.

In the following example, Nemo describes how to give the impression, in a particular effect, that "the sequence of events is . . . contingent upon the audience's behavior,"[55] not on the will of the magician. In the effect, the magician writes a secret prediction on a piece of paper, and then places a number of cards on the table. A volunteer selects one, which turns out to be precisely the card that the magician predicted. The key to the effect, Nemo explains, is that the spectator must believe that the prediction would have proven correct *regardless of which card had been chosen*. While the procedure itself is easy, instilling this conviction in the spectator is not. Nemo uses hypothetical inner speech to illustrate what spectators must be led to think.

NEMO: People must say to themselves, *"The same thing would have happened* if I picked another number. He would have done the same thing, we just wouldn't have landed on the same card." That's where it's magical.

STUDENT: But do you follow up quickly with another trick? It's— If you let them think—no, I don't know—

NEMO: Exceedingly quick!

ALL: [*laugh*]

NEMO: Il faut que les gens se disent, *"Ça aurait été la même chose* si j'avais pris un autre numéro. Il aurait fait la même chose, simplement on serait pas tombé sur la même carte." C'est là que c'est magique.

STUDENT: Mais est-ce que tu t'enchaines vite avec un autre tour? C'est—Si tu les laisses réfléchir—non, je sais pas—

NEMO: Excessivement vite!

ALL: [*laugh*]

Here, Nemo employs hypothetical reported speech to verbalize the perspective of a spectator or volunteer satisfied with the authenticity of his or her own agency in determining the outcome of the trick (*"The same thing would have happened* if I picked another number").

In voicing the hypothetical spectator's thoughts, Nemo shifts the pronominal frame of reference from an egocentric to an allocentric perspective. Thus, in the quoted utterance, the "I" is the spectator and the "he" is Nemo (or the magician performing the effect). Nemo's use of the first person plural ("we just wouldn't have landed on the same card") points to the reality co-constructed by actions jointly undertaken by the magician and the spectator.[56] Without explicitly invoking the intersubjective dimension of magic performance, Nemo uses language to allow novices to perceive a sequence of actions from an intersubjective viewpoint. One of the students, registering the importance of spectator psychology, asks if it is necessary to quickly move on to another effect so that spectators don't have time to think about what just happened. "Exceedingly quick," Nemo jokes.

In other instances, Nemo also used hypothetical inner speech to illustrate not only what spectators should be led to think, but also what they must be discouraged from thinking. Audiences can approach magic with certain general notions about how a magician might fool them. For instance, in a trick where a volunteer is asked to select a card that the

magician will subsequently identify or reveal by magical means, spectators could suspect the magician of influencing the selection by "forcing"
a particular card. The magician must establish that this is a false solution, impressing upon spectators that the choice is utterly fair and free of
influence. Even the way the magician extends the cards for the spectator
to select from can enhance (or detract from) this impression.

To teach us this, Nemo demonstrated the difference between two different ways of "fanning" a deck of cards from one hand to the other: the
proper method, in which one continues moving through the cards after
the spectator has made a selection, and the improper method, in which
one stops the motion of the cards as soon as the spectator has selected.
Here he demonstrates the improper method.

NEMO: [*demonstrates*] The fact of
continuing after the card . . . it's
psychological, it's very strong. It
really gives the impression, "You
could have picked *whichever* you
wanted." If you stop, look at the
difference. . . . [*fans cards*] Pick a
card.

STUDENT: [*points*] That one?

NEMO: That one?

STUDENT: Mhm, that's it.

NEMO: [*Stops fanning*] It'll—
Somewhere one says to oneself,
"Oh, yeah sure. But it suited him
that we didn't pick further on."
It's—

ALL: [*laugh*]

NEMO: No, but it's like—*People
won't say it*, but they *can* say to
themselves, "Ummm, why'd he
st—" You know? "He forced the
card."

NEMO: [*demonstrates*] Le fait de
continuer après la carte . . . c'est
psychologique, c'est très fort. Ça
donne vraiment le côté, "Tu aurais
pu prendre *celle* que tu voulais." Si
vous vous arrêtez, regardez la
différence. . . . [*fans cards*] Choisis
une carte.

STUDENT: [*points*] Celle-là?

NEMO: Celle-là?

STUDENT: Mhm, voilà.

NEMO: [*Stops fanning*] Ça va—
À quelque part on se dit,
"Ah ben oui. Mais ça
l'arrangeait qu'on prenne pas
après." C'est—

ALL: [*laugh*]

NEMO: Non, mais c'est genre—*Ils
le diront pas* les gens, mais ils
peuvent se dire, "Euhhh, pourquoi
il s'a—" Tu vois? "Il a forcé la
carte."

Nemo is making the argument that continuing to fan the cards after allowing the spectator to make a selection tacitly conveys, "You could have picked *whichever* [card] you wanted," even a subsequent one. He uses hypothetical inner speech to represent the undesirable thoughts that spectators might have if the magician does not continue to fan the cards after the selection ("Oh yeah, sure. But it suited him that we didn't pick further on").[57] This contrast leads apprentices to a heightened understanding of the logic behind a preferred technical practice.

In the above example, Nemo explicitly differentiates between what people could internally think and will externally say (*"People won't say it,* but they *can* say to themselves, 'Ummm, why'd he [stop]?' "*). On one level, this suggests that considerations of politeness generally discourage spectators from making face-threatening challenges to a magician's authority, even if they privately entertain negative assessments (a fact that magicians are well aware of, and at times use to their advantage). On a deeper level, I think Nemo means to distinguish between preverbal or nonverbal intuitions that might arise in a spectator's consciousness and fully verbal, propositional thoughts. This can be an important distinction for magicians, as Tamariz suggests: while tricks generally unfold too quickly for a spectator to consciously analyze, the slightest lingering suspicion can lead the same spectator to subsequently mull over the effect, attempting to "reconstruct" (*remonter*, in French) its underlying method. Whether or not they guess correctly, the mere act of trying to explain an effect away can be inimical to the magician's objectives.

Magicos not only use hypothetical inner speech to construct the perspective of laypeople. They employ the same verbal strategy to imagine the perspective of an expert audience by voicing the hypothetical thoughts of fellow magicians. For instance, Jérôme taught us a version of a well-known trick in which a particular card moves inexplicably between the top and bottom of a pile of cards. The version of the trick that most magicians know, Jérôme said, involves the use of additional cards secretly introduced into the pile, which remain there after the effect is finished. This means that spectators cannot examine the cards at the end of the performance. Instead, he taught us a version using a ploy that makes the addition of extra cards unnecessary. Jérôme advocated staging the effect so that knowledgeable spectators couldn't fail to remark on the absence of additional cards, tacitly defying them to find another "solution." In the following example, he uses hypothetical inner speech to illustrate how a magician might react to this version of the trick.

JÉRÔME: It's a trick by Ackerman that I find really devious because—in fact, there's a ploy.

[. . .]

JÉRÔME: So, there laymen don't see the difference, but for a magician? You—you'll fool him. The dude who doesn't know this version of—In any event, as far as I'm aware, nobody knows it.

[. . .]

JÉRÔME: It's really deceptive because . . . those who know the version with the added cards, here you have—you really have three cards. That's what's strong. . . . So at the end people say to themselves, [*pretends to look for extra card*] "It's not possible, there must be one that's—" That's it.

JÉRÔME: C'est un truc d'Ackerman que je trouve vachement vicieux parce que—en fait, y a une ruse.

[. . .]

JÉRÔME: Bon, là les profanes y voient pas la différence, mais pour un magicien? Tu—tu vas l'avoir. Le mec qui connaît pas cette version du—De toute façon, à ma connaissance, personne ne la connaît. [. . .]

JÉRÔME: C'est très bluffant parce que . . . ceux qui connaissent la version avec les cartes rajoutées, là t'as—t'as vraiment trois cartes. C'est ça qui est fort. . . . Donc à la fin on se dit, [*pretends to look for extra card*] "C'est pas possible, il doit y avoir une qui est—" Voilà.

This is a wonderful example of "magic for magicians." Jérôme makes clear that the revised method to the well-known trick would make no difference for an average spectator's experience of the illusion ("laymen don't see the difference"). The true appeal of employing the "devious" ploy is to "fool . . . those who know the version with the added cards." Magicos often incorporate features they call *anti-magicien* (anti-magician) or *baise magicien* (magician screwing) into their routines, seeking the added glory of fooling experts along with laymen, though, as we shall see in Chapter 4, some professionals regard a fixation with this kind of metamagic as a sign of amateurism.

In all three of these examples (and in virtually all of the other cases I recorded), the verb used to introduce hypothetical speech is *se dire*, "to say to oneself." I have evidence of magicos employing other verbs of thinking such as *penser que* (to think that), *croire que* (to believe that), or *soupçonner que* (to suspect that) in indirectly describing spectators' mental states, without voicing them as quotations. However, *se dire* is the overwhelming verb of choice for presenting those mental states in the form of directly quoted utterances, as if they were speakable. Sociolinguistic research suggests that, in spoken French, *se dire* is the verb of thinking most commonly used for presenting thoughts in the form of directly quoted utterances.[58] Because it inherently encodes thought on the model of speech, *se dire* allows magicos to present spectators' probably nondiscursive mental states (belief, disbelief, uncertainty, doubt, surprise, suspicion, etc.) in propositional form, demonstrating as opposed to merely describing a spectator's process of reasoning by literally acting out an internal monologue.[59] In so doing, they render complex thought processes such as induction from evidence available for scrutiny and analysis in talk and as talk.

In the following example, for instance, Stefan uses the verbs *se dire* (to say to oneself) and *dire* (to say) in alternation to enact demonstrations of spectators reacting favorably to the particular approach to presenting magic effects he advocates.

STEFAN: If I want you to remember at least one thing from my classes it'd be—let it be that, you know.

GRAHAM: Yeah.

STEFAN: It's to split things apart to clarify effects as much as possible.

GRAHAM: Mhm.

STEFAN: After you say, "*But where can the magic be hiding?*" when you work like that.

GRAHAM: Yeah.

STEFAN: People say to themselves,

STEFAN: Si au moins je veux que tu retiennes un truc de mes cours ce serait—que ce soit ça, quoi.

GRAHAM: Ouais.

STEFAN: C'est de découper pour clarifier au maximum les effets.

GRAHAM: Mhm.

STEFAN: Après tu dis, "*Mais où peut se cacher la magie?*" quand tu travailles comme ça.

GRAHAM: Ouais.

STEFAN: On se dit, "Mais tout était

"But everything was *totally* clear!"

GRAHAM: Yeah.

STEFAN: People say to themselves, "It's—He didn't do anything!" People often say it to me, "But—you didn't do anything!" Of course! [. . .] It's always guiding their attention that makes the—the spectators think they saw everything—

GRAHAM: Yeah.

STEFAN: whereas . . .

hyper clair!"

GRAHAM: Ouais.

STEFAN: On se dit, "C'est—Il n'a rien fait!" On me le dit souvent, "Mais—t'as rien fait!" Mais oui! [. . .] Toujours c'est du guidage d'attention qui fait que les—les spectateurs ont l'impression d'avoir tout vu—

GRAHAM: Ouais.

STEFAN: alors que . . .

Here, Stefan is teaching me that, by making every step of a performance as clear as possible, a magician can give spectators a false sense of following along. Quoting the thoughts of hypothetical spectators, he demonstrates exactly the kinds of reactions he wants to elicit ("he didn't do anything"). Quoting purportedly real people, he demonstrates how spectators do respond to his performances ("you didn't do anything"). Ironically, the allegation "You didn't do anything" is one of the highest compliments laypeople can pay to a magician's skillful artistry, for magical illusion comes to life when, as Ovid says, "art hides art," [60] falsifying every solution.

Whenever the verb *se dire* is used, it is never entirely clear if the quoted utterance is thought silently or uttered verbally, directed at oneself or directed to other auditors. This is because "in the case of the verb *se dire*, we are dealing with the possibility of a double meaning: reflexive meaning (to say to oneself) or reciprocal meaning (to tell one another)." [61] This ambiguity is, in fact, productive for magicians engaging in staging talk. Consider the following example. Nemo is teaching us an effect in which, under the cover of misdirection, the magician transfers a spectator's selected card from the deck of cards to a nearby location, where it will be revealed at the end of the trick. He cautions us that this transfer must be done without making any noise at all.

NEMO: If you allow the—the slightest suspicion about the fact that you *might have tossed it*, you're dead. People will say, "OK, he tossed it, we didn't see it go." It's too easy to say. That—that happened to me once, someone said that. And he says, "Oh, yeah, in fact." You [*inaudible*] you—you know it's good, but no. The dude he thinks that—"Oh, yeah! You tossed it and we didn't see it go." If there's a *"clack"* at the last moment, people say to themselves, "OK he tossed it."

NEMO: Si vous donnez le—le moindre doute sur le fait que vous *l'avez pu lancer*, c'est mort. Les gens vont dire, "OK, il l'a lancée, on l'a pas vue partir." C'est trop facile de dire. Ça m'est—ça ce m'est venu une fois, quelqu'un me l'a dit. Puis y dit, "Ah, oui, au fait." Toi [*inaudible*] tu—tu sais que c'est bon, mais non. Le mec y pense que—"Ah, oui! Tu l'as lancée et on n'a pas vue partir." Si y a un *"clac"* au dernier moment, les gens se disent, "OK il l'a lancée."

The hypothetical quotation at the beginning of this example suggests the intellectual work of a spectator endeavoring to reconstruct a magician's methods ("OK, he tossed it, we didn't see it go"). The subsequent quotation, using the nonreflexive verb *dire*, is an explanation of the effect Nemo reports that a spectator *actually* verbalized to him in front of a tableful of other spectators ("Oh, yeah! You tossed it and we didn't see it go"). In the final quoted utterance, Nemo imagines what hypothetical spectators say to themselves if they hear a suspicious noise at an inopportune moment: "OK he tossed it."

In practice, the boundary between reflexive speech (what is said to oneself) and reciprocal speech (what is said to one another) is a slippery threshold for magicians; as we see in this example, inner speech is also always potentially external speech. Spectator challenges are not only face threatening for the magician. Made within earshot of other spectators, they are potentially damaging to the overall experience—particularly insofar as spectator reactions are often an integral part of the performance (for an illustration of this, see Figure 12). Magicians therefore must approach spectators' negative assessment as possible sources of disruption. In this sense, the referential ambiguity of *se dire* is generally not a liability, but rather an expressive resource that speakers use productively to accomplish specific kinds of verbal projects.[62] Within the genre of staging talk, this ambiguity calls attention to the permeable boundary between what spectators say to themselves and what they say to each other.

Furthermore, it becomes clear in this example that when Nemo voices spectators' hypothetical inner speech, he is pointing not only ahead to future moments of performances, but also retrospectively back to previous performances. His ability to predict what potential spectators might think under certain conditions emerges from his experience of what actual spectators have said in similar situations. By invoking his past experience, Nemo establishes that spectator reactions to particular effects follow predictable patterns. In connecting his instructions about discouraging certain possible thought processes to verbal assessments he has received while performing, Nemo highlights his authority as a seasoned professional, also reminding us that even professionals must learn from their mistakes.

The capacity to talk about talk is a property all languages share, and that all speakers use in referring to conversations past, present, or future.[63] Magicians' ability to voice spectators' hypothetical perspectives, however, is a specialized and acquired skill based on experiences performing, watching other magicians perform, and conversing with colleagues. Pedagogically, such voicings give those learning magic insights into why a trick must be performed in a certain way.[64] Insofar as Nemo, Stefan, and Jérôme were "modeling"[65] a kind of expert speech practice prevalent in magicians' staging talk, their instructions can also be viewed as instances of "language socialization," learning through language and to use language,[66] which takes specialized forms in settings of skilled apprenticeship.[67] The ability to voice the viewpoint of hypothetical or possible spectators is a skill that novices will in turn acquire, by imitating their mentors and by gaining experience interacting with spectators themselves.

An important final consideration concerns temporality. Performances are ephemeral, and illusions fleeting. Magicos appreciate not only that audiences attempt to interpret illusions by reconstructing events in narrative form, but also that narratives allow performances to live on as reminiscences. They strategize to make their effects memorable as stories, and take feedback from spectators very seriously. For instance, one day Loïc told me about a frustrating experience he had testing out a new close-up effect the evening before. He had a spectator select a card and sign his name on it, and then shuffled it back into the deck. Loïc told the spectator he would deal the cards facing up, one by one, and asked him to put his hand over his own card before the next one was dealt. The spectator did as instructed, but when he looked under his hand, the card had vanished. Then Loïc took the card from inside his own zippered wallet. The amazed spectator brought a gaggle of friends to see Loïc later that evening, begging him to repeat the trick: " 'It was amazing! I put my hand right on the card,'" Loïc recalled him telling his friends, " 'but it had vanished. Then he found it somewhere else!' " Loïc was dejected. " '*Somewhere else?*' " he repeated in disbelief. He didn't know if the discovery of the card in the wallet complicated what was already a sufficiently powerful effect, or if he hadn't done enough to call attention to the wallet itself. Either way, he saw the previous performance as unsuccessful because the spectator could not produce the desired narrative, and vowed to continue experimenting until his presentation was sufficiently "storyable."[68]

· · · · ·

After me, multitalented Jean-Jacques took the stage. He not only performed a skillful comedy magic act, but also went on to juggle no less than six balls. Our youngest classmate, Antoine, had adopted the most risqué shtick: in the persona of a dissolute middle-aged businessman (with penciled-on five o'clock shadow), he performed a collection of effects involving alcohol, cigarettes, and gambling.

In my second turn, I stuck with the considerably more family-friendly theme of baked goods, performing a trick inspired by Mimosa (who happened to be in the audience that evening). At a meeting of the CFI earlier that year, he performed an effect called the Dancing Cane, in which the magician's walking stick flies in dizzying loop-de-loops around his or her body. Mimosa, a world-class juggler, infused it with a buoyant exuberance that left me utterly spellbound. "That's for me!" I thought. But rather than performing with a cane, I envisioned a French baguette defying gravity, and sailing gracefully through the air. (This would effectively be a visual pun: in French, the word baguette *designates both a loaf of bread and a magician's wand.)*

In order to learn the secret, I purchased a Dancing Cane from my favorite shop, Paris Magic. The knowledgeable clerk, Ratcékou, taught me how to perform the effect, and explained the underlying principle. Initially, I assumed I could simply outfit a real baguette with the same gimmick employed for the Dancing Cane. I gleaned further information from the technical forums on VM, and began experimenting with bread from my corner bakery. In an effect where less than a gram can make a world of difference, real bread was far too heavy to fly. I tried different procedures for making my baguettes more air-worthy—hollowing them, drying them, filling them with polystyrene foam—but still couldn't perfect the weight. I tried working with the fake plastic loaves used as decoration in Italian restaurants, again without success. Over the course of two months, I made dozens of trips to the hardware store, transforming my apartment into a mad scientist's laboratory—now I understood why Gaëtan Bloom said his favorite magic shop was the mammoth hardware store in the Bazar de l'Hôtel de Ville! When I finally unveiled the prototype at a meeting of the CFI, everyone assured me I had the world's first flying baguette. Several people even offered to buy it from me, but I refused to sell.

The night that I walked onstage with a baguette under my arm, I fancied I looked a real Parisian. I explained that I had found a boulangerie *whose imported Belgian yeast made their loaves so light that—and here the sound of a wistful saxophone cut me off. I let go of the baguette, and it began to sail through the air, up, down, and around and around my body. I danced with it briefly, then caught it in my hands.*

I found this performance to be such an intense high that the subsequent emotional crash knocked me out for days. Talking about the experience with other magicos, I learned that it was not uncommon to experience a welter of emotion progressing from stage-fright before, euphoria during, and depression after a performance. "Now you know what it's like," Nemo said. "With time, you learn to deal with it better, but it never goes away."

While the performance at Les Halles was, without a doubt, the emotional high point of my research, its symbolic culmination came a few weeks later, when I performed the same routine before a panel of five expert magicians—the admissions committee of the FFAP. After my performance and oral examination, the committee deliberated before informing me I had been admitted to the club. I leapt for joy, but my sense of legitimization didn't last for long.

None of the magicos I was closest with were members of the FFAP, and they looked bemusedly on my proud achievement. "Congratulations," one told me over the phone the next day. "You're now a card-carrying amateur." And he was right. Years later, videos of these performances seem glaringly amateurish. The awkward body language, the poor sense of timing, the inelegant handling of props—it all makes me cringe. But for the chance to experience some of the challenges magicians face every day, any embarrassment I may now feel was entirely worth it.

IDEOLOGIES OF LEARNING

The pathway to magicianship unfolds through dialectics of imitation and innovation. In a practice of overwhelmingly self-directed learning, magicos selectively take advantage of all the resources available: classes, lessons, lectures, clubs, peers, mentors, merchants, books, videos, and the Internet. By assimilating tricks created and performed by others, novices learn not only techniques but also ways to apply them to the production of illusion and strategies for presentation. Decisions about how to present effects in an act or in association with a stage persona comprise an essential part of creativity. I learned that magicians display cunning not just by deceiving people, but also through the inventive appropriation of tradition. Accordingly, in my Dancing Baguette routine, I appropriated a well-known effect, imitating established precedents and emulating Mimosa's stellar performance. But in changing the cane into a baguette and weaving a story about a fairy-tale bakery, I brought some degree of individuality to the interpretation of the canonical effect.

Magicos value both fidelity to conjuring traditions and originality in the presentation of effects. Given the way that novices progress, these two values sometimes seem at odds. A riveting discussion of this subject began when a fourteen-year-old novice with only four months of experience in magic addressed the following question to the VM forum: "What's wrong with copying a routine in its entirety (with the author's consent)?"[69] Sébastien Clergue was prompt to respond: "Quite simply because, within a trick, it is your personality, your style, your patter, your personal imprimatur that renders the magic your own. . . . By reproducing someone else's trick AS IS you will only succeed in erasing yourself, renouncing your personality, and becoming someone else's clone." Philippe expressed a contrasting opinion: "Before you can create, you need to have copied a lot. To find your personality, you need to have tested different styles, imitating your favorite magicians. That's how all learning unfolds; magic is no exception. . . . Telling beginners to start out by creating their own tricks is just bad advice. You might as well toss someone a violin and say, 'Go ahead, create. Come back when you've composed your first concerto.'" Philippe implied that the pathway to the mastery of technique entails the systematic imitation of exemplary routines.

Magicos voice strong beliefs about proper and improper pathways of apprenticeship, particularly at a moment when patterns of knowledge transmission are rapidly evolving due to novel information technologies as well as changing commercial practices. In the course of lifelong learning, most magicos today take advantage of all the resources available to them, but don't regard these resources as equivalent in terms of the learning outcomes they promote. Generally speaking, they esteem forms of knowledge transmission that require hard work and individual initiative or ingenuity, and many pride themselves on being autodidacts. Nevertheless, direct instruction or advice from experts is an essential feature of novices' informal apprenticeship (see Figure 4). Formal apprenticeship, in which a novice develops a privileged relationship with an individual master who imparts technical knowledge, an aesthetic sensibility, and a vocational ethic, remains a highly valorized mode of learning.

Those lucky enough to be taken under the wing of a distinguished expert in a relationship of formal apprenticeship speak with pride of their "master" (maître). One such person was Pallas, a retired engraver and a highly accomplished semiprofessional magician. Drafted to serve in the Algerian War, the slight, good-humored, and artistic young man caught the eye of a magician in his platoon whose assistant had been recently killed in combat. After three years of traveling war-torn Algeria

Figure 4. Arthur Tivoli (*right*) explains a balloon sculpture. Photo by the author.

entertaining the troops as the magician's new assistant, Pallas was discharged and moved to Paris. Seeking to continue his apprenticeship, he contacted the local branch of the FFAP (then AFAP). "Back then, there were only twelve or fifteen guys meeting in the back of a café." In sharp contrast with today, he recalled, "They all addressed each other as *vous!*"

Through the club, he began taking lessons from one of its members, René Gysin, whom he still refers to as "Master." Several years passed, and his master began charging him less and less for lessons. Finally he gave him his wand and said, "I'm going to teach you everything I know, with the one condition that you transmit it, in turn, to those who you deem worthy." For the next 30 years, Pallas studied with Gysin. "It was a lot like the apprenticeship (*compagnonnage*) I experienced as an engraver," he told me. "There was transmission from old to young, a spirit of the trade that went beyond professional rivalry, and an expectation of mutual assistance." On the day that I interviewed him in his home, Pallas showed me the wand his master had given him—a beautiful object of ebony and ivory that he still uses on special occasions. Before I left, he said that he wanted to "give me a gift" and imparted three secrets inherited from Gysin, including a card sleight called the Hofzinser Move. "With that you can kill a man," Pallas cautioned.

Though highly esteemed, privileged relationships of master-apprentice transmission can also engender anxieties of influence. For example, at one point or another, many Parisian close-up magicians have sought guidance from Bébel. Some ultimately find the gravitational pull of his idiosyncratic style too strong. "At one point I was taking lessons from Bébel," Loïc told me. "When I performed, people started to say I reminded them of him. It got me worried, so I called off the lessons." A virtuoso cardician in his own right, Loïc did not want to copy Bébel, but develop a signature style of his own. While magic is a kind of folk tradition in which virtually every performance relates intertextually to others, magicos seek to establish a personal approach to referencing, inflecting, and appropriating that tradition—similar to the way "saying something" in jazz improvisation involves the creative embellishment on an established repertoire and crafty "intermusical" references to other performances.[70]

Given the premium they place on originality, it is not surprising that magicos also value self-instruction as a privileged mode of knowledge acquisition. Older magicians, in particular, often boasted that, starting out at a time when instructional materials were hard to come by, they had no choice but to devise their own solutions to the effects they saw other magicians perform (a process that often results in the development of altogether new methods). Gaëtan Bloom told me how hard it was to find magic books in the Paris of his youth. "When I started out, you had to look high and low to find books. Now they're publishing a hundred a month!" Despite the availability of books today, the most popular instructional medium is by far video. "Books are great by comparison," Bloom said. "It's a medium that lets you use your imagination. The problem with DVDs is that the image is so strong it's virtually irresistible. The DVD is the best way to create clones." From Bloom's perspective, the uncertainty involved in coordinating the various aspects of performance—gesture, body language, timing, patter, spoken intonation, and so on—can make it difficult to learn from a book. Yet the resultant hysteresis or "free play" leaves room for innovative individual adaptations.[71] Instructional video, on the other hand, eliminates much of this ambiguity: one sees the trick performed in real time, generally with live audience reactions (real or simulated), and the technical explanations leave little doubt about executing the sleights. Most magicos agree that the danger of such an efficient mode of instruction is, as Bloom said, unreflective mimesis—or "cloning."

Copying without understanding can lead to other problems besides imitation. Even Loïc, barely half Bloom's age, complained, "When I started out, I just had a little magic book—and it was really hard! Now you've got dudes who buy a DVD to learn a few routines that they never really master, and after six months they blow it off to take up knitting or building model boats. Or else they post a question on VM like, 'I need to make the four aces disappear at the end of "Twisting the Aces." How do I do it?' First off, there's no point, but even if there were, there are a million ways it could be done. Figure it out for yourself!" The trick Loïc mentions, "Twisting the Aces," is one of the most famous card tricks in all of magic. Created by Canadian magician Dai Vernon, it uses only the four aces, which magically turn from face down to face up, one by one.[72] Loïc says there is "no point" to making the aces vanish, because this additional effect is an extraneous addition to Vernon's elegant routine.

Similarly, in my magic class with Jérôme at the Musée de la Magie, a student demonstrated a version of this trick that ended with the red aces in one hand and the black aces in the other. This infuriated Jérôme. "The end's no good," he said. "Separating the colors just adds meaningless confusion. Dai Vernon didn't write it like that! The effect is that the aces turn over one by one, period. What are you going to do next, have pictures of rainbows appear on the cards, then families of rabbits? No one gives a damn!" This concern about the modification of Vernon's routine, I think, reflects less a donnish devotion to tradition than the conviction that certain landmark tricks are so harmoniously coherent that they achieve a kind of aesthetic perfection. For magicians, "Twisting the Aces" is like a Bach fugue. To appreciate this, however, a novice needs to acquire something beyond virtuosic skill, that which magicos call *culture magique* (magic culture).

Magic culture can be defined as familiarity with and appreciation of the artistic and technical heritage of conjuring. It entails both knowledge of the origin and development of tricks and techniques, and insight into the theoretical bases of magic as an art. Possessing magic culture can bestow a reputation of expertise, for which a magician might be sought out and sometimes paid for technical advice or asked to adjudicate intellectual property disputes. Conversely, lacking magic culture can be a cause for derision. For instance, Nemo told me that several magicos we knew from the Illegal, all skilled cardicians, came to see him perform at a Pigalle cabaret. At the beginning of his routine, he stretches his arms to "warm up," using a simple party gag to create the blood-curdling sound of snapping bones. "They came up to me after and said, 'That was great— but how'd you do the arm?' You see? Cards, cards, cards, cards—and then you totally blow them away [*tu leur niques la gueule*] with an old gag like that! It's a lack of magic culture, plain and simple."

CONCLUSION

Performing magic successfully involves both mind and hand. In acquiring manual skills, magicians seek to imprint sequences of gesture so deeply that they become entirely unconscious automatisms, an ideal reflected by Stefan's pedagogical concept of the magical *kata*. Magicos revel in achieving high levels of skill, and invest countless hours in rehearsing techniques and training their bodies. "Practice is pleasure," Jérôme told me. "It's a pleasure to practice card sleights. Even if I tire myself out for two hours working on a [sleight], I don't care, because I know if I do it thousands of times I'll be perfect." While learning new material sometimes requires undivided attention, he said he often practices card manipulations while watching movies or listening to music. "I even practice with my eyes closed. If I go blind, I can perform my act just like I do now. Everything is tactile. By practicing, practicing, practicing, it becomes your second nature." Tireless practicing in pursuit of technical excellence paradoxically culminates in the concealment of all traces of skill; magicians strive for an ideal something like the notion of *sprezzatura* that Castiglione describes in the *Book of the Courtier*: "to practice in all things a certain nonchalance which conceals all artistry." [73]

Robert-Houdin wrote, "Although everything that we say during a performance may be nothing but—let's not mince words—a tissue of lies, you must inhabit your role so deeply that you believe yourself in the truth of the falsehoods you spout. Your conviction will inevitably inspire conviction in spectators." [74] To accomplish this paradoxical state of believing in deceptive actions that one knows to be false, covert manipulations must be rendered as unconscious as possible. "You have to forget that you're a cheater," Jérôme explained during the course of one lesson. "If you're hiding something in your hand, you can't think, 'There's a card, there's a coin, there's a trick.' You have to believe your hand is empty. Otherwise people will intuit that something's wrong."

This ideal of an estranged perspective on one's own actions is the apogee of the kind of allocentric orientation to spectators' experiences that magic instructors seek to instill. In the examples discussed in this chapter, expert magicians design instruction to highlight the importance of moving from a subjective to an intersubjective perspective on performing magic. They enhance novices' capacity for "audience design" [75] by building the audience perspective into the form of instruction itself through the extensive use of hypothetical reports of inner speech. The ability to see magic through spectators' eyes is particularly important given the role of audiences in co-constructing illusion. "Magic," Nemo was fond of saying, "is like an empty present you give to people. It's beautifully wrapped, but there's nothing inside. The spectators themselves fill it up."

Acquiring the cunning intelligence and magic culture necessary to think like a magician is not easy. For some veteran magicos, the novel modes of knowledge transmission ascendant in magic today—video and the Internet—appear to be largely at odds with an artistic ethos that values hard work, individual initiative, and originality in the appropriation of tradition.[76] In the accelerated circulation of magicians' secrets that has developed with new forms of consumerism and new mediating technologies, some magicos see agents of dissipation and decline that may ultimately imperil the practice of magic itself. "We're in a period when the secret is less and less deserved," Gaëtan Bloom told me. "Not long ago, the notion of secrecy was something much more powerful than it is now among magicians. Today it seems like everything is open and accessible. But magic still needs the notion of secrecy. So of course magicians go chasing after new discoveries and unknown things. But something has been lost."

TWO The Social Life of Secret Knowledge

Entertainment magic's first ethnographer was not a modern anthropologist but a freethinking sixteenth-century English lawyer. Appalled by witch hunts sweeping across Europe, Reginald Scot set out to prove that witchcraft was not a diabolical conspiracy against Christendom but a mass delusion. To document public credulity about apparently supernatural phenomena, Scot conducted fieldwork in London fairgrounds and markets among illusionists (or "jugglers," as he called them) and peddlers of magic tricks. In the process, he claimed to have acquired conjuring skill sufficient to make witch hunters "sweare [he] were a witch, and had a familiar divell at commandement." [1] Instead, in 1584 he published *The Discoverie of Witchcraft*, a book explaining magicians' secrets, that he "might proove [witch hunters] fooles."

While King James had copies of the book burned, it remains, in the minds of many magicians, one of the first manuals on the art of magic. Its pages resonate with Scot's sense of wonder at magicians' astounding ingenuity. Upending associations of magical trickery with diabolical forces, he identified a spark of divine intelligence in conjurers' crafty illusions. "It hath pleased GOD," he wrote, "to shew unto men that seeke for knowledge, such cunning in finding out, compounding, and framing of strange and secret things, as thereby he seemeth to have bestowed upon man, some part of his divinitie." [2]

Like Scot, my research inclines me to marvel at the special kind of intelligence magicians marshal to beguile the eye and ensnare the mind. As we have seen in the previous chapter, it is a form of intelligence both embodied and abstract, connecting the meticulous virtuosity of imperceptible gestures with a devious grasp on the mechanics of cognition, perception, and desire. A vast, transnational system of expertise with a wide range of specialized subfields, it flourishes with little institutional support. Cultivated in social gatherings where magicians engage in staging talk, it is imparted from expert to novice through face-to-face or mass-mediated instruction, objectified in commercial props and gimmicks, and ultimately mastered in the proving ground of live performance. It is also an inevitably guarded intelligence, keenly attuned to the pressures and pleasures of secrecy. Spectators can't help but sense its presence when a magician fools them, but laymen rarely catch more than a glimpse of its elusive form.

Secrets are the distillation of magicians' ingenuity, the locus of their surprising skill, and their principal mechanism for promulgating illusion in the world. In this chapter I explore what Scot called magicians' "cunning in finding out, compounding, and framing of strange and secret things," [3] and their traffic in secrets more broadly. Secrets are complicated things, and those of magicians especially so. Because concealing knowledge produces value through the exclusion of outsiders and revealing knowledge produces value through the incorporation of insiders, centripetal and centrifugal forces pull and push on the secret. In his germinal essay, Simmel writes that "out of the counterplay of these two interests, in concealing and revealing, spring nuances and fates of human interaction that permeate [the secret] in its entirety."[4] It is not uncommon for possessors of secrets to flaunt them, revealing the existence of concealment but not its object.[5] Tricks are, in this regard, ingenious mechanisms for flaunting secrets in performance.

Although magicians, as a rule, never reveal secrets to laymen, they circulate secrets widely—but not freely—among themselves. In many ways the delicate equilibrium between magicians' knowledge and spectators' ignorance is sustained simply by the curiosity of the former and the lethargy of the latter. While many spectators profess intense curiosity about magicians' secrets at the moment of performance, few subsequently avail themselves of the Internet, a bookstore, or a library to find out how a magician's tricks were actually accomplished. Those who do may be well on the road to becoming magicians themselves. Thus, while much of magicians' "secret" knowledge is widely available, the acquisition of it is largely on a self-selecting basis.

Many of the skills that magicians employ and the tricks they perform emerge from an international folk tradition of shared knowledge that constitutes a vast public domain. Yet magic is also a generative system of technical knowledge, developing and expanding through innovations that constantly produce new objects of concealment. The circulation of knowledge whose value fundamentally depends on exclusivity raises a paradox neatly summed up in a fortune cookie I recently received in my favorite Chinese noodle joint: "A secret is no longer a secret by the time it gets to you." *So how do magicos sustain an aura of exclusivity even as they put secrets into circulation?*

This chapter traces what we might imagine as the "life cycle" of a secret among magicians, from creation to circulation and, in some cases, destruction. I show that creating a secret is both a technical and a social accomplishment involving calculated revelations to other magicians. While magicos routinely share secrets with each other, as we shall see, they carefully manage circulation in order to avoid the dispersal of precious knowledge. The ultimate form of dispersal—the divulgation of secrets to laymen—is so repugnant that magicos characterize it as a form of desecration.

CREATING SECRETS

Innovation in magic follows a variety of paths and manifests itself in different ways, but always exhibits certain key characteristics. Renowned British magician Nevil Maskelyne defines invention as "the production of some novelty, in either principle, construction, method, or purpose, not merely put forward as a vague idea, but worked out in a practicable form."[6] The arenas of innovation Maskelyne identifies correspond to different facets of conjuring as a technical system. What magicians call "principles" are general illusionary procedures that can be variously configured for use in a range of tricks; for instance, many magicians would consider "misdirection" one of the art's most basic principles. Principles can be instantiated in what Maskelyne terms "constructions" (i.e., technologies) or "methods" (i.e., techniques). Novelty of "purpose" involves the application of previously known constructions or methods in the production of unprecedented effects. Most innovations in magic—close-up magic at least—are new effects involving old techniques. New methods or constructions are less common. New principles are so seldom seen that Maskelyne called them "the most desirable discovery" in magic.[7]

In the course of my fieldwork, I met someone who made just such a discovery. His name is Christian Girard. Among magicos, I commonly heard him referred to as a genius. Identifying himself as a *pure* researcher with little interest in applying his inventions to performing, Girard has a scientist's eye for discerning hidden patterns in formal systems and an artist's ability to modulate those patterns in creative ways. Trained as a painter at the École Nationale des Beaux Arts in Lyon, he now makes a living teaching magic and acoustic guitar. When I visited his home in a cozy Paris suburb, the boyish, forty-something Girard took me on a tour of his creative pursuits that began with student paintings, seriated according to the styles of modern masters from Cézanne to the abstract expressionists. Then he took out his guitar and played a rollicking blues improvisation in the fingerpicking style of Big Bill Broonzy.

"Whenever something exists, I try to do it," Girard said by way of explaining his rigorous dilettantism. His entire house seemed like a giant laboratory with his so-called experiments unfolding in every nook and cranny. In his bedroom, he showed me a stack of newly discovered palindromes. In his office, a pile of scrap paper with portmanteau neologisms scrawled by the hundreds, for instance: *dionysauce*, "an aphrodisiac preparation used to garnish food at Bacchanals;" and *monopolyp* "a tumor afflicting people allergic to board games."[8] The basement revealed an immense collection of puzzles, brainteasers, and mechanical toys piled in several dozen overflowing cardboard boxes. As we haphazardly excavated, Girard alighted upon a Rubik's cube whose colored squares had been replaced with words such that, however the cube was manipulated, sentences remained legible in every direction. "For me, this is worth as much as a Vermeer," Girard said, tossing it back into his treasure trove. Finally, the subject turned to magic. I knew Girard's inventive prowess from a widely circulated 2001 instructional video called *Scrunchy Magic*, containing hours of effects with an improbable medium: the brightly colored elastic hair ties popular with teenage girls in the 1980s.[9] But this didn't prepare me for what he showed me that afternoon—one of the most ingenious card tricks I'd ever seen.

Girard gave me a card with a picture of a bearded maharaja, and asked me to insert it into the middle of a normal deck of facedown playing cards. "Wouldn't it be amazing if, by chance, you inserted the Indian king between two Western kings?" I agreed it would be. Girard carefully removed the maharaja, sandwiched between the cards on either side of it. He placed all three cards on the table and turned them over. In fact, I had placed the Indian king between two Western queens: spades and clubs. "You know, in India they have queens as well," Girard said. He turned the queens face down, and rotated the remaining card. In place of the bearded maharaja, I now saw the face of a lovely young woman. Further examination revealed that the image on the card was, in fact, reversible: one way it looked like a maharaja, but inverted, it looked like an Indian queen. "So you've figured out the trick!" Girard smiled. "It's an optical illusion that depends on the orientation of the card." At this point, I relaxed, assuming Girard was explaining the trick to me as a fellow magician. Then things took a strange turn. "The illusion is so strong," he continued, "that the Western queens are also susceptible." He turned over the other two cards, which had never left my sight. Instead of queens, they were the kings of spades and clubs. My head swam with wonder.

Girard explained that he awoke one morning with the idea of this new principle—using reversible images in card magic—fully formed in his mind. Eventually, he had the cards manufactured and published a book, *Désillusions d'optique* (*Optical Disillusions*), with routines created by internationally known magicians like Gaëtan Bloom, Max Maven, and Jean-Jacques Sanvert. He stipulated that spectators must always know the principle of the cards' reversibility, challenging the authors to locate the magic somewhere else in their routines. As he demonstrated by performing his own routine (entitled "They Play Cards in India, Too"), the results were astounding.

Girard's creative process reminded me of the beautiful observation that, among Hausa weavers, "innovation is a skill. It is the refinement of curiosity."[10] His mind seemed to be constantly scanning for new perplexities to embellish upon. Like computer hackers and scientists,[11] magicos evaluate innovations on aesthetic grounds, and consider particularly cunning sleights, gimmicks, or routines things of great beauty. Girard was rightly proud of the subtle new principle and its elegant application in a startling effect. Indeed, he had created a new tool for magicians to use, and hoped they would employ it in creative and unforeseeable ways. Though he is not religious, Girard told me he believes in "survival of the soul through the transmission of information," less through the genes you pass on to your children (he has two daughters) than through the cultural information you pass on through your creations (see Figure 5). "I have a huge stockpile of magic tricks. I feel bad for them until they're published. The most important thing is what happens after the creation of something—how people make use of it. Creations need to live and propagate."

"Publishing," in the context of magic, means putting a new idea into circulation by marketing it as a trick, writing about it in a book or periodical, explaining it on an instructional DVD, including it in photocopied notes to sell on the lecture circuit, or posting it on the Internet. On the last two days of its annual magic convention, the FFAP even al-

Figure 5. Christian Girard (*center*) watches an exchange of secrets. Photo by the author.

lows participants to record new ideas for release on a *Secrets of the Year* DVD, "as a way of inscribing themselves in history," one of the organizers said. Before an idea is objectified or inscribed in a format that will allow it to circulate independently, the only way to learn it is from the inventor directly. If the inventor elects not to share it with other magicians, then he or she theoretically can enjoy sole use of a new discovery. However, another magician who came to possess the same idea, through either independent invention or plagiarism, could publish it and gain full credit. Indeed, it is not uncommon to hear complaints about unscrupulous magicians seeking attribution for innovations they did not originate. But what does it mean to *own* a secret in the first place, and what kinds of advantages does ownership confer?

While there is some direct economic interest in claiming an innovation to package for sale in a trick or instructional materials, most of the secrets that preoccupy close-up magicians are essentially valuable as symbolic capital, as extensions of an inventor's reputation. A reputation for creativity, cunning, and magic culture—all important components of innovation—is tremendously valuable. It can establish a magicos as a prominent figure, sought out by others for his or her expertise. An increase in one's reputation can thereby lead to participation in more dynamic networks of knowledge exchange, helping to secure access to rarefied spheres of cutting-edge technical knowledge. Furthermore, having a reputation as an inventor can open up doors for going on lecture tours, domestically and abroad, and create a market for one's tricks and publications.

Déposer is the verb magicos use for the action of establishing ownership of a newly invented trick or technique. It translates as "to register," and outside of magicians' argot, it refers to the procedure of legally filing a patent for an invention. Stage magicians sometimes submit legal patents for illusions that can involve millions of dollars in research and development, or contractually bind their crews to keep trade secrets. However, few of the things close-up magicians call inventions would qualify for patent protection—certainly not a principle or a sleight. Most secrets of this sort are initially established as inventions simply by showing them off. I asked Nemo to explain the process to me. "In the magic world, when you say *déposer*, it means officially showing a technique to certain people," he said. "That way, people know it's yours. You have to show it to influential people, magicians who are relatively representative and trustworthy, so that, if they see other people using the technique, they can say it belongs to you. It's like registering a patent for a new idea so that no one can touch it, but for magicians it's basically an ethical code."

Openly showing a new invention to other magicians can be a risky affair, and requires an element of trust. Before it has been definitively established as *someone's* property, an invention can be plagiarized or stolen, or it can simply lapse into the public domain detached from any claims of authorship. Thus, when Gaëtan Bloom showed me the footage of his "human vacuum cleaner" routine, he said, "When I show this effect to magicians, I'm going to have to perform all over the place, as fast as I can. Otherwise someone will steal the idea." Ultimately, the surest way to register an invention is by publishing it in an article, book, or video, or by including it in a trick made available for sale, but this maximally diffuses the secret among magicians, decreasing its novelty. However claims of ownership are secured, they make a secret a kind of "inalienable wealth" [12] that continues to remain an extension of its inventor even as it circulates.

Like a legal patent, the registration process that magicos follow produces ownership of knowledge through the disclosure of secrets. Marilyn Strathern explains that "the patent attaches the invention exclusively to the inventor. In doing so it also detaches it in the form of knowledge: the patent agreement compels the inventor to yield information to the world about how to re-create the artefact. Patents simultaneously produce private property and public(ly available) information." [13] As with industrial patents, the promulgation of new secrets potentially can spark ripple effects of innovation, as other magicians incorporate them into original effects or build upon them to generate other new techniques. Once a secret has been made public in the magic world, its spread is hard to control. For this reason, an inventor may want to keep a new discovery for personal use before registering it. When the decision has been made to register a secret, it must be done perspicaciously, before unauthorized circulation can begin. An inventor may stipulate how recipients can use and circulate secrets, and may authorize other magicians to publish or market a secret as part of a trick or routine.

The nature of innovation in magic leaves ample room for conflict and confusion over intellectual property (IP) rights. While there are profoundly original thinkers in magic, no one invents *ex nihilo*. Conscious and unconscious influences stream in. Inventions often begin as improvements on existing techniques, or emerge from the search for innovative methods for existing effects. As Strathern writes, "at the point of patenting, an invention becomes a 'place' or passage point at which diverse expertise, all the knowledge that went into creating it, is gathered together and condensed into a single entity." [14] Ultimately, the magic community may come to regard some putative innovations as too derivative or too superficially different from their sources to constitute real inventions. Furthermore, as we have seen in the previous chapter, innovation in magic, as in other fields, often takes a collaborative form. Indeed, small groups of magicians often spend hours on end "sessioning," that is, working together to refine their skill and develop new ideas; magicos call these working groups *ateliers de réflexion* (brainstorming workshops), or simply use the verb *bosser* (to work). Claims of invention can unintentionally—or intentionally—efface this kind of collaborative work, just as patenting a new technology "[truncates] the network of scientists behind the invention into those who claim the final inventive step that leads to a patentable product." [15]

Innovators can use a variety of strategies to maximize the value of their innovations. As part of a super-secretive stratum of close-up innovators and cognoscenti magicos refer to as *l'underground*, Daniel Rhod was well positioned to explain these strategies to me. "Some magicians like to show their inventions all over the place," he told me. "I wait for the perfect conditions. One year, at a convention, [a famous close-up magician] came up and asked me to show him something that would fool him. I got a deck of cards and said, 'Last night I dreamt I met a well-known magician at a convention and asked him to think of a card. I woke up and placed that card on top of my deck. What card do you think it was?' He named a card. I told him to turn over the card on top of the deck. He jumped back! It was the one he named. He begged me for an explanation. I told him it would be in my next book. 'How much is the book?' he said. I told him it would be 100 euros. 'I'll take three and pay you on the spot, just please explain it to me now!' I told him he'd have to wait. The next day he came back and said he had told everybody at the convention about the amazing trick and begged me to do it again, but I refused. The last day of the convention, he came back and told me he thought he had the solution—and he was almost right, save one crucial element. All this serves to create demand, so people talk about your tricks, but can't get an easy explanation."

In this way, Rhod and other inventors use extreme secrecy to increase the value, longevity, and reputation of their inventions. This strategy of adding value by engineering scarcity is reminiscent of the system of initiatory metaphysical knowledge that Fredrik Barth documented among the Baktaman of Papua New Guinea, for whom "the value of information seemed to be regarded as inversely proportional to how many share it. From this, it would follow that if you seek to *create* highly valued information . . . you must arrange worship so that few persons gain access to these truths. But there is also a paradox in these premises: if the value of information is greater, the fewer persons have it, its value is greatest when it stops being information at all: when only one person has it and he does not transmit it." [16] Rhod seeks to restrict the circulation of his inventions to approach these conditions as nearly as possible; paradoxically, sharing secrets can expand reputation, while also diminishing the intrinsic value of the secret as property.

Rhod explained that when he publishes more esoteric material, he only produces his books in limited runs, numbering each copy. "That way, they retain a higher value for a longer period of time." In fact, they often increase in value: one book sold out of its initial run in a year, and listed for three times its original price two years later. Similarly, while the French National Library owns a full collection of *Imagik*, the magic journal he edited for several years, he had the title cataloged as "confidential," hence unavailable for consultation in the near future. When he wants to keep a secret but at the same time protect it from unauthorized use, Rhod might also publish it in a restrictive fashion. For instance, he showed me an astounding coin sleight he developed called the "ideal vanish" whereby a coin disappears from inside a closed fist. He included it on twenty videotapes with a copyright protection system linking each copy to the purchaser's name. He also published a written description of the sleight, without illustrations, in the last issue of *Imagik*. Without visual cues, it can be extremely difficult to achieve a satisfactory "handling" (that is, the embodied execution) of a sleight. Rhod said, "Someone who works hard will figure out a satisfactory handling independently, but most people will not put in enough effort. So it's registered [*déposée*] without being diffused [*diffusée*]."

Another strategy that inventors use to extend their influences involves constituting oneself as what scholars in science and technology studies call an "obligatory point of passage," that is, a junction in a network of skilled practice that actors must move through in order to accomplish their personal projects.[17] For instance, when Rhod published *Techno Pièces*, a manual of sleight-of-hand technique for coin magic that quickly became an indispensable reference work, he strategically placed a sleight of his own alongside the canonical antecedents, staking a credible claim to a position in the pantheon of close-up innovators.[18]

Innovators commonly begin with an idea for an effect and develop new techniques or applications of extant techniques as they search for an adequate method to enact the illusion they imagine. Often this entails some trade-offs. Bloom told me that, when he imagines a new effect, "the magical reflex is to say, 'Yes, it can be done.' Then it's a question of compromises. There's a joy in arriving at the end and having a solution of pure simplicity." Rhod said his method is to imagine the "ideal effect" and then work as long as it takes to make it possible. Sometimes inspiration comes from other magicians. For instance, he told me that, watching television one evening, he saw a magician do an incredible trick: the performer had a spectator shuffle a deck of cards, then name any four of a kind. As soon as the spectator indicated her choice, the magician did a single manipulation and produced the four cards. "I asked around," Rhod said. "No one knew who the performer was or how he did the trick. I spent three years trying to figure out the principle. When I did, it represented the culmination of twenty-five years of research in magic. One evening I was giving a lecture, and explained the effect. Someone in the back of the room said, 'I'm the one who did that trick on TV, but your method is so much better! I just used an accomplice.' "

Like cinema, music, or architecture, magic employs techniques and technologies that can be said to advance, creating new expressive opportunities.[19] This may mean that the distance between an "ideal effect" and the technically feasible effect decreases with time.[20] Rhod illustrated this for me with the example of levitation: "The ideal effect is that a person flies, period. Robert-Houdin developed the technique of levitating his son on a rod. Eventually somebody said, 'That's good, but it would be great if there was no visible support.' Next, someone said, 'It would be great if the levitated person could be moved in two dimensions.' Then three dimensions. Finally, we arrived at David Copperfield's flying illusion [an effect in which the magician soars freely around the theater]. It's as close as you can get to realizing the eternal dream of flight. That's progress!" Of course, Copperfield performs illusions on a scale that few magicians can hope to emulate; but even in the realm of close-up sleights, progressive improvement is possible. For these magicians, techniques are themselves technologies.

In 1991, Rhod founded an organization called the Société Internationale des Arts Magiques (SIAM), which he directed for five years. "The SIAM was created in order to establish a database of magic inventions and to inform its members about how to protect their creations," he explained to me in an email. "It got involved in a number of conflicts to protect the rights of members whose work was copied by magic dealers or other magicians. The ultimate goal was to create a company that would manage magicians' intellectual property rights, like recording artists have." While the SIAM dissolved in 2004, magicos continue to register their inventions by informally presenting them to each other. A network of sufficiently influential magicians who can corroborate an inventor's claims to have developed a technique in a particular form at a particular time is necessary for securing IP rights. These adjudicating parties should also have an adequate level of expertise for judging whether the technique is sufficiently different from its sources to constitute a real innovation, and for determining if it has unknown precedents in magic's long history. As Bruno Latour argues, innovation is both a technical and a social accomplishment.[21]

While magicos primarily secure IP claims by publishing or informally registering their inventions, and augment the value of secrets through intertwining strategies of concealment and revelation, they sometimes turn to the legal system to protect their property interests. According to legal experts, French patent law extends protection to magical technologies, such as a novel apparatus for making an assistant disappear, but not to magical techniques, such as a novel sleight for vanishing a coin.[22] While sleight of hand falls into a category of technical procedures, including recipes for food and perfume, that cannot be patented, the published description of such procedures can be copyright protected. A magic effect— the disappearance of an assistant or the vanish of a coin—cannot, in principle, be protected under regnant IP law, but a specific *presentation* of an effect can be copyrighted, and many magicians have indeed registered descriptions and recordings of their routines. As the property relations most important to close-up magicians—those associated with the ownership of sleights—are not legally recognized, the informal system of registration, enforced by moral sanction, functions effectively to protect their IP claims.

American attorney and magician Jacob Loshin has recently shown "how the magic community has developed a particular set of informal norms and sanctions for violators, which go some distance toward protecting intellectual property in the absence of law" and which is "uniquely suited to the special demands of the magic community."[23] Generally speaking, the norms that Loshin identifies among American magicians are the same as those I encountered among French magicos; indeed, magicians perceive their IP prerogatives as having a global reach. As in other communities of cultural producers where norm-based IP systems function as alternatives to legal regimes, the consequences of violating magicians' moral code can be permanent ostracism. For instance, elite chefs share information with colleagues who respect the culinary community's IP norms, while "violators . . . are punished by a refusal to provide further information and by a lowered reputation."[24] Stand-up comics refuse to share a billing with colleagues known to steal others' material, making it hard for anyone who violates IP norms to succeed in the comedy business.[25] In magic, those who violate IP norms—be they performers or merchants—not only will suffer from a diminished reputation, but also will no longer be trusted with secret information, and may even be forced from the magic business altogether.

In the section that follows, I look in greater detail at the preferred practices that sustain magicians' informal IP regime in the absence of legal enforcement. In particular, I consider how experts instill an ethos of respect for IP norms in novices in the course of routine instruction. While these norms seldom are enumerated explicitly, old-timers tacitly reinforce them through the deference they exhibit, and in their responses to newcomers who fail to adhere to customary standards of behavior. Furthermore, like any close-knit community, magicos gossip incessantly. From the stance and tone of the stories one hears about magicians who violate IP norms, one quickly learns the difference between proper and improper modes of conduct, for, as Lave and Wenger argue, "apprenticeship learning is supported by conversations and stories about problematic and especially difficult cases." [26] For instance, hanging out in a magic shop one afternoon, Christian Girard told a group of magicos about someone who was showing off one of his techniques around Paris without permission. When confronted, the other magician denied the allegations. To make matters worse, he said that, on tour in the United States, he had shown the technique to some top American magicians who thought it was extraordinary. "He said he always cited me, of course. You expect me to believe that? If he didn't cite me in France, you expect me to believe he cited me on the other side of the Atlantic? And even if he did, two days later, each of those American magicians is going to have derived three variants and claimed them as their own."

Participating in the exchange of secrets, one gradually assimilates rules governing concealment and revelation in the world of magic. Conforming to community norms seems to maximize the long-term profitability of exchange: attributing secrets to innovators and teachers can be a way to build one's reputation by proclaiming membership in prestigious networks of reciprocal exchange, and to establish one's credentials as a trustworthy exchange partner. At the same time, magicians also master strategies of play for calculating and maximizing personal advantage through exchange. In a general sense, the self-interested goal of exchange is to give as little as possible and receive as much as possible. If secrets are given too freely, they lose value, but one cannot receive secrets without giving something. Tallying relative gains or losses for every act of revelation, magicians learn to be chary of their secrets. As we have seen, even when they appear to give, they are also often keeping by withholding personal handlings. In this way, novices inevitably acquire what I will call the secretive *habitus*—the "durable, transposable dispositions" [27]—of a magicos, just as apprentices in other fields are transformed as persons through the acquisition of skill.[28]

CIRCULATING SECRETS

When I visited amateur magician Pierre Guédin in rural Burgundy, the members of his tight-knit local magic club prepared an elaborate initiation ceremony for me: first, they escorted me through the heart of Dijon, revealing hidden mysteries of the medieval city in Old French verse. Then, in an ancient courtyard, we donned wine-red druidic cloaks. They gave me initiatory emblems and bestowed upon me the Latin name Veterum Domum (Figure 6). This ritual, while undeniably impressive, was atypical; indeed, the Burgundian magicians created it for the occasion. Just because a ritual is invented or improvised, however, does not make it inauthentic.[29] Guédin and his friends channeled an ambient nostalgia for a time, real or imagined, when magic functioned along the lines of a medieval guild—with a strong sense of corporate identity and elaborate rituals of initiation. Above all, the ceremony playfully underscored the cultural importance of secrecy in conjuring, and very real parallelisms between the world of magic and a secret society.

Unlike secret societies, the magic community does not have widely recognized initiation rituals, but rather multiple points of entry accessed through the acquisition and display of skill. In magic, initiation is not a decisive event but an overwhelmingly self-directed journey of enskillment, punctuated by transformative encounters with other wayfarers. Today, many secrets are simply purchased. Virtually any bookstore or public library offers instructional literature on magic. Most magicians assimilate secrets alone, in the privacy of their home, practicing manipulations in the mirror, trying to recreate illusions from the pages of a book, or watching instructional videos. In addition to the half dozen magic shops in Paris, scores of online dealers are only a click away, offering not just instructional material but also professional-quality apparatus to anyone with a credit card.

Shopping for magic supplies on the Internet is a profoundly different experience from visiting a brick-and-mortar dealer. For a beginning magician, entering a magic shop can be a harrowing rite of passage: to examine any of the materials in forbidding display cases, one must generally ask for assistance. At first, I struggled to work up the courage to go

Figure 6. Pierre Guédin (*far right*) and his secret society of Burgundian magicians induct the author, aka Veterum Domum (*center*). Photo by Dorothée Guédin.

into a magic shop, then hurried in and hurried out, hoping not to attract attention to myself. As I gained in experience, I came to appreciate that magic shops are not just retail outlets. They are the caravanserai of the magic world, places to go to meet other magicians, share gossip, get news about recent innovations, and examine apparatus firsthand. The ultimate success of a magic dealership depends in no small part on the personality of the shopkeeper, who is sometimes also the owner: for artists who are primarily self-trained and self-produced, they furnish vital technical and creative input. The bonds of trust are fragile, however, since the customers must believe that the dealer isn't just trying to make a sale, and the dealers must believe that a customer isn't just seeking free advice.[30]

There was a time when dealers could afford to be exclusive. Bloom told me that, when he was starting out as a boy, there was only one magic dealer in Paris, Mayette, the oldest magic shop in Europe. "The owner was a magician, and if he didn't want to sell to you, he wouldn't. 'Are you a professional?' he'd ask. 'No? Then beat it!' You could beg and plead: 'But I've got money! I can pay!' 'No! I said beat it!' It was a complete dictatorship." With the gradual evolution of magic from a predominantly professional entertainment industry to a predominantly amateur leisure activity, however, dealers now actively court amateurs and novices, particularly as heightened competition from the Internet continues to force brick-and-mortar shops out of business.

As novices gain gradual acceptance as legitimate participants in the magic scene, they will inevitably enter into exchange relationships with other magicians. Old-timers will welcome them with offers of secrets. With increasing expertise, these novices eventually will be able to reciprocate with secrets of their own, forging lasting exchange partnerships with other magicians. Revealing a secret to another magician—"tipping" in the parlance of American magicians—is a token of recognition, a gesture of inclusion, a microritual of initiation, and a move in a system of exchange. Tipping a secret means crossing a threshold, as an excluded party joins a network of people who possess a particular bit of restricted knowledge. For a beginner receiving basic knowledge, that network could be so vast that it encompasses most of the magicians in the world. For innovators like Bloom, Girard, or Rhod sharing an esoteric or newly originated technique, that network could be very small, comprising just a handful of peers. Either way, recipients of a secret become custodians of restricted knowledge shared with a constituency of other stakeholders whom they may or may not know. They, in turn, will decide when and where to conceal or reveal the secret invested in them. These decisions are not made in a moral vacuum, but rather within a "moral economy" [31] that successive transactions perpetuate.

When a magicos tips a secret in a public manner, for instance at a lecture or in print, there is a tacit understanding that it is being made available for use and circulation among members of the magic community at large. However, when tipping is directed to an individual or a select group, it is not uncommon for magicos to verbally qualify the offer of knowledge, stipulating how a secret should and should not be used or circulated. In this section, I look closely at several instances of tipping in which I took part as a recipient, and which I recorded and subsequently transcribed. My interest here is not in the secrets revealed, but rather in the manner of revelation. Examining the way magicos characterize, qualify, and verbally transact the act of tipping offers crucial insights into their underlying attitudes toward and understandings of secrecy. Focusing on the social and verbal life of secret knowledge, I consider how magicians' secrets are made—and made valuable—through the talk that surrounds their exchange.

Consider the following example. A self-proclaimed tinkerer (*bricoleur*), Cocodenoix (or Coco for short), is known among Paris magicians for his resourceful craftsmanship as well as his generosity. One day, I was at his apartment with Kalifa, a North African magicos seeking a procedure for manufacturing playing cards that would match his dark skin (to better dissimulate them). Coco had a perfect solution, which he demonstrated in detail. He warned Kalifa, "Keep this to yourself. It mustn't be disseminated too quickly because that lets us have something that other magicians don't have." The next month, a fellow student in my magic class at Les Halles needed a similar technique. When I called Coco to ask if I could pass his method on, he left this message on my answering machine: "There's no problem if you want to share it with your friend who's stuck. No problem—share, share. But just as long as it comes out slowly [*que ça arrive doucement*] so that not too many of us will know how to do it at first. That lets us have effects before other people, you know."

At the same time as he gave us a secret technique to use and even authorized its further circulation, Coco reiterated, on two separate occasions, a request that we reveal it sparingly so that we could "have effects before other people." By requesting that we limit circulation, Coco called attention to the exclusivity of the secret he was sharing, implicitly reaffirming a kind of commensality between us. His request is a reminder that the magic world is essentially a field of ideas in which uncommon knowledge is valuable intellectual capital that can be converted into social capital through the process of exchange.[32] In what follows, I consider the process of revealing secrets in greater detail, examining how structures of attitude and affect emerge from the texture of talk.

The next example is drawn from the magic class I took with Stefan. Before the transcript begins, I had shown Stefan a card sleight I had recently learned from a magic video by Jean-Pierre Vallarino. This initiated a discussion about other interchangeable sleights (that is, different methods for producing the same effect), which culminated with Stefan tipping a technique of his own devising. He begins by reassuring me of the unprecedented nature of the revelation.

STEFAN: So *this*, I can even tell you that I've [*laughs*] taught it to no one so you're the first. . . . Plus, you just traded me a beautiful one there, um, by—by—by Vallarino [*laughs*].	STEFAN: Donc ça, je peux même te dire que je l'ai [*laughs*] appris à personne donc t'es le premier. . . . En plus, tu viens de m'en échanger un beau là, euh, de—de—de Vallarino [*laughs*].

The assurance that he has "taught it to no one" signals that Stefan is putting a technique developed for his own personal use into circulation for the first time. This means that, in terms of scarcity, its value is relatively high, as is the risk of its revelation: should it escape my control, Stefan would most likely forgo any proprietary claim he might have otherwise enjoyed.

According to Simmel, the moment of revelation "constitutes the acme in the development of the secret; all of its charms are once more gathered in it and brought to a climax—just as the moment of dissipation lets one enjoy with extreme intensity the value of the object: the feeling of power which accompanies the possession of money becomes concentrated for the dissipator, most completely and sensuously, in the very instant in which he lets this power out of his hands."[33] Certainly, tipping a secret activates the latent pleasures of possessing exclusive knowledge, but it is not purely dissipative in the way Simmel seems to imply. Because of normative IP regimes among magicos, revealing secrets according to accepted conventions materializes and extends the reputations of inventors and engenders or perpetuates relationships of reciprocity. Thus, even though I was paying him for lessons, Stefan identifies this act of tipping as a reciprocal *exchange* of gifted knowledge, not a money-mediated transaction ("you just traded me a beautiful one there"). Furthermore, it is important to note that Stefan identifies the technique I gave him with the name of its inventor, Jean-Pierre Vallarino. When tipping a secret that one does not own, magicians consider attribution or citation to be the rule, and continue to circulate the technique with the name of its originator.

Following his preliminary remarks, Stefan taught me his technique. He didn't have a name for it (something essential for constituting of property), but devised one on the spot: "Multi-Cut Total False Cut." After making sure that I had retained the technique and properly written it down, Stefan follows his unbidden offer of a valued secret with the following request.

STEFAN: So that one try, ummm—Keep it kind of to yourself, huh? Um—

GRAHAM: Yeah.

STEFAN: I mean, if you have one or two, um, *close* magician friends, you can show them, huh? It's not—

GRAHAM: OK.

STEFAN: I'm not—I—I'll never publish things like that, it's . . . But, um—All I mean to say— Don't spread it in a way that's, um [*long pause*] well, too extensive, you know. . . . Keep it kind of to yourself?

GRAHAM: So that it stays—

STEFAN: So that it stays—

GRAHAM: unique?

STEFAN: Right. So that it stays unique, yes.

STEFAN: Bon c'lui-là t'essaies, euhhh—Tu le gardes plutôt pour toi, hein? Euh—

GRAHAM: Ouais.

STEFAN: Bon, si tu as un ou deux amis, euh, *proches* magiciens, tu peux leur montrer, hein? C'est pas—

GRAHAM: OK.

STEFAN: J'suis pas—Je—Je publierai jamais des trucs comme ça, c'est . . . Mais, euh—Tout ce que je veux dire—Tu diffuses pas d'une manière, euh [*long pause*] bon, importante, quoi. . . . Tu le gardes plutôt pour toi?

GRAHAM: Pour que ça reste—

STEFAN: Pour que ça reste—

GRAHAM: original?

STEFAN: Voilà. Pour que ça reste original, oui.

Notice that Stefan expands upon this request over several turns, offering a variety of modifications and qualifications. Rather than issuing an outright order (e.g., "Don't show anyone"), which would leave me few options between "compliance or confrontation,"[34] Stefan requests that I limit the circulation of "Multi-Cut Total False Cut" in a way that attenuates his proscriptive demands and reaffirms my freedom of action. For reasons I explain below, this suggests an awareness of the potential for conflict, and an effort to avoid it.

Because it entails an imposition on someone else's freedom and presupposes that the speaker has the authority to so impose, a request of any sort is what Brown and Levinson call an inherently "face threatening act."[35] They argue that, across languages and cultures, people making requests use "politeness strategies" to mitigate the potential for conflict. Stefan's request exhibits a number of such strategies. First, it expands over several utterances, in which Stefan repeats and rearticulates the core directive, a strategy that can be used "to create vividness and/or to indicate tentativeness."[36] Stefan modifies the initial articulation of the request with *plutôt* (kind of), a hedge word that diminishes certainty or commitment, conveying that the directive is not categorical, but rather affords some latitude ("keep it kind of to yourself").[37] He goes on to further attenuate the request, offering possible exceptions ("if you have one or two *close* magician friends, you can show them"). Then he downplays the seriousness of the request, claiming, "I'll never publish things like that," a statement that implies he is not seeking public recognition for this invention. Next he reformulates the request in a variant form ("don't spread it in a way that's too extensive"), before reiterating it in its original form. The expansion of the request allows Stefan to add vividness while simultaneously minimizing face threat by offering exceptions and downplays that reaffirm his addressee's freedom of action.

In addition, Stefan's request employs so-called hesitators, which "occur when the speaker is uncertain of the impact of a request on the addressee. This real or conventional concern can be expressed by employing various means of hesitation, such as simple stuttering, repetition, or a combination of the two."[38] We can see stuttering and repetition, alongside other markers of hesitance like long pauses and the filler word *euh* (um). Stefan further modifies his initial request with a tag question *hein?* (huh?), which can imply uncertainty and avoidance of imposition on an addressee ("Keep it kind of to yourself, huh?").[39] The tag question *hein?* parallels the use of another sentence-final discourse marker, *quoi* (you know), which Stefan also employs ("Don't spread it in a way that's . . .

too extensive, you know"). Used like this, *quoi* "flags tentativeness," serving either to signal "inadequacy of expression . . . or to hedge an over-exaggerated claim."[40]

The clustering of so many verbal features associated with politeness indicates that the request to limit circulation is a very serious matter, but that Stefan is taking care to avert any conflict that it might occasion. Similar mitigating strategies are used in the next example I consider. The following conversation occurred during a weekend-long workshop on card magic Nemo offered to five adult students, including myself. At this point in the transcript, we are discussing a well-known sleight called the "Charlier Shuffle" (named for its inventor). Nemo introduced a variant ending that added a delightfully devious twist to the technique, and attributed it to his friend Christian Girard. Again, such attributions don't just credit inventors, but also refer to social relationships, evoke a sense of tradition, and propagate a system of mutual recognition. They express a *warrant* for transmission, and constitute an oral record of circulation.

The exchange below immediately follows Nemo's demonstration of the procedure.

NEMO: That, however, ummm, is something of Christian's, so we—

STUDENT: No.

NEMO: To you, I'll give it to you, alright, but well, um, I'm—we're not gonna make it official or whatever, um, that's it. It's—it's—it's—it's his—it's his—No, but—

GRAHAM: Make it official?

NEMO: No, but like, I—I—I don't want there to be traces of it everywhere—because it's—it—it—Afterwards who knows, huh? People learn it, that's it, they [*makes a gesture of something flying away and whistles*]

NEMO: Ça, en revanche, euhhh, c'est un truc de Christian, donc on—

STUDENT: Non.

NEMO: Je vous le donne, vous voilà, mais bon, euh, j'vais—on va pas l'officialiser ou quoi, euh, voilà. C'est—c'est—c'est—c'est à lui—c'est à lui—Non, mais—

GRAHAM: Officialiser?

NEMO: Non, mais genre, je—je—j'veux pas qu'il y ait des traces partout—parce que c'est—ce—ce—Après on sait pas, hein? On l'apprend, v'là, on le [*makes a gesture of something flying away and whistles*]

Here, Nemo essentially requests that addressees limit circulation of the secret he has tipped using a politeness strategy Brown and Levinson call "indirection," which mitigates face threats by conveying a directive in a roundabout manner.[41] To "ground"[42] his request, he establishes that the technique belongs to Christian, and that there is a danger of other magicians circulating it in a way that would compromise Christian's rightful ownership. He says that he is not giving the technique "officially" and that he doesn't "want there to be traces of it everywhere." Without explicitly going "on record" with the request,[43] Nemo is effectively directing us never to show the technique to other magicians.

At the time, I assumed Nemo was proceeding cautiously because this variation had not yet been publicly registered as belonging to Christian (who, I subsequently learned, had already published it). When he says, "I'll give it to you" but that "we're not gonna make it official," he's authorizing us to use the technique in performing, but not to transmit it to other magicians. By extension, this means that we should not use it in performing for other magicians because they could so easily reverse engineer it, "stealing it with their eyes."[44] (In the presence of a sufficiently expert colleague, any performance becomes a potential, even an inevitable, revelation.) Nemo expressively demonstrates what would happen if the secret fell into the wrong hands: it would fly away like a bird taking wing, entering into uncontrollable circulation. In addition to indirection, Nemo's request is densely modified with strategies of attenuation, similar to Stefan's: expansion of the request over several utterances, qualifications ("I'll give it to you, alright, but [. . .] we're not gonna make it official"), hedging ("we're not gonna make it official or whatever"), stuttering ("it's—it's—it's—it's his—it's his"), hesitation ("well, um, I'm—we're not gonna make it official"), filler particles ("That, however, ummm"), and tag questions ("Afterwards who knows, huh?").

While Brown and Levinson view the type of verbal "elaborations"[45] that surround face-threatening acts as strategies of politeness oriented toward preserving social harmony, psycholinguists might describe them as simply reflections of a speaker's emotional state. For instance, Levelt classifies repetitions, self-corrections, pauses, and hesitations as "disfluencies" (i.e., the opposite of fluent speech) arising from the "self-monitoring" of speech, as speakers attend to questions like "Is this the message/concept I want to express now? . . . Is this the way I want to say it? . . . Is what I'm saying up to social standards?"[46] From this perspective, the volume of disfluency in the examples examined above suggests that these speakers are attending closely to their compliance with a normative standard or anxious about the consequences of their speech.

Whether we view these elaborations as sociocentric politeness strategies or egocentric expressions of anxiety, I argue that they function as "affect keys," that is, "linguistic features that intensify or specify affect function" in talk.[47] When magicians verbally restrict the circulation of the secrets they tip, politeness modifications do not simply mitigate face threats, nor do disfluencies simply point to heightened self-monitoring; they key an affective stance of anxiety vis-à-vis the secret itself. The requests I have analyzed are iconic, conveying the appropriate attitude toward secrets by performing it. In qualifying their acts of tipping with requests for secrecy, Coco, Stefan, and Nemo make proscriptive statements and also model a culturally appropriate attitude of precaution toward magical secrets. Their qualifications simultaneously reaffirm the sacred nature of the secret and activate a sense of moral duty and personal accountability within exclusive lineages of transmission. Over time, the cumulative impact of such transactions profoundly affects the way magicos view secrecy, inculcating a vocational habitus viscerally attuned to its moral and practical imperatives.

In initiatory secret societies, a sense of danger surrounds the revelatory transmission of esoteric knowledge. Among the aforementioned Baktaman, for instance, the "novice develops a fearful awareness of vital, unknowable, and forbidding power behind . . . secret and cryptic symbols. . . . He comes to recognize the futility—and danger—of speculation and curiosity about ritual knowledge, how his own ritual acts have meaning only by virtue of the deeper knowledge of the seniors, who provide him with a set of instructions for action and an (unknown) wider context which assures that these acts are not dangerous and destructive."[48] Initiates in Liberia's Poro secret societies come to appreciate the danger of initiatory knowledge through the strategies of indirection and avoidance that initiators use to reveal secrets without speaking them aloud.[49] As the above examples illustrate, there is an identifiable set of iconic verbal practices that accompany the exchange of secrets among magicos, setting it apart from surrounding activity, and keying an affective stance of anxiety. Recurrent instances of this kind of marked speech in magic lessons signal that it too is a kind of expert performance that is being transmitted to novices.

In magic, the sense of danger surrounding secrets is not merely activated through elaborate protocols of tipping but also reinforced through the policing of deviance. Stories about transgressions of secrecy or IP norms remain in circulation for years, and a victim of plagiarism or theft will never forgive an unremedied transgression. In this talkative community, gossip can quickly spoil an unethical magician's reputation. Policing deviance is an important component of social cohesion in any community, and not only because the deviant act is intrinsically harmful. As Kai Erikson writes, paraphrasing Durkheim, "the deviant act . . . creates a sense of mutuality among the people of a community by supplying a focus for group feeling," making them "more alert to the interests they share in common."[50] Furthermore, hearing gossip about the violation of secrecy protocols reinforces the importance of respecting community norms in the mind of a novice. It may be difficult, however, for a novice to entirely avoid violating those norms, which are seldom if ever dispensed in the form of explicit maxims. I discovered this myself—the hard way.

At the Illegal one evening, a small group of magicos including Nemo and myself were exploring different techniques for making brightly colored Styrofoam sponge balls vanish. Sébastien Mossière, an affable young professional and costar of *Magicien(s), Tout est écrit*, one of France's most successful magic shows in recent memory, demonstrated a sleight that surprised us all for its audacity and inventiveness (see Figure 7). Word quickly spread to surrounding tables, and before long, several more people joined our group, commenting on the new technique. Over the course of the rest of the evening, Sébastien patiently instructed me and a few others in the execution of the counterintuitive procedure, never mentioning issues of ownership. In the coming days, I continued to work on it in conversation with Nemo.

Figure 7.   Sébastien Mossière (*left*) teaches a coin sleight. Photo by the author.

That weekend, I interviewed professional magician Jan Madd on board his riverboat theatre, moored on the Quai de la Seine. Madd was relaxing after a show in his red robe, absentmindedly manipulating a set of sponge balls as we talked. "Sébastien Mossière showed me an incredible vanish the other day," I said. "What do you think?" Borrowing one of his balls, I performed the improbable vanish to the best of my ability. Madd's sat up straight, eyes wide. "Do it again!" I did, and showed him the technique from another angle to make the hidden movements visible. "That's a keeper. It's really impressive," he said, beginning to practice the move on his own in slow motion. I was thrilled to have conveyed a piece of useful knowledge to someone like Madd, a revered elder in the French magic world.

As soon as I left Madd's theater, I called Sébastien to tell him what an impression his unique sleight had made on Madd. My enthusiastic story met with an awkward silence. "I mean, I *cited* you, of course. I hope you don't mind that I showed him. . . ." I said, trailing off. "No . . . not too much," Sébastien replied unconvincingly. "By the same token, don't show it off too much either. . . . I'm hoping to make a DVD with a bunch of sleights like that." I immediately realized that I had transgressed some unspoken rule, though Sébastien was too nice to tell me so outright. I apologized profusely, and, luckily, there didn't seem to be any hard feelings. I eventually grasped what I hadn't understood about the nature of Sébastien's revelation at the Illegal. I mistakenly assumed that in tipping the sleight without any explicit directives, he was giving it to everyone present for free use. I hadn't yet learned the rule that one never tips another magician's unpublished material without explicit permission.

As we have seen, sharing secrets in the magic world produces solidarity and yields advantageous access to new knowledge. Bloom, for instance, who has a reputation for generously offering ideas to other magicians, told me, "The more you give, the more you receive." But becoming a social person, Bambi Schieffelin argues, entails learning culturally appropriate ways not only of sharing but also of not sharing.[51] Because access to magical knowledge is differential, the circulation of secrets establishes inequalities of expertise and authority.[52] Indeed, magicos conceptualize the culture of conjuring not just in terms of their inside-outside relationship with the lay public, but also in terms of an up-down pyramidal hierarchy of expertise among insiders themselves. Refusals to share secrets are, in this regard, enactments of difference in respect to privileged access expertise. Explicit refusals do not happen as frequently as one might expect. As in most contexts, there is a dispreference against refusing requests;[53] novices learn not to make requests for disclosure, to avoid putting others in the uncomfortable position of refusing.

There are some contexts in which refusals to share are the norm. For instance, it is expected that a lecturing magician will perform some tricks without an explanation (as I witnessed on one occasion, however, a lecturer who offers paying attendees too few explanations may provoke displeasure). Generally, magicos are ambivalent about refusals to share secrets, as evidenced by a 2002 discussion on a VM forum, ignited when prolific user Gilbus posted the following question: "Secrecy vis-à-vis muggles [i.e., laymen][54] is normal, and aims to protect them and preserve their sense of wonder. . . . But what should we think of secrecy in general vis-à-vis other magicians?"[55] Gilbus was particularly concerned with cases in which a magician performs a trick for fellow magicians, but refuses to give an explanation. "Does this make magic progress?" he wondered. "Isn't secrecy in such cases just about flattering the magician's ego at the community's expense? Is there even a community to begin with, or is it just individuals who want to show off for each other?" Gilbus implied that excessive secrecy among magicians is not only symptomatic of endemic megalomania but also harmful to magic as a community and as an art.

Respondents, from beginners to some of France's most respected magicians, offered a range of provocative views. Dominique Duvivier, widely regarded as one of France's most innovative—and secretive—close-up magicians, described tipping as a kind of gift giving that the recipient must deserve: "I think that giving a secret . . . is a good thing as a general rule. By this, I mean one or two secrets, not everything one knows. Secrets should be given with parsimony as a token of recognition among magicians. A common currency, like a form of exchange, even a 'calling card' that has circulated since magic became a world of its own. . . . The force of the gift one makes of oneself is sometimes proportional to an individual path." An anonymous user then endorsed and extended Duvivier's characterization of tipping as gift giving: "Giving a detailed explanation of a routine to someone who has done no work of their own is, from my perspective, a denaturalization of the gift. The recipient will not understand . . . the depth and value. . . . Giving certain keys that will allow those with the will and determination to progress, is a much more precious gift than any thoroughgoing explanation. . . . The gift, the real gift, will enrich the person who receives it. But this can only emerge from a dialogue, not a monologue."

The connection these VMistes make between tipping and gift giving is an important reminder that, as Marcel Mauss argues, through exchange, individuals stabilize solidary relationships based on reciprocity, encompassing each other in projects of self-making.[56] For magicos, gifting secrets is a way of extending reputations, engendering reciprocal exchanges that increase one's own stock of knowledge, and cementing bonds of friendship. Secrets circulate with what Mauss calls *hau*: the piece of oneself that one transmits in any act of giving.[57] Magicians' connections with their secrets are especially strong because, so often, those secrets literally become part of the person as embodied knowledge. In exchanging such secrets, magicians come to share the physical substance of skill, as the focused mimeticism apparent in so many scenes of transmission suggests (see Figures 1, 3–5, 7). Each person within the system has a different initiatory trajectory—and skilled identity—because they participate in different networks of exchange with different exchange partners. For all these reasons, secrets are not just magicians' tools of the trade; they are symbols through which magicians generate value and meaning,[58] and whose loss or destruction imperils more than merely the ability to produce illusion.

DESTROYING SECRETS

In 1998, the French television network FR3 purchased a program from the Fox network entitled *Breaking the Magician's Code: Magic's Biggest Secrets Finally Revealed*. The program, in which a masked magician performs and then thoroughly explains some of magic's best-known tricks—including the Sawing a Lady in Half illusion—had already raised an outcry from magicians in the United States.[59] French magicians mounted an impressive offensive. On September 7, two hundred magicos met in Paris, establishing the Collectif des magiciens francophones.[60] Members of this group contacted media outlets championing what they brilliantly dubbed the public's "right to dream."[61] They organized a letter-writing campaign, urging politicians to stop FR3, a public television station, from broadcasting the program. Ultimately their strategies worked, but the victory was short-lived. While FR3 did not air *Breaking the Magician's Code*, to magicians' horror, a private cable network soon did.

   This was one relatively dramatic example of what appears to be a never-ending problem: the revelation of secrets to the lay public, or "exposure" in the parlance of Anglophone magicians. Exposure, the destructive revelation of secrets, is the converse of tipping, initiatory revelation that reproduces secrets. Magicos call it *débinage*, and someone who does it a *débineur*. The use of the verb *débiner* with the meaning "to divulge [a secret]" arose in the French criminal argot of the mid-nineteenth century.[62] To my eyes, this usage seems closely connected to the verb's earlier (and now standard) meaning, "to denigrate," suggesting an equivalence metaphorically between divulging a secret and speaking ill of it, and metonymically between divulging a secret and speaking ill of one's accomplices. The English expression "to betray a secret" similarly connotes disloyalty, but does not have the same association with slanderous speech.

The first instances I have found of the term *débinage* in French magic literature date to the early 1900s, and magicos continue to use it widely today with the specialized meaning of "divulgation" unknown to the laity.[63] That they should preserve a term, borrowed from an otherwise forgotten underworld argot, and which gives references to exposure such strong moral shadings, suggests the importance that secrets have for them. For magicos, the illegitimate revelation of secret knowledge is a kind of defilement, a desecration of cultural sacra forming the basis of the magic community. Paradoxically, *débinage* not only dissipates secrets but also conveys a distorted sense of their importance. As we have seen in previous chapters, magicianship involves a tremendous amount of skill beyond simply knowing how a trick is done; *débinage* denigrates magic by suggesting that there is nothing to it beyond knowing secrets.

The initial vogue for *débinage* as a form of entertainment à la Masked Magician began in the midst of what is now thought of as the "Golden Age of Magic," the period from around 1880 to 1920 when magicians were among the top-billed entertainers in the swelling sphere of show business celebrity. Illusionist Abel Blanche described the 1890s as the "the golden age of exposure," when specialists in *débinage* could be found on music hall stages throughout Europe explaining the secrets behind magicians' tricks.[64] For Blanche, this dubious form of entertainment was a byproduct of the music hall business model that demanded maximal novelty for the minimal price. Music hall managers preferred to hire artists who could perform two entirely different acts. Thus, a juggler or a mime might put together an exposure act in order to play both the first and second half of a review. At the same time, artists subjected to the vagaries of public taste found exposure routines relatively easy to concoct. Would-be *débineurs* could apprise themselves of magicians' secrets easily through mail order services and the many new magic boutiques. The situation ultimately became so dire, he recollects, that in the same music hall, one might see a magician with a *débineur* following on his coattails explaining all his tricks. With the public's curiosity piqued by these "professional exposers," it even became common for professional magicians themselves to offer explanations of a few "little" tricks in the course of their normal performances. But one magician's little trick is another magician's livelihood, and controversy soon erupted.

By the dawn of the twentieth century, when magicians in France began to form professional groups and found the first magic periodicals, the fight against exposure quickly became a collective rallying cry. In 1905, the fledgling *Journal de la Prestidigitation* ran an article lamenting the scourge of *débinage*: "We are pained to observe that a certain number of individuals who were generally only able to enter within the Temple of Magic through the service entrance think they can avenge themselves by throwing its front door wide open. More bluntly, these people, after managing to understand the workings of a few tricks, can't think of anything better to do than reveal them in public. . . . Behold the *débineurs.*" [65] The author urged readers to band together in order to "cauterize this putrefaction . . . with a red-hot iron."

Letters were sent threatening music hall directors and magicians themselves who ran afoul of magic's cardinal interdiction upon revealing secrets to laymen. In one of many letters he claimed to have sent to *débineurs*, Jules Dhotel, president of what is now the FFAP, wrote, "We demand that you cease these *débinages*, and give us your word thereon, for many members of our Organization, actively mobilized against *débineurs*, have sworn not to let them continue, be it by creating noise, interruptions, or scandals whenever and wherever they might perform." [66] Nor were these idle threats. Parisian magicians staged a number of guerilla-style attacks on theaters or music halls where *débineurs* were performing. "In these *puni-*

tive expeditions," one participant recollected, "the President [Dhotel] him-self and his intimates led numerous members of our Association on a mission to jeer, niggle, and otherwise interrupt these indecent perfor-mances. . . . Of course, we were usually carted off to the nearest police station." [67]

While turn-of-the-twentieth-century illusionists seemed to achieve a ready consensus about the inherent evil of theatrical divulgation, dis-agreement soon arose about whether or not other forms of revelation should be classified as *débinage* as well. Commentators began to use the term *débinage* to describe all forms of revelation that they found objection-able, for example, the sale of instructional manuals in department stores and the availability of magic props through mail order catalogs.[68] Was this also *débinage* as critics asserted?

One of the most interesting early commentators on the problem of *débinage* was Édouard Raynaly, the freethinking and poison-tongued editor of *L'Illusionniste*. Although he was himself arrested after leading an anti-*débinage* expedition against Hermann the Great, he cautioned against confusing *destructive* and *constructive* exposure. In a 1904 edito-rial he expressed "absolute condemnation" for any magician who, "in-stead of contenting himself with the production of illusion . . . publicly reveals the methods used to perform his tricks." [69] He went on, however, to differentiate this type of exposure from another, salutary form—instructive publication: "The book is . . . not harmful. Readers who un-derstand nothing don't matter, and those who do understand are, in fact, our allies, our apprentices, our admirers and . . . eventually our clients and spectators. They will take an interest in performances whose ingenuity, artistry and skill they are uniquely able to appreciate." [70] For Raynaly, while gratuitous public exposure was an obvious ill, the transmission of secrets to interested novices was an inherent good. He cautioned against a too liberal construal of *débinage*, warning that if no secrets were revealed—be it by giving lessons, publishing, or selling tricks—magic would cease to exist altogether. In a later article, he went further still, contending that most magicians are, in fact, responsible for some form of exposure—from the "vandals" who gratuitously divulge, to the bumbler who inadvertently botches a trick and even the careless magician who describes a prop as "normal in every way," thereby implanting in the audience's mind that it could be gimmicked.[71]

Raynaly's wariness toward the ambiguity of the notion of *débinage* proved prescient. Over the century separating these early diatribes from the present day, skirmishes about the category and consequences of *débinage* have erupted at regular intervals, generally in connection with technological changes affecting the way magicians' secrets circulate—most recently, the advent of the Internet. Raynaly recognized that in an age of mechanical (and later digital) reproduction, secrets would come to circulate more freely and more widely than they ever had before, and that the consequent challenge for magicians would be to find a way to manage this circulation so that magic could remain a sustainable activity.

A key issue for magicos has been differentiating between gratuitous *débinage* serving only to satisfy spectators' fleeting curiosity, and productive revelation responding to an authentic interest in magic. Some have argued that *débinage* is inevitable, and that magicians should take steps to control it and render it productive. "We have no choice but to recognize that *débinage* continues to spread and that everything we have tried to stop it has been utterly ineffective," wrote magician Maurie Gauthron.[72] "Bismarck said socialism comes from the state not being socialist enough. I'd say *débinage* comes from us not doing enough *débinage*." For his part, Gauthron went on to found the introductory magic course that allowed me and countless others to become a member of the FFAP.

In the mid-1970s, two widely popular television programs brought the problem of *débinage* again to a head. The first, *Y a un truc* (roughly, *There's a Trick*), was a game show in which contestants attempted to explain tricks performed by the host, Gérard Majax. Most of the so-called tricks fell squarely within the realm of scientific recreations or dinner table amusements. Magicians remain ambivalent about the program to this day. Some argue that, while the principles revealed were generally not drawn from magicians' actual repertoire, the program stimulated public interest in magic and, indeed, inspired many young magicians. Others argue that the show demeaned the art of magic by suggesting that magicians were not skilled artists but rather exhibitors of clever little parlor amusements. To their chagrin, three decades later magicos still are reminded of this program by spectators hooting "Majax!" or parroting the phrase "Y a un truc!" during performances.

During the same era, the magician Jacques Delord created a program entitled *Les Ateliers du magicien* (*The Magician's Workshop*) on a competing network. He told me that the show was conceived to give a "more distinguished image" of magic than the one presented in *Y a un truc*. Delord offered young audiences a virtual apprenticeship in magic, teaching the standard tricks in the magicians' repertoire, along with principles of presentation, and an overarching, somewhat mystical, philosophy. One middle-aged magician whose first encounter with the art was through *Les Ateliers du magicien* told me that, as a child, after watching Delord manipulate billiard balls on the show, he ran out and bought the accompanying workbook. He turned excitedly to a chapter on making balls appear and disappear. "It said, 'You should form a bond with your objects, a lasting relationship.' It said to choose a ball and keep it in your hand at all times and to sleep with it under your pillow. I thought, 'Oh geez, just teach me the damn trick!' But I did it."

Today, many magicians remember Delord's program as an amazing achievement, but at the time, it sparked an outcry. Writing in the *L'Illusionniste*, a critic praised *Y a un truc* for being "amusing and instructive" in equal measure.[73] "In respect to the art of magic, a program like *Y a un truc* not only presents no danger to professional artists, but cannot but inspire spectators' interest in real prestidigitation, towards which they will devote their entire faculty of amazement." Meanwhile, the same critic singled out Delord's *Ateliers du magicien* as wantonly destructive. "This program represents . . . an actual course in prestidigitation, with the demonstration and explanation of fundamental principles of many manipulations and effects, the revelation of which deprives the trick of its necessary mystery. . . . [These revelations] are all the more gratuitous because television viewers will quickly forget the sequence of sleights necessary to create the illusion and give the trick its value and beauty. Conversely, they will retain, thanks to the power of the moving image, an undying memory of the basic principle—sufficient knowledge to destroy the illusion's charm forever."

Despite simmering concerns about *débinage*, I was surprised to hear a number of professional magicians describe it as a "false problem." Notorious firebrand Jean Merlin probably went the furthest in this regard, publishing an editorial proclaiming that "the magician's Oath of Secrecy is like the Legion of Honor: something dreamed up to keep a bunch of dipshits happy." [74] Merlin, a specialist of cabaret magic, argued that successful magicians are not only immune to the problem of *débinage*, but also too busy working to worry about it in the first place. He attributed the worry about *débinage* to amateurs and unsuccessful professionals blaming others for their failings *male fide*, rather than trying to come up with original material.

Mimosa similarly concurred that *débinage* is a false problem. He told me about a new act in which he literally explains to audiences fundamental principles of magic like misdirection and then illustrates their use in tricks. "When you explain how misdirection works and then turn around and fool them with it, they begin to appreciate how powerful magic really is," he told me. "They're spellbound." When asked about *débinage*, magician Abdul Alafrez questioned the very premise of the concept. "The secret in magic exists to titillate people," he told me. "But it's only a convention between the magician and the spectator. Spectators ask the magician, 'How'd you do that?' and the magician says that he can't reveal the secret. But spectators don't *really* want to know the secret and, in a certain way, the magician doesn't *really* care about keeping it. But theatrically, this is precisely the convention that justifies the magic show."

CONCLUSION

One evening, I was chatting over coffee at the Illegal with Bébel and his friend Thomas, an amateur in his mid-thirties. Someone at our table brought up a recent American indie film called *Shade* about professional card hustlers. In a bonus section of the French DVD release,[75] David Stone explains how to perform the three-card monte con game, which involves techniques that magicians employ not to fleece rubes but to entertain spectators. Bébel winced. "Is it any good?"

Thomas reacted violently. "More *débinage*? It's criminal." Thomas feared that heedless divulgation would render the lay public impervious to magicians' time-tested illusionary techniques. "For me," he said, "becoming a magician was a deal with the devil. I made a conscious choice to sacrifice all the pleasure of magic's mystery to know how it works. And now you've practically got planes flying overhead pulling banners and dropping pamphlets explaining tricks. And all our sacrifices? And all our hard work? You can shove it."

As a child, Thomas had been delighted by the magic tricks of an elderly family friend. When he asked for instruction, though, the magician issued a stern admonition: "Be careful, sonny. Magic is secret. It can only be passed from magician to magician." Recalling the incident that evening, Thomas snorted grimly. "Can you imagine that? You're eleven years old, and you've got this seventy-year-old dude telling you that magic is secret, so be careful. You *believe* it." Thomas went on to a career in music, but after a long stay in the hospital due to a sudden neurological illness, he began to contemplate pursuing close-up magic as a form of rehabilitation.

Thomas finally worked up the courage to enter a magic store near his apartment. He was amazed that he was able to buy a magic book, no questions asked, and even received an invitation to a magic lecture that afternoon ("There are magic lectures?" he remembers asking himself in disbelief). In the coming months, Thomas made other startling discoveries: instructional videos to speed his learning, magicians' clubs where he was welcomed with open arms, and websites where he could exchange knowledge and information with other magic enthusiasts. He had come to a startling realization. "I thought that magic was like a secret society," he recalled. "When I figured out that wasn't the case and that *anybody* can get involved, it was like an enormous shock. The openness allowed me to become a magician, but it still irks me that our secrets are disseminated so freely. Without secrecy, there's no illusion. Without illusion, there's no magic." For Thomas, it seemed that, because of *débinage*, magic might be a moribund art.

After listening to Thomas's story, Bébel expressed a different opinion. "The real problem isn't *débinage*," he said. "To do magic you've got to *respect* the secret. To create mystery you've got to *respect* mystery. Now you've got so-called magicians who don't respect the secret at all because it's so easy to access information on DVDs and over the Internet or whatever. Today people do disposable magic: *What's the latest trick? What's the latest effect?* And as soon as they've got their trick, they go looking for the next one and throw out what they've already got. It's like any other kind of consumerism." He sighed. "And the paradox is that the fewer magicians there are onstage, the more people there are with secrets for sale."

In an information age and a consumer culture, the magic world might appear to be hemorrhaging secrets. Thomas was rightfully concerned about the way the increased circulation of secrets might affect laymen, but Bébel shifted the topic to the effect on magicians themselves. His construal of "consumerism" as antithetical to "respect" for the secret can be read on multiple levels. As we have seen in this chapter, the circulation of secrets among magicians produces value. In instances of face-to-face tipping, magicos verbally constitute secrets as valuable by honoring inventors, reaffirming scarcity, asserting moral obligations, and restricting circulation. In these interactions, transmitters of secrets take care to both *conform* to IP norms and *inform* recipients about those norms.[76] The directives they address to recipients enact and induce an affective stance regarding secret knowledge, rooted in personal bonds of intimacy and trust, and grounded in deference to the prerogatives of expertise. Similarly, the fight against *débinage* also authenticates the sacred nature of the secret even if, as some magicos contend, exposure is a false problem. For these reasons, magicos often construe "initiation" and "gifting" as prototypes for the normative circulation of secrets.

Treating a secret as a commodity rather than a gift could have serious consequences. Mauss viewed settings in which gifting is a primary mode of exchange as very different from the modern condition of "purely individual contract, of the market where money circulates, of sale proper, and above all of the notion of price reckoned in coinage weighed and stamped with its value."[77] For Mauss, money-mediated transactions depersonalize exchange. Unlike a gift that engenders lasting reciprocity while producing solidarity and identity, purchase and sale culminate when a commodity changes hands. While the commercialization and mediatization of magic can expand the system of value production described above, allowing inventors and authors to extend their reputations around the world, it may also threaten to supplant face-to-face knowledge transmission that moors the circulation of secrets in strong affective relationships.

This dynamic is nothing new. In early modern Europe, the proliferation of how-to manuals after the advent of the printing press similarly overturned the monopoly that late medieval guilds enjoyed over their craft knowledge: "for a growing number of people, including artisans as well as nonartisans, literacy, not membership in a guild or a formal apprenticeship, became the precondition for knowing the secrets of the arts." [78] At the same time, this reconfiguration of knowledge shifted the locus of intellectual property from the corporate group to the individual inventor. As in magic today, the dissemination of new ideas in print became a way for early modern inventors to consolidate intellectual property claims. Paradoxically, while printing hastened the movement of new ideas into the public domain, through judicious publication, "an author . . . could at least be assured that his discoveries would be publicly acknowledged, since his name would be prominently displayed on the title pages of his books." [79]

In recent years, the most alarming vector of increasing circulation has not been commodification per se, but rather the traffic in freely distributed secrets over the Internet. While access to VM's technical forums is password protected and relatively restricted, there are many other ways of acquiring secrets online. Pirated videos and scanned versions of magic books are now widely available through file-sharing sites. One talented teenage amateur bragged to me that, other than buying playing cards, he had never spent a cent on magic. "I download all the videos with BitTorrent [a file-sharing application]," he said. Other magicos were more scrupulous. "I only download stuff by Americans," one told me. "For French magicians, I always try to pay." A simple search of YouTube turns up countless homemade magic videos—many with explanations—in multiple languages. Amazed by the changes in the way magicians acquire secrets, Sébastien Clergue said, "When I was a kid, we'd say, 'I bought the book.' Today they say, 'I downloaded the MPEG.' "

Even if mercantile and mass-mediated forms of circulating secrets may pose new challenges to established patterns of knowledge acquisition in magic, for the moment, they don't seem to be undermining the art as a whole. Loïc, who is very troubled by increased circulation (he said that magicians who make mass-market videos are "spitting on the very thing that lets them live"), admitted that it hadn't created much of a problem for him as a close-up magician—yet. "You encounter spectators who think they understand what you did because they watched a few magic DVDs. Then they bust your balls with half-baked explanations cobbled together from the little they know, and ruin the magic for all their friends. It hasn't happened to me much, maybe five times in my life, but I'm worried it's going to happen more and more." (I recently saw a spectator using a smartphone to search YouTube for explanations of tricks *during* a magic performance.) For his part, Daniel Rhod told me that rising tides of consumerism and mass divulgation in magic were the inspiration for the super-secretive practices of *l'underground*: "some authors of high-quality tricks are returning to a more confidential outlook aligned with the respect of secrets and the ethics of magic. Their tricks are more exclusive, sold in smaller copies and at higher prices," not unlike high-quality artisanal goods that discriminating consumers might prefer to mass-produced commodities.

Magic tricks fascinate because secrecy makes "everything mysterious" appear "important and essential," demanding that we "pay attention to it with an emphasis that is not usually accorded to patent reality." [80] The illusions that magicians craft through the exhibition of secrets in performance give people the thrill of the mysterious and the uncanny. At best, these performances can be intensely moving, constituting memories that spectators will carry for a lifetime. Indeed, I'm always surprised by the number of laypeople who, upon learning that I study magic, recount in vivid detail a magician's performance they witnessed many years before. At worst, magic shows are fleeting distractions, or even minor annoyances. Approaching secrets as plentiful commodities or indifferent articles of conspicuous consumption, Bébel seemed to be saying, is not conducive to performing magic at its highest, most ennobling level. [81] To lead an audience to wonder, it follows, the magician too must remain alive to the preciousness and fragility of the secret itself.

THREE Potency and Performance

One evening at a meeting of the Illegal Magic Club, I was chatting with several male regulars when someone introduced us to a female newcomer in her late teens. She had piercing eyes, tomboyish baggy jeans, and, like most everyone else, a deck of cards, which she casually manipulated. Someone asked her to do a trick. She promptly had a card selected and returned to the deck, then exhibited her dexterity with a series of impressive, acrobatic "cuts," splaying the cards in small packets between her outstretched fingers in a kaleidoscope of abstract geometric configurations that would make the location of the card seemingly impossible to determine. Suddenly, she ejected a card from the deck, sending it spinning in a high arc over her head and into her awaiting free hand. It was the selection. While she didn't quite manipulate with the effortless confidence of a seasoned magician, the young woman appeared well on her way to becoming a formidable cardician. She was already able to perform sleights far more difficult than anything I would ever dream of, and had a clear penchant for what magicians call "flourishes," ostentatious displays of virtuosic technique. I clapped encouragingly, but was surprised that the other magicians I was with didn't seem as impressed. "Not bad," one said, "but that's a dude trick [*tour de mec*]."

"Yeah, that's dude magic [*magie de mec*]," the other concurred. "Can't you do something where you express yourself, something poetic?"

"But this is what I enjoy . . ." she said defensively, edging away from our table.

Until then, the concept of tricks for *dudes* had never surfaced in my conversations with magicos. "What do you guys mean by *dude magic*?" I asked once we were alone again. By way of response, one went immediately into an impersonation: "Here we have the four aces, but no! It's not the aces, it's the kings! And the aces are in my pocket!" We all laughed knowingly at this caricature of the kind of pyrotechnic performances that particularly appeal to adolescent boys. "It's athleticism, its virtuosity, it's 'Hey, look at me!' It's screwing the spectator." If the novice had been male, I am almost positive that same magicians would have criticized technical aspects of the performance rather than questioning his aesthetic proclivities. Indeed, magicians generally admire demonstrations of technical prowess, even if they consider flourishes inappropriate for lay audiences (this is a subject that inspires endless polemics).[1]

To my mind, this brief incident crystallizes prevalent but unspoken articulations of gender and illusion within the culture of magic. Because they are so rare, female magicians almost inevitably stand out. The way a group of seasoned male magicians reacted to the impromptu performance of a female novice at the Illegal spoke volumes. As I show in Chapter 1, when magicians meet for the first time, they establish "what level they place themselves on" by performing representative material. Through an ostentatious display of dexterity, this young woman clearly evinced a commitment to cultivating virtuosic skill. Yet her expert audience did not ratify the legitimacy of this self-presentation. They agreed that a woman could not "express herself" through demonstrations of virtuosic skill like the card acrobatically flipped from one hand to the other, and encouraged her to embrace a suitably "poetic" style that would presumably feature feminine props and sentimental themes. To be fair, if the female novice was aspiring to a professional career, the advice from more experienced male counterparts may have been perfectly germane. Magicians must remain constantly aware of what kinds of images will appeal to potential spectators, and it is quite possible that mainstream audiences in France would balk at the image of a woman displaying virtuosic conjuring skill. But this begs the question. Why would a female magician performing so-called poetic routines be more culturally credible and, therefore, an easier sell?

This incident reveals an awareness that performances of magic are also performances of gender, in which aesthetic choices serve as iconic features of gendered self-display. Judith Butler famously argues that "gender performativity . . . is a matter of reiterating or repeating the norms by which one is constituted. . . . Gender norms operate by requiring the embodiment of certain ideals of femininity and masculinity, ones which are almost always related to the idealization of the heterosexual bond." [2] In the incident at the Illegal, the female novice clearly ran afoul of an unspoken norm equating the ostentatious display of technical skill with an ideal of heterosexual masculinity, making it relatively "unperformable," in Butler's terms,[3] for members of the female sex. The reaction of male magicians to this performance of the unperformable suggests that they carefully monitor each other's compliance, if not with norms of sexuality offstage, then with standards of gendered self-display onstage.

Kulick and Schieffelin write that it can be difficult to study the socialization of what they term "bad subjects," that is, "subjects who do not recognize or respond to calls to behave in particular, socially sanctioned ways."[4] According to their analysis, bad subjects—like a young woman who does virtuosic card tricks—raise provocative questions: "how do individuals come to perceive the subject positions that are available or possible in any given context? How is the taking up of particular positions enabled or blocked by relations of power? How do particular positions come to be known as intelligible and desirable, while others are inconceivable and undesirable?"[5] In this chapter, I consider symbolic linkages established within the subculture of French magic between particular aesthetic features and certain essentialist notions of gender, and the way magicians—male and female, queer and straight—negotiate gender norms in conjuring. I do not mean this to be an exhaustive discussion of gender in magic; there are many performers whose work complicates these issues in ways I cannot address here. What I am proposing is an analysis of what I see as some recurring emphases that I encountered repeatedly during the course of my research.

Articulations of gender and magic run deep. Scholars have argued that cultural anxieties about occult female power made it historically difficult for women to perform as magicians: they "could not easily succeed as stage magicians" because "the unforgotten history of early modern witchcraft panics perpetuated the fear that females who practiced magic would enter into dangerous alliances and acquire powers that might upset the gender hierarchy."[6] Further, many famous magic tricks have a strong gendered subtext. A trick like the famous Sawing a Lady in Half illusion not only projects imagery of antifemale violence; it also obscures the skilled labor of the female assistant placed inside the box: "the display of power is such that the weak (female) assistant cannot even be imagined as laboring. The narrative of weakness and passivity is essential to the trick" because "the woman's talent and effort is part of the secret, part of the magician's misdirection."[7] Similarly, the popularity of Vanishing Lady illusions in Victorian England has been described as a misogynistic expression of anxieties about women's social position.[8] The historical marginalization and symbolic subjugation of women in magic constitute a cultural backdrop against which my discussion unfolds.

Of course, discussing gender performativity raises questions about the other kinds of identities that magicians enact when they perform (e.g., race, ethnicity, class, ability, and age). It is important to note that Robert-Houdin endures as "the model magician"[9] in the modern West not only because of his conjuring talent but also because the configuration of his magical persona in terms of white, heterosexual, bourgeois, masculine potency continues to resonate (see Chapter 5). Thus, in the mainstream "magical assemblage,"[10] people of color have traditionally occupied niches of exoticism, while people with disabilities often have been relegated to sideshow attractions.[11] Magicos with immigrant and working-class backgrounds or those with disabilities know they must grapple with stereotypes; for some, doing magic becomes a tool for confronting stereotypes.[12] Much could be said about magic and the performance of identity broadly speaking; here I focus exclusively on gender as the dimension of performativity that emerged as most salient in my research.

In making decisions about styling their personae and staging their effects, magicians articulate individual artistic proclivities with established cultural conventions. In the following section, I discuss some of these conventions and describe their implications for gendered self-display. I go on to describe the experiences of female magicos today, and discuss persistent linkages of magic performances and the imagery of heterosexual masculinity. The continuing predominance of masculine images and themes, I argue, makes it especially difficult for women to credibly enact the role of magician, but it also constrains the male magicians' opportunities for self-expression; their performances are also instances of gender display that can be more or less successful. However, these enduring conventions do not only limit expressive possibilities. They also provide expressive resources open to resignification. In the final section, I examine the way that seemingly conventional performances of gender roles can encode powerfully subversive messages.

PRESENTING MAGIC

Magicians operate on the cusp of authenticity and illusion. While their trickery makes the unreal appear deceptively real, they conventionally do not claim authentic supernatural ability. What these honest deceivers do profess is authentic mastery of otherwise mysterious skills. They present themselves to audiences not as indifferent purveyors of magical illusions but, rather, as the "type of person"[13] who is good at doing

magic. Thus, magic performance is an occasion for displaying master-
fully mysterious skill and for displaying oneself as a master of mystery.
"To *be* a given kind of person," Goffman writes, "is not merely to possess
the required attributes, but also to sustain the standards of conduct and
appearance that one's social grouping attaches thereto." [14] The presentation of magic tricks is only one part of magicians' overall strategy of self-
presentation as magical kinds of persons. They style and enact personae
in respect to cultural expectations about the kinds of people magicians
are; these expectations both create and constrain opportunities for self-
expression in and through magic.

Magical kinds of persons typically display a range of seemingly paranormal abilities, which the effects they perform illustrate. Magic theorists since Robert-Houdin have been seeking an exhaustive taxonomy of
magical effects.[15] Although there is still no generally accepted system of
classification, in everyday staging talk, magicians do classify effects into
a small number of relatively uncontroversial categories such as *appearance, disappearance, penetration,* and *transformation.* A trick could comprise
just one effect, but routines often combine effects of different types into
a coherent sequence of magical events. For instance, in the Cups and Balls
routine described in the Introduction, Bébel makes the balls he manipu-
lates appear, disappear, penetrate solid metal, and transform into objects of a different color and size.

Magicians can frame the same effect in a variety of ways, depending
on the "alignment" or "footing" [16] they adopt. They term this dimension
of performance *presentation.* As I discuss in Chapter 1, decisions about
presentation are a crucial part of any magician's creative process. In an
activity where most performers draw on a common stock of effects, presentation is what differentiates one performer from another. Plagiariz-
ing another magician's presentation ranks with stealing secrets as a
moral outrage. While intellectual property law generally does not protect secrets, magicians have fought and won cases of copyright infringe-
ment over plagiarized presentations, and I know a number who have
filed for copyright protection. In some cases, presentations—even entire
acts essentially comprising a series of presentations—can be exchanged,
gifted, bought, and sold.

It is an oft-repeated truism among magicos that "presentation is more important than technique" for successful performance (because technique exerts such a powerful attraction as an end in itself, they constantly remind themselves and each other to attend to other dimensions of magic). With the full emotional palette at their disposal, they may choose to approach an effect in a humorous vein, to swathe it in otherworldly mystique, or to infuse it with elegance and romance. One presentation might emphasize the performer's incommensurable prowess; another might poke self-disparaging fun at the performer's self-importance. Depending on the type of performance, elements like costume, patter, props, music, and décor can all complement particular presentations; sometimes stage magicians will adapt all these elements to individual tricks in their shows. From "abracadabra" to "hocus pocus," even the magic formula that magicians may utter to summon their power and signal their feats can play an important role in a making a memorable presentation; every French magician knows (and some even imitate) cardician Bernard Bilis's trademark "bloubloublou!"

Presentation can also be thought of in terms of what Bauman and Briggs call "recontextualization." [17] As I described in the previous chapter, tricks can be "entextualized" and "decontextualized," circulating as secrets among magicians on a variety of platforms. Every performance is a recontextualization of an effect in a situated moment of interaction co-constructed with an audience. When learning a trick, novice magicians acquire not only an entextualized routine but also knowledge concerning the process of recontextualizing it as a performed effect.[18] According to Bauman and Briggs, all performances involve "'contextualization cues' that signal which features of the settings are used by interactants in producing interpretive frameworks." [19] In making choices about presentation, magicians are deciding what kinds of contextualization cues to provide when performing to encourage particular interpretations of effects and magical personae. To give an extreme example, the effect of predicting what card a spectator will select could be presented as an amusing parlor trick or as evidence of extrasensory perception depending on how the performer cues it.

Performers align themselves in different aesthetic schools of thought about issues of presentation. For instance, in recent years, "bizarre magic" presentations that blend esoteric imagery and narratives to create eerie effects have emerged as one of the most salient currents in European and North American conjuring. Magicos often disagree about aesthetic questions. When I went with Nemo and Loïc to see Philippe performing at a Paris café, the two friends got into a heated debate about presenting card tricks. Nemo self-identified as a proponent of "figurative" presentation, while Loïc voiced a preference for "abstractionism." Figurative presentations personify playing cards in order to tell a story, in which, for example, the kings stand for gangsters, cannibals, or some other characters. Abstract presentations do not frame the cards as representations of some other reality, but focus attention on the formal relationships between them (e.g., the appearance of aces where one expects kings).

As their discussion intensified, the two friends improvised ironic caricatures of each other's patter. "These jacks are two brothers from Marseilles," began Loïc, "and they are going to screw these four prostitutes, represented by the queens of course, and then gorge themselves on this pile of frogs." His impersonation ingeniously used clichés about French concupiscence, embodied by characters from a stereotypically coarse city in southern France, to imply that storytelling trivializes the intellectual interest of magic effects in and of themselves. Nemo then performed an equally scathing imitation of his abstractionist counterpart, one suggesting that without a narrative framework, magic tricks degenerate into vacuous displays of dexterity: "If I take these four kings, and make this magic gesture, and then this one, and finally this one, automatically they are transformed into aces!" He hinted that such patter, at best, serves to underscore the incomprehensibility of the magician's technical prowess; at worst, it is an insult to the audience's intelligence.

Popular presentational styles often draw on the register of cabaret or nightclub humor, whether the performer is working in those settings or not. Of course, close-up magicians need to have a stockpile of one-liners at the ready, both to get laughs and to deal with unexpected situations, but jokes that sound too much like an old shtick may fall flat (often magicos will use such lines ironically, as if poking fun at themselves). Sexual innuendo ("Please examine my balls—make sure they're solid") and ridiculing spectators ("Pick a card and show it to your friends—that shouldn't take long") are easy ways to get laughs, but tread a razor's edge of poor taste; spectators have reported to me finding jokes in this vein off-putting. Generally speaking, the presentational conventions (patter, clothing, music, etc.) prevalent in magic sometimes seem out of sync with trends in popular culture (at least as defined by the entertainment industry). A number of laypeople told me they consider magic kitschy (*ringard*, in French). Magicos are aware of this, and constantly work to update presentations and incorporate contemporary references. As I describe in Chapter 5, exponents of the new magic movement respond to this cultural predicament by positing a radical break—discursively, if not aesthetically—with modern magic.

However they choose to present their material, successful performers strive for consistency of mood and style in the selection and staging ("routining" in the parlance of Anglophone magicians) of their effects. All things being equal, these decisions have an enormous impact on the way audiences receive and evaluate a performance. In styling their self-presentation, magicians may draw on a number of stock personae that audiences can readily recognize: the elegant gentleman in the mold of Robert-Houdin, the oriental magus, the leather-clad rebel. . . . World champion magician Norbert Ferré straddles extremes, flipping between the split personalities of a loveable buffoon and a cocksure virtuoso. They must also decide how to incorporate readily apparent personal attributes like race or sex. For instance, Antillean magician Filaos—a middle-aged computer engineer—told me he begins his amateur stage act wearing fake dreadlocks and joking about voodoo to confront stereotypes about Afro-Caribbeans.

German magician Topas has influentially argued that there are three ideal typic personae that magicians can adopt.[20] Insofar as magic is a violation of the laws of nature, he writes, a magic performance is the *scene of a crime* in which the magician can be a *killer*, *victim*, or *witness*. The killer "commits the effect . . . willingly fooling someone" and defying others to understand; the victim is "blown away by the effect;" and the witness "plays innocent," taking the effect in along with the audience. As Topas defines them, these three personae hinge on the alignment or footing the magician takes up toward the magical effects he or she produces. Before saying more about these roles, I want to bring in visual evidence to better illustrate them.

Perhaps no one is better positioned to understand the artifice of magicians' personae than Zakary Belamy, one of the few photographers in the world who specialize in work with magicians. The child of Algerian immigrants, Zakary traded a career in computers for one combining his two hobbies—photography and magic. It is hard to convey the experience of a magical illusion in a single image, but Zakary is able to rely on his insider's knowledge of the genre to capture iconic images of magicians onstage (see Figures 2 and 14, for example).[21] In the studio, he works for hours, and sometimes days, to produce images that are disarmingly honest yet dramatic, often enhancing them with eye-catching artwork. A penchant for provocation suits him perfectly for photographing constitutionally cagey subjects like magicians. "You have to be tyrannical when you work with magicians," he once told me. "They're so self-conscious about their image."

Although he excels at artistic portraiture, magicians mostly commission Zakary for publicity materials. Publicity photos must be simultaneously generic and individuating so as to convey both performers' competence in doing the types of things normally expected of magicians, along with their uniquely marketable talents or traits. For instance, even someone unfamiliar with Gaëtan Bloom's signature cut-and-restored microphone cord routine would immediately recognize his loony humor and mad scientist inventiveness (Figure 8). Like many comedy magicians, Bloom is positioned in this photo as a laughable "victim." A portrait of the masterful Laurent Beretta in dramatic chiaroscuro, effortlessly balancing a homonymous firearm on his fingertip, suggests a different type of magician—a "killer," virtuosic and dangerous, but also elegant and even sensual (Figure 9). Both portraits intimate contact with a kind of force: Bloom humorously succumbs to the electric current he foolishly unleashes; Berretta smiles slyly, in absolute control of the perilous power he wields. In that sense, both images point to the unique kind of liminal charisma that is the hallmark of all good magic performance.

Figure 8.   Gaëtan Bloom, portrait of a *victim.*
Photo by Zakary Belamy.

Looking through hundreds of photos, Zakary and I had no trouble
finding examples of killers. As Topas writes, "most [magicians] are killers" and want to project an image of potency and even subtle hints of
danger. From the perspective of the subculture of magic, the killer is
the most valorized persona a magician can adopt. Victims, while more
difficult to find in Zakary's archive, nevertheless abounded, particularly among comedy magicians. However, we could not agree on a single image to illustrate the figure of the witness, the passive, contemplative persona. Why did instances of this persona seem to be in such short
supply?

My strong suspicion is that Topas's category of witness largely coin-
cides with the notion of a poetic—feminine—style in magic. Consider

Figure 9.   Laurent Beretta, portrait of a *killer*. Photo by Zakary
Belamy.

this poster for a recent magic show at the Maison de la Magie in Blois
(Figure 10). Entitled "Magie poétique" (Poetic Magic), the program features four illusionists, three male and one female, Alice. At the center of
the poster, which is entirely suffused with the color pink, an elegantly
dressed Alice holds a white dove. Note that she is neither depicted in a
pose of producing the dove (which could be the mark of a killer) nor
grappling with it (as a comedic victim might), but rather contemplating
it in an attitude of engrossed reverie.[22] More than any other image in my
corpus, this poster emblematizes cultural connections between the role
of the witness, femininity, and the so-called poetic style in magic.

During the course of my research, I saw no evidence of the active exclusion of women from magic. Subtle and not-so-subtle pressures to

Figure 10.   Poster for the *Magie poétique* (*Poetic Magic*) show at the Maison de la Magie. © Dr. Peche and Mlle. Rose, Laboratoires CCCP. Used with permission.

conform to heterosexual ideals of femininity in their presentational style could nevertheless function to distance female magicians from the most culturally esteemed images of potency in performance, namely, the role of the killer. Research has found similar dynamics in other communities of expressive practice. For instance, Rebecca Bryant finds that women who play the saz, a stringed instrument emblematic of Turkish national identity, are expected to perform in a "soothing" and "modest" style, far different from the culturally iconic style of "heavy" and "deliberate" improvisation characteristic of the top male soloists.[23] "The association of saz playing with masculinity," she writes, "is not a simple exclusion of women. Rather it is an entire domain of learning marked in the body through gendered signs" of appropriately masculine and feminine bearing. Similarly, a recent study of the French jazz world reveals that, in a practice where playing an instrument is the privileged means of asserting technique, virtuosity, and creativity, instrumentalists are over-whelmingly male, and women are overwhelmingly singers—a role that conforms to traditional norms of feminine self-display.[24]

In the following section, I continue this discussion of gender by con-sidering the experiences of a handful of women active in the French magic scene today as both amateurs and professional magicians. His-torically, women have often figured as male magicians' assistants, placed inside boxes for vivisection or dematerialization. The women I discuss here work outside the box—literally and figuratively—as magicians themselves. How does gender affect their involvement in the male-dominated community of magicians and in a cultural practice that places a premium on forms of expression that it construes as "unper-formable" for women? Does their approach to performing reflect differ-ent thematic or stylistic emphases? Do their experiences of contextual-izing magic for audiences differ from those of their male counterparts, and what might this suggest about the gendered content of magic per-formance more generally?

OUTSIDE THE BOX: FEMALE MAGICIANS

In March 2005, I attended a lecture at the Cercle Magique de Paris by the professional magician and quick-change artist Valérie. She had re-cently won first prize in a national magic competition for a ten-minute act in which she makes eight virtually instantaneous costume changes. Valérie advised the forty-odd attendees to make their own costumes suited to their bodies, holding forth on the relative merits of Velcro and metal snap closures, the advantages of Lycra fabric, and the impor-tance of alternating colors and cuts between changes. "My goal isn't to sell you my own effects; I hope you can use my ideas to create your own acts," she said by way of conclusion. "That goes for all magicians who reveal their secrets. My real goal is to share my philosophy of magic. When you change a costume, it's like working with a gimmicked deck of cards or a big box illusion—the gimmick alone won't produce a miracle."

With her presentation over, Valérie continued answering questions from the corner of the stage, as her husband did brisk business selling some of the accessories and materials she had discussed during the lecture. As I made my way to the door, I noticed Maeva was leaving as well. I had long admired the literary rhyming verses the youthful septuagenarian composed to accompany her manipulations of ropes, fans, linking rings, and colored thimbles (Figure 11). I asked if I could walk with her to the subway.

Outside, a light snow was falling. I commented how nice it was to see a female lecturer for a change. Maeva agreed. "You know, it's much easier for a man to get into magic than for a woman," she said. "A woman has to stay in her *category*. And maybe we aren't any exception. Valérie is a woman, and she does clothes—very well, I might add. I'm a woman, and I recite poems. A man will get up and slice through his arm or cut off some poor girl's head! All this business with knives and violence, it's not exactly . . . suited to a woman."

As Maeva suggested, much of magic is dominated by a system of heterosexual masculine signs in which women, when they do appear, figure as the objects rather than the agents of illusion. Indeed, of all the questions nonmagicians (on both sides of the Atlantic) ask about my research, "Did you learn how they saw a lady in half?" is by far the most common. That the metonym of this one legendary illusion saturated with imagery of male potency and female vulnerability is still able to emblematize the entire practice of magic suggests the extent to which it remains an activity dominated by men. For every fifty or so male magicians I encountered in France, I met roughly one *magicienne* or *prestidigitatrice*, as female practitioners are called. Given the prevalence of masculine motifs and the continuing ascendency of men, I wondered what drew women like Maeva to magic and how their experiences as performers and members of the magic subculture differed from those of the male majority.

As we were walking, Maeva suddenly stopped short. "A Japanese dancer," she said matter-of-factly. I looked all around the deserted intersection before I realized she was staring down at the wet sidewalk. At first all I saw was a pile of litter and leaves the wind had blown together.

"Don't you see him?" Maeva asked. Suddenly, in the pinkish glow of the streetlights, I did see: a plastic sack forming a kimono, draped around the body in a sinuous "S" curve, a candy wrapper the head cocked backward, and a leaf the fluttering fan. It couldn't have been more obvious. "There is a world within our world that not everyone is able to see," Maeva said. "Magic can open it to you. It transforms your relationship to everything."

Like so many amateur magicians, she had been a doctor. "I worked hard my entire life caring for others, my patients, and my own family," she would later tell me over coffee and cookies in her comfortable Paris apartment. "My work raised all kinds of troubling questions: *Why is man born to suffer? Why must innocent children die?* When I retired, I felt I needed to answer these questions for myself." She turned to Judeo-Christian and Hindu theology, learning both Hebrew and Sanskrit, and ultimately earning bachelor's and master's degrees in Indian civilization—while also learning to play the harp. "Then I discovered magic." For its Christmas party in 1991, an association of retired doctors she belonged to invited Antoinette Marteret to perform. The widow of doctor-magician Étienne Marteret had been giving volunteer performances weekly since her husband's death in 1968. "Madame Marteret was extraordinary. She performed dove productions, everything, with incredible brio. By the time she left the stage, I knew that's what I wanted to do."

Maeva enrolled in a magic class at the FFAP and began visiting the magic shops in Paris. "You've seen how magicians are—they all know each other. I did my homework, and I knew what I wanted. When I showed up asking for a specific style of copper goblets for my Cups and Balls routine, everyone said, 'What planet is she from?' But they were wonderful. They all helped me." Meanwhile, she became a regular at the local club meetings. "All my life, an incredible number of men have told me, 'This isn't for girls.' At first when you show up at the magic clubs, they say things like 'She's just here to pick up a guy.' But when they saw that I was really interested, their opinion changed. I had to prove I was *really* interested. I didn't know anything at first! I had to attach myself to people who would teach me."

Figure 11.   Maeva performs a magical effect set to verse with her harps in the background. Photo by the author.

With lightning speed, Maeva passed the test to become a member of the FFAP—a mere nine months after discovering magic. Like many magicians, she used competitions as incentive to push her growth as a conjurer. Several years later after starting magic, she won third prize at a local magic competition, doing manipulations and reciting couplets. Over the years, Maeva befriended a number of experts who helped her acquire different skills or learn specific tricks. In turn, she has become herself an expert, transmitting the knowledge she has acquired to newcomers such as myself. "Magic is such a friendly world, and you meet people from so many different backgrounds—very open-minded people." Although she has seldom performed for money, she often performs voluntarily for friends or for charity. "When you're with people you don't know very well, you can do a few tricks. People love it. Do you think they want to hear about your suffering and hardship? Much less your philosophy of life."

A small but growing number of female magicians are changing the face of magic today. Like Maeva, other female magicians I spoke with agreed that women face added challenges in pursuing an activity so closely associated with men, and must continuously prove their commitment and competence. Despite changing norms, venturing into this male-dominated world still is symbolically and socially risky for a woman. In recent years, Alexandra Duvivier, the daughter of Dominique Duvivier, has emerged as a close-up star in her own right. When I asked her why there were so few *magiciennes*, she was reluctant to construe magic as different from other traditional professions: "It's just like any other field that's been male-dominated for a long time, but it's growing more open every day." She conceded that because female magicians still occupy a marked category, their performances are subject to additional scrutiny. "When you're a girl, you already have extra pressure. You have to do the tricks perfectly or people will just laugh at you."

When we met in 2005, Marie-Odile Langloÿs, who performs stage and close-up magic solo and with her husband, Laurent, told me that the perceptions of women in magic are changing quickly. "When I started out as a professional doing close-up in the late nineties, there were lots of people who assumed women shouldn't touch cards or money. Spectators would tell me those weren't feminine objects. They would actually say things like, 'A magician should be a man.' In part, I think they were testing me because I was young, just to see what they could get away with. But some really believed it. Even employers would sometimes say, 'We don't want a woman, we'd rather have a male magician.' But times have changed. Now we have customers specifically requesting female magicians. There are only five or six professional female magicians in France, so we're definitely hot commodities. People tell me that they're happy to see a woman doing magic. Other women are especially thrilled to see a woman succeeding in a male-dominated career."

Despite the great success she now enjoys, it took Marie-Odile some time to perfect her close-up act. She has always performed in an evening gown—suitable attire for the kinds of fancy soirées where she often works. She told me that she initially received icy responses from many female spectators, perhaps because of an implicit sense of rivalry. That all ended when she struck upon the idea of coupling her

gown with a signature top hat, making her role as an entertainer perfectly clear (see Figure 13). She said that her relationship with male and
female spectators is still very different when she performs close-up.
"Men will flirt with me, but they'll also try to trip me up. I have some
tricks where I pretend to make a mistake. Men react by making fun of
me, but women will console me or encourage me to try again. It's
funny."

For their part, many male magicos I spoke with were troubled by the
small number of women in magic, and struggled to understand why it
remains, unlike other genres of art and performance, such a male-
dominated field. At one point in the 1970s, the FFAP even established an
annual "feminine magic" competition to promote female magicians, but
the project was quickly scotched after Polish magician Michaël Vadini
won first prize dressed in drag.[25] Clearly this was not what the organizers had in mind, but Vadini raised a troubling point about how concepts
like "femininity" and "magic" may or may not relate. Reflecting on the
disappearance of "feminine magic" as a category in competitions, Mimosa would write years later that "savagely sticking two unrelated concepts together gives birth to a monster that nature, in its great wisdom,
quickly eliminates." [26]

I observed that male magicians were generally eager to encourage female beginners who found their way to a magic club—often to the point
of solicitude. Unfortunately, I also saw female participants in club meetings constantly reminded of their minority status as, over the course of
any given evening, male magicians repeatedly invited the handful of
women present onstage as volunteers. Furthermore, the locker-room at-
mosphere of some clubs imbues many interactions with unpleasant sexual overtones. For a time, an attractive young woman aspiring to a career in magic began frequenting meetings of the Illegal. I often heard
sexual remarks directed to her or about her. "If she wants to become a
professional, all she needs to do is sleep with me," one magician lewdly
muttered to a table of other men.

For female beginners, the lack of female peers and role models can
make the magic world a lonely place. The incident that best dramatized
this for me occurred in my introductory class at the FFAP. After a year of

monthly meetings, our last session was devoted entirely to student performances. In a class of nearly thirty, there were only two female students who stuck it out to the end of the year: an adult woman and a girl in her early teens, whom I admired for holding her own in a roomful of mostly middle-aged men. For her final performance, she had prepared a loosely autobiographical trick. She stood up with a deck of cards, and began to tell a story. "Once there was a magician," she said, holding up a card. Taking additional cards, she continued, "and he taught everything he knew to a second magician and a third, and so on, until together, they formed the FFAP. Then one day a little girl came to the club and said she wanted to learn magic too." She held out the deck to a spectator. "Will you pick a card to represent the little girl? Memorize it and put it back in the deck." She cut the deck and continued her story. "At first the little girl was lost among all those magicians. . . ." Then she paused. I could tell something was wrong. She had really lost the card. Flummoxed, she excused herself and sat down, refusing to try again.

After the student show ended, I saw her sitting sullenly in the corner with her parents, while the rest of our classmates enjoyed cookies and champagne. I went over and told her how much I liked her routine, and appreciated her ability to tell a story in magic—not something everyone can do. I asked if she would consider performing her trick again for me, because I sincerely wanted to know how her story would end. To my dismay, she burst into tears. I encouraged her to continue in magic and asked if she thought she would come back for the second year of the course. "I don't think so," she replied. "There's no one else my age, and I haven't made any friends." Sadly, it seemed, the "little girl" would be lost forever in the deck of cards.

Without question, female novices entering magic face challenges their male counterparts do not: feelings of isolation, the added scrutiny that comes with minority status, sexual harassment, and cultural pressures to conform to feminine ideals. However, I did not come away from my fieldwork with the impression that the glaring gender disparities in magic result primarily from the active exclusion of women. Like most magicos I spoke with, I think the disproportionate appeal that magic seems to exert for men and boys is a crucially operative factor. Elizabeth

Amato, who raised two children as a close-up entertainer and now tours with a successful one-woman stage show (and who is also a trained psychologist), stated bluntly, "There aren't many women in magic because women don't need magic the way men do. Woman are inherently magical because they can create life." As a performer, Amato considers her gender empowering. "I can bomb a trick. A man can't, because the trick is all he has to show off his power. For me, it's something else. It's a communion with the public. It's bringing to life the magic that inhabits us all." At the end of her show, she performs a torn-and-restored cigarette paper routine with patter about "the natural cycle of life." She told me that one evening, try as she might, she couldn't manage to restore the paper and, in frustration, she burst into laughter and tossed the torn bits into the air like confetti. "That's life too!" she told the audience, and received a standing ovation.

Film historian Lucy Fischer arrives at a strikingly similar interpretation of the symbolism of magic based on a semiotic analysis of the Western magical repertoire: "when one begins to examine those sleights-of-hand so characteristic of magic tradition, one is struck by how so many of them center on the theme of *creation*: men pulling rabbits out of hats, making flowers grow from canes, bringing mechanical automata 'to life.' All of these acts seem like symbolic representations of *birth*, and their occurrence at the hand of the *male* magician seems to bespeak an envy of what is, essentially, the *female procreative function*." [27]

Many other magicians I spoke with cited womb envy as a reason why men are attracted to magic more than women. [28] I am in no position to assess the psychological validity of this ethnotheory, but I would like to point out for the purposes of this analysis that it corresponds to a cultural construction of creativity through an analogy with heterosexual reproductive functions. Whether or not male magicians experience sublimated womb envy, the view that women are inherently magical whereas men's magic is merely prosthetic correlates with aesthetic views about gender-appropriate artistic styles. Most of the male and female magicians I spoke with believe that a "feminine touch" sets women's magic apart, and female novices are encouraged to cultivate a "poetic" style, emphasizing supposedly inherent qualities of grace and beauty rather than the acquired technical skill that "killers" foreground. Understanding why one presentational style might seem more culturally appropriate for people of a specific gender requires that we take a closer look at what actually happens when a magician performs a trick. All tricks involve deception, hence someone fooling and someone being fooled. In the next section, I examine how magicians' staging talk construes this relationship in terms of powerfully gendered roles.

DISCOURSES OF DOMINATION

Skillful magicians provoke strong reactions. The promise of deception implicit in any magic performance arouses different forms of engagement: excitement, curiosity, skepticism. Enacting tricks, magicians enlist spectators in the active co-construction of imaginary worlds as both voluntary assistants and firsthand observers.[29] When magicians produce unexpected effects, spectators may gasp, laugh, shout, or—I have seen it—even cry. It is important to recall that whatever reactions the magician elicits also become part of the co-constructed performance, particularly when a volunteer is onstage as an emissary from the audience.

Successful tricks build up interest and discharge energy. Magicians thrive on that energy, which amplifies their charismatic presence. Face to face with spectators, they personify the principle of the unknown, dislodging uncertainty from the cozy folds of everyday life. Producing the frisson of mystery is one of the great pleasures of performing magic. While magicians love to experience it themselves, they watch each other perform with expert eyes that can't help but anatomize the sinews of illusion. But they can and do experience the mental and emotional impact of their own performances vicariously, reflected back to them in the wondering eyes of spectators.

Magic, in this sense, may not be so different from masked performances in which secret societies intimate hidden powers. Anthropologist Andras Zempléni, himself an initiate of a secret society among the

Senufo of West Africa, writes that "initiates' belief . . . in the power of their secret is constantly reinforced by the belief of . . . uninitiated others. . . . Having worn one in public, I can confirm that the mask—with its ears that hear, and its eyes that see and are seen—attentively follows the effects of its exhibition. It knows perfectly well, but still . . . it needs to know how others signify to it that they don't know and that they want to know." [30] I could describe my own tentative experiences performing magic in similar terms: the awe spectators express literally reawakens the performer to the power of secrets that have grown otherwise familiar, even habitual. Doing a trick not only intimates the value of secrets but also replenishes that value.

The excitement of exhibiting secrets is inseparable from risk: every performance can become an unintended revelation. Whatever precautions magicians take, tricks can always fail. If spectators glimpse a gimmick or a sleight, not only is the illusion shattered, but the principle on which it relies is compromised as well. Like their Anglophone counterparts, magicos call this mistake a *flash* (verb: *flasher*). Avoiding it is one of the basic requirements of their craft. When they practice together, magicians helpfully call flashes to each other's attention. While practice and experience diminish the probability of failure, the *possibility* of catching a magician out remains part of the thrill of spectating. Magicians expect and indeed require that spectators will skeptically scrutinize their every move; otherwise, there would be no interest in fooling them. In this sense, risk is a precondition for magic, not an obstacle to overcome.

In at least one respect, the acquisition of conjuring skill, paradoxically, can allow magicians to augment rather than minimize dimensions of risk. Near the end of our yearlong class, Nemo took the Les Halles magic students out to a café. After dinner, he taught us several effects that relied on probability—in other words, effects that wouldn't always work as hoped and that perforce required contingency plans for various possible outcomes. In the best-case scenario, these effects were astonishing; in the worst-case scenario, they were still perfectly salvageable. "You have to learn something," Nemo said, as if inducting us to a new initiatory level. "Sometimes in magic you have to tempt the devil."

The capacity to fascinate through the display of secret skills compensates magicians for the risks they run. It confers them with charisma, making them objects of attention and desire. This is consistent with Simmel's assertion that "the secret . . . operates as an adorning possession and value of the personality. This fact involves the contradiction that what recedes before the consciousness of . . . others and is hidden from them, is to be emphasized in their consciousness; that one should appear as a particularly noteworthy person precisely through what one conceals."[31] Exhibiting secrets can serve the function Simmel terms "personal emphasis," which paradoxically mixes "superiority to others with dependence upon them, and their good will with their envy."[32]

Another way of thinking about this dynamic is in terms of power: producing magical effects colors the interaction between a performer who possesses secrets and spectators who do not with connotations of power. According to Alfred Gell, "Artistic agency, especially of the virtuoso character . . . is socially efficacious because it establishes an inequality between the agency responsible for the production of the work of art, and the spectators."[33] This "incommensurability of creative powers," as Gell calls it, is an inherent feature of magician's illusions, feats of performance designed as demonstrations of staggering skill. Even when that skill is prosthetic—distributed across gimmicks or apparatus—the impression of virtuosity is still the magician's principal creation and mark of prestige.

Power is central to the way contemporary conjurers conceptualize the history of their art. In influential works of magic historiography written in both French and English, magicians generally portray themselves as the reputable modern heirs of disreputable ancient priests and tribal shamans who purportedly used conjuring trickery to convince benighted followers of supernatural abilities.[34] Magician and magic theorist Eugene Burger argues that, while there is no reliable historical evidence to support this theory—widely accepted as fact among Francophone and Anglophone magicians—invidious comparisons with purportedly dishonest wonder workers provide a foundational charter myth for contemporary magical entertainers. "Do you think that there might be a connection between this picture of the early magician as an unscrupulous scoundrel and the character or persona adopted by many contemporary magicians when they perform?" Burger asks.[35] "Much contemporary conjuring is performed as little more than a power struggle between performer and spectators. The ultimate aim of this endeavor is for the performer to deceive the spectators and thereby win the battle," which is why "we find in much contemporary conjuring performance the recurring themes of *power* and *challenge, humiliation* and *oneupsmanship.*"

Themes of potency pervade the culture of magic today. One has simply to look at any catalog of magic paraphernalia, like one from the Société Française de Prestidigitation mail-order boutique that I received in the mail.[36] Inside, the advertisement for a Card Sword (which allows the magician to toss a deck of cards in the air and impale a spectator's selection) claims, "Your reputation as a swordsman will be assured. D'Artagnan look out." The copy for a poker trick called "Royal Flush" promises that "with this trick you can prove that casinos should tremble with fear when they see you coming." An advertisement for an effect in which a spectator's signed card instantaneously transforms into a card of another value with the same signature ventriloquizes an audience's response: "How can the card's instantaneous appearance on top of the deck be explained? There are only two possible explanations for this miracle: either you are as fast as lightning with incredible precision, or you are a real magician." The catalog's language invites consumers to imagine themselves exhibiting secrets that will make them objects of admiration, awe, and even fear.

Many male magicians I've spoken with acknowledge the allure of this kind of prestige as an initial motivation for their involvement with magic. "I used to be shy," one said simply, "and as soon as I started doing magic, I was suddenly an interesting person." A teenage boy relatively new to magic volunteered, "I used to be really shy. When I had to meet new people, I realized that if I just did a few minutes of magic, the worst would be over. It's a great way to make yourself look good and draw attention to yourself." Although an extreme case, Pierre Brahma's autobiography provides one of the most poignant versions of this motif. After suddenly going deaf in his early teens, Brahma found magic among his sole means of connecting with the hearing world: "I had become a secretive and taciturn young man, a victim of circumstance. To protect myself from harm, I fled contact with others, and my peers did nothing to stop me. Solitude was my lot. This is why I threw myself into presti-digitation like a drowning man clutches at a buoy. Performing magic, I escaped my engulfing darkness. Once again, I became an object of inter-est and admiration."[37] Alex, an auto mechanic in his late fifties and an accomplished amateur magician, confessed that practicing magic turned him into an unwitting egoist. After several years of involvement, he said, "I always find myself trying to turn conversations back to me. I wasn't like that before starting magic!"[38]

In the pursuit of attention, magicians eye each other as potential com-petitors. When a small dinner among magicians turned into an im-promptu show for the handful of laypeople present in an otherwise empty pizzeria, a half dozen professionals and semiprofessionals vied for the spotlight. Walking to the bus afterward, Nemo complained to me that another magician had not left sufficient time for the spectators to take in one of his tricks before launching into a trick of his own. "I love it when there's jousting [*quand ça joûte*]," he said. "But there are certain basic rules you have to respect." Among magicians, calling attention to oneself invites challengers to advance. One professional magician told me about watching an amateur "show-off" (*frimeur*) doing tricks at a vacation resort: "[T]his guy was showing off with a bunch of card tricks. He didn't know I was a magician. He was doing a trick I knew, some-thing basically mathematical. He asked me to deal the cards. I knew my card was the fifth card, so when I got to the fifth card I substituted it for another. All proud of himself, he goes, 'Is this your card?' Bam! When he turned it over, he couldn't understand what happened. It was an *auto-matic* trick, and he blew it. He was lost. 'Don't worry,' I said. 'The card's right here!' I know it's mean, but he was a show-off." (The subtext of this story is that the show-off was doing tricks that did not involve sleight of hand; the storyteller tripped him up using a sleight that reflected his own superior skill.)

However fleeting the relationship might be, in the midst of perform-ing, magicians' skill places them in a position of social preeminence in respect to the spectators they deceive. Connotations of power point to a subtext of symbolic violence in magic, one that Thomas Mann famously explores in the sinister character of Cipolla, a hypnotist-magician who so humiliates spectators onstage that one ends up killing him.[39] Peter Nardi writes that performing a magic trick entails "a kind of deceit that involves power, control, and one-up-man(sic)ship."[40] According to this perspective, the inherently agonic dimension of magic performance makes it particularly amenable to an idealization of heterosexual masculinity in terms of the competitive pursuit of social ranking. Furthermore, because magic performance requires an audience's acquiescence, Nardi hypothesizes that individuals from groups to whom positions of status or authority are less commonly accorded—women or certain minorities—could encounter added resistance in the context of performance.[41]

In terms of its imbrications of gender and power, magic can be likened to humor. In Western societies, there is a "traditional incompatibility between displaying femininity and active, and, in particular, aggressive joking."[42] As I argued in the Introduction, magic tricks and jokes both involve building up misleading expectations in order to enact a gratifying surprise that often elicits laughter. And both seem to involve power. Humor, like magic, "creates new, unusual perspectives on the object and thereby communicates sovereignty, creative power, and the freedom to intervene in the world. Such demonstrative displays of subjectivity and their potential to define normality have been less accepted by women."[43]

Magicos tell each other stories about performing that celebrate the agonic nature of deception in terms that make gendered connotations readily apparent. Talking among themselves, magicos often construe tricking others as a form of symbolic violence. Like English-speaking magicians, they praise performances that "kill" (*tuer*) spectators and call an especially potent performer a "killer" (*tueur*).[44] I also heard magicos use words like *assassiner* (to assassinate) and *niaquer* (roughly, to maul) in describing the activity of tricking someone. But while Francophone and Anglophone magicians share this aesthetic idiom of physical violence, in France the register of sex provides the preferred metaphor for evoking potency in magic performance (perhaps therein lies the crux of Franco-American cultural difference). Recounting successful performances, they commonly use the transitive verb *baiser* (to screw)—and less frequently *niquer* (to fuck)—to characterize the act of fooling spectators. By extension, they describe tricks that are powerfully deceptive as *baisant* (roughly, liable to screw).

Examples proliferate in the flow of everyday talk (as in this chapter's opening vignette). For instance, during the course of giving a lecture, a magicos describing a technique he invented for instantaneously locating a series of selected cards in the deck said, "I admit this makes me particularly proud because I've screwed a lot of dudes with it [*j'ai baisé pas mal de mecs avec*]!" A magicos fresh from a session with a photographer told me and other magician friends that he had taken some great "I'm really going to screw you [*j'vais vous baiser la gueule*]" publicity shots. On another occasion, I was conversing with a pair of magicians, one of whom had just completed filming a commercial for a candy manufacturer in which he performed a series of manipulations with the company's products. Given the unaccustomed nature of the manipulations, he was understandably proud of some of the innovative sequences of sleights he had devised. "Watch this," he said to the other magician. "Try to understand this with your magician's eye." He transformed a large cookie into a slender piece of candy before our eyes. We laughed approvingly. "It's extremely *baisant*," he commented on his own manipulation. Magicos also use the idiom of screwing to praise one another, complimenting a fellow magician with the proclamation, "You really screwed me."

Etymologically, the verb *baiser* originally meant "to kiss." In modern French, it came to mean "to copulate" through a euphemistic extension that led to a third meaning, "to deceive" or "to hoodwink," by a "metaphoric transfer" that equated fooling someone with an act of sexual conquest.[45] In everyday French, the original meaning of *baiser* has been almost completely displaced by these colloquial usages, which are both covered by the English gloss "to screw." Linguist Suzanne Romaine furthermore notes that the verb *baiser* "used colloquially to refer to sexual intercourse enters into a different type of grammatical construction when the subject is male, for example, 'a man has sex with a woman' (*un homme baise une femme*) than when the subject is female, for example, 'a woman is had sex with' (*une femme se fait baiser*). . . . The verb *baiser* behaves transitively when the subject is male. When the subject it female, there is no object . . . . This suggests the woman is passive and the male, active. Intercourse is something done to women rather than something they actively participate in."[46] I argue that magicians' use of the verb *baiser* illustrates that these gendered implications carry over from the domain of sex to the domain of deception.

The idiom of screwing calls attention to a subtext of symbolic violence in magic, and points to the kinds of gendered meanings that magic performances can promulgate in the cultural setting of contemporary France. Drawing an implicit parallel between tricking a spectator and sexual penetration, the notion of screwing portrays tricking in terms of heterosexual masculinity and being tricked as correspondingly feminine. Anthropologists have noted similar patterns of verbal behavior in other male-dominated domains of expertise. In an ethnographic study of American nuclear strategic analysts, Carol Cohn documented "the ubiquitous weight of gender, both in social relationships and in the language itself; it is an almost entirely male world (with the exception of the secretaries), and the language contains many arresting metaphors" equating weapons with phalluses and warfare with sexual conquest.[47] My own experience of language socialization was similar to Cohn's: by the time I became aware of the implications of this metaphorical idiom, I realized that I had already adopted it, unselfconsciously, as a natural part of speaking about magic with other magicos. I therefore agree with Cohn that "individual motivations cannot necessarily be read directly from imagery; the imagery itself does not originate in . . . particular individuals but in a broader cultural context."[48]

Likewise, Joan Cassell found patterns of gendered meanings in the shoptalk of American surgeons. She writes that the "values and symbolism" of the surgeon's ethos "are culturally masculine: hardness; cold brilliance; an intense, narrowly focused drive."[49] The stories that surgeons circulate about "saves"—heroic interventions that snatch patients from the brink of death—reinforce ideals of technical prowess, impassive intelligence, and sheer stamina as the hallmarks of excellence. Cassell further remarks that "not only are dramatic macho 'saves' valorized over compassionate, empathetic, clinically informed surgical care, but when women *do* perform dramatic saves, the male audience assumes that something inevitably must have been done wrong." [50] Magicos' talk about screwing may play a similar role in the French magic subculture as sexual metaphors among nuclear physicists or gendered stories of saves among surgeons. It not only reflects an emphasis on the expression of a heterosexual masculine ideal within the cultural practice of magic, but also creates a discursive arena in which corresponding forms of behavior involving power, competition, or aggression become the object of verbal elaboration and even exaltation.

To be clear, many magicos explicitly reject the idiom of killing and screwing, and its associated ethos. "I don't like the expression [*baisant*] at all," Loïc told me. "It connotes a twisted state of mind. It's unhealthy to equate performing a routine well with *screwing* somebody, even if it's just an abuse of language." On another occasion, he said of his former magic teacher, "Bébel would never say, 'If you do such-and-such, it will be more *baisant*.' He always says, 'If you do it this way, it will be more magical.'" Similarly, Abdul Alafrez lent me a booklet in which American magician Whit Haydn, quoting Bobby Fischer, argues that the essence of magic is "to crush the mind of the opponent" by creating "a problem that the logical mind cannot solve. Like chess, magic is a purely cerebral art form." [51] "If that's really the essence of magic," Abdul said, "I'm stopping immediately. I don't want to be in perpetual opposition with my public, and I definitely don't want to end up like Bobby Fischer."

Even those magicos who reject connotations of competition and symbolic violence must nevertheless be mindful of these potential associations when they perform. In the next section, I consider the way professional close-up magicians use contextualization cues to establish a ludic play frame. Many magicians I spoke with say that their favorite part of magic is the opportunity to "share something" with spectators, in terms of both proffering material they cherish for the enjoyment of others, and creating new experiences and memories. To achieve this, they must approach every performance ready to disarm whatever antagonism spectators may project onto the encounter with a magician. Ultimately, I suggest that play frames in magic constitute a liminal space in which nonnormative constructions of gender can be explored and enacted, particularly through metatextual commentary on familiar conventions of gender display in magic.

PLAY SIGNALS

Sensuous experiences, tricks are also social accomplishments. Particularly in close-up magic, the intimate involvement of spectators in co-constructing the course of performance means that magicians must carefully manage social interaction. Cultural connotations of power and competition establish conditions in which spectators may react defensively to a magician's illusions, particularly in a national setting where performers steadfastly believe that audiences are "too Cartesian" to enjoy being deceived. Furthermore, a table-hopping or strolling magician who arrives at a table or among a cluster of people threatens to undermine the established balance of power or to intrude at an inopportune moment. Succeeding in demonstrating feats that people do not understand without insulting them or provoking conflict is one of the essential skills of the table-hopping magician's trade.

A table-hopping performance potentially risks the face of everyone it involves, from the spectator who cedes control of the social situation and acquiesces to being deceived, to the magician who submits his or her professional artistry to direct public scrutiny and critique. Goffman proposes the term "face-work" to describe everything people do to ensure that their actions do not cause anyone, including themselves, to lose face.[52] Table-hoppers are painfully aware of the imperative of mitigating the potential for power struggles with spectators, and cultivate expert "knowledge of face-work" and "experience in its use."[53] A striking feature of magicians' staging talk is their refined insight into the subtle dynamics of social interaction. Performing the same effects literally thousands of times, professional magicians learn not only to anticipate spectator reactions but also to manage aspects of technique and presentation that can contribute to producing the desired outcomes. Gleaned from experience and transmitted informally between colleagues, this knowledge of face-work is ultimately codified in expert discourse and imparted through trade publications and videos.

In essence, table-hoppers must, through their manner of self-presentation and contextualization of magical effects, constitute indifferent restaurant goers or guests at a special event as an audience for magic. Professional table-hoppers have many strategies for making spectators receptive to magic, even if there is some disagreement about the best ways to go about this. In a bestselling, 400-page treatise on professional table- hopping, David Stone explains that when potential spectators do not know who the magician is or expect his or her arrival, there is always potential for conflict. "One thing's for sure," he writes, "if you appear out of nowhere like a Greek god, brushing aside glasses to make way for your magnificent card mat [a piece of thick fabric on which close-up magicians sometimes perform], there's a good chance people are going to tell you to beat it. . . . You'll be met with confused, uncomfortable, or even hostile looks. It's a boorish entrance and a dubious start. You have to approach the tables intelligently and politely. Remember, if the first table refuses you, you've already dug yourself into a deep hole." [54] Here, I explore some of the strategies that magicos employ to establish themselves as legitimate entertainers and minimize the risk of conflict when table-hopping.

During a lecture to a roomful of novice magicians, Peter Din, then president of the Cercle Magique de Paris (and currently president of the FFAP), attempted to shatter the myth of the "problem spectator"— the incorrigible audience member who magicians dread and who is referred to in French as a *spectateur chiant* (roughly, shitty spectator) or a *casse-pieds* (heckler; literally, foot breaker). "There are no problem spectators," Peter said, "only problem magicians." He argued that by contextualizing an encounter as a demonstration of magic, table-hoppers risk eliciting hostile responses.

PETER: We all make the mistake of saying . . . "[*superciliously*] I am a magician."

ALL: [*laugh*]

PETER: The spectator's response? "[*standoffishly*] Oh yeah? Prove it!" You're necessarily—you're necessarily in a dangerous position at that point. By contrast, if you do things naturally, without specifying that you're doing magic, then it becomes really magical because spectators aren't on the defensive. It's very disagreeable for a spectator to have someone in front of him, someone who does things that people don't understand. It's practically unbearable.

PETER: On fait tous cette erreur de dire . . . "[*superciliously*] Je suis magicien."

ALL: [*laugh*]

PETER: Réponse du spectateur ? "[*standoffishly*] Ah ouais? Prouve-le!" On est forcément—on est forcément en danger à ce moment-là. En revanche, si on fait les choses naturellement, sans préciser qu'on fait de la magie, là ça devient vraiment magique parce que les spectateurs sont pas sur la défensive. C'est très désagréable pour un spectateur d'avoir quelqu'un en face de lui, quelqu'un qui fait des choses qu'on ne comprend pas. C'est à la limite de l'insupportable.

In this example, Peter highlights the initial moment of self-presentation to spectators as potentially problematic. He cautions against explicitly claiming a status ("I am a magician") that spectators may or may not endorse. According to Peter, if a performer is seen as boasting of being "a magician," spectators will consequently be "on the defensive," because magicians confront people with things that no one understands. Peter implicitly links the magician's supercilious self-presentation as a master of mystery with the connotations of power and agonism implicit in the very act of tricking someone. He warns that keying a performance in this way could provoke spectators to respond with defensive strategies of their own: insults, jibes, recalcitrance, and refusal. By contrast, he recommends approaching spectators, particularly in the context of table-hopping, "without specifying that you're doing magic."

Generally no one in a restaurant or banquet announces a magician is performing, nor do table-hoppers enjoy the immediate legitimacy that performing on a stage confers. In approaching each table, the magician has to performatively constitute himself or herself as an entertainer and the dinner guests as a receptive audience. The particular characteristics of this kind of entertainment service employment render the dynamics of face-work particularly fraught, as Peter went on to explain.

PETER: When a guest bothers you, it's that what you're doing doesn't seduce. He's the one you have to seduce. And to seduce, there are techniques. It's your sincerity, it's your gaze, it's your sympathy, it's a form of—of self-derision too. You come across a spectator who wants to take you down a notch because he doesn't like having someone stronger than him at the table. Well, you have to prove to him that, "[*obsequiously*] You are after all so much better than me. Me, I'm just a funny little guy, but you! You, you're so wonderful." Who gives a damn? It's a game! Me, on stage, I often have occasion to say—to make fun of myself. To say [*rubs his belly*], "Look! I'm a magician. I'm not the world's biggest magician, but I am the fattest!"

PETER: Quand un client vous embête, c'est que ce que vous faites ne séduit pas. C'est lui qu'il faut séduire. Et pour séduire, il y a des techniques. C'est votre sincérité, c'est votre regard, c'est votre complicité, c'est un moyen de—d'autodérision aussi. Vous tombez sur un spectateur qui veut vous casser parce qu'il n'aime pas avoir quelqu'un qui soit plus fort que lui à la table. Ben, il faut lui prouver que, "[*obsequiously*] Tu es quand même beaucoup mieux que moi. Moi, je suis qu'un petit rigolo, mais toi! Toi t'es vachement bien." On s'en fout! C'est un jeu! Moi, sur scène, il m'arrive très souvent de dire—de me moquer de moi-même. De dire [*rubs his belly*], "Regarde! Je suis magicien. Je suis pas le plus grand magicien, je suis le plus gros!"

The reality of table-hopping is that magicians seldom, if ever, are entertainment attractions, but rather service entertainers who have to "seduce" spectators one by one, table by table. Peter advocates self-effacement in order to appease a spectator who "doesn't like having someone stronger than him at the table." Neophyte table-hoppers have to accept, according to Peter, that performing magic is only a "game" in which effective play may require overt displays of self-derision.

All seasoned table-hoppers have different ploys they use to build rapport with the public (particularly the initial tables, since subsequent tables know to expect the magician's performance). Peter juxtaposes a magician who contextualizes performance as a form of self-aggrandizement with one who demonstratively positions him or herself as a deferential status inferior, offering the example of a self-deprecating joke about his own weight ("I'm not the world's biggest magician, but I am the fattest"). To avoid overt symbolic combat, the magician must tacitly convince spectators that the performance is not a show of force or an affront to their intelligence. Gregory Bateson calls this kind of message a "play signal." Play can only occur, he writes, "if the participant organisms [are] capable of some degree of metacommunication, i.e., of exchanging signals which . . . carry the message 'this is play.' "[55] From the jokes they tell to the costumes they wear (Marie-Odile's top hat, for instance) and icebreakers they use, table-hoppers can send a variety of play signals to contextualize their performances as non-threatening fun.

In the third example I examine here, two experienced close-up magicians discuss strategies of signaling play when table-hopping. I was spending the evening in Philippe's basement as he and Bruno prepared for a gig the next day. During the course of rehearsal, Philippe brought up an idea he had for initiating a close-up performance while table-hopping.

PHILIPPE: You know, even in table hopping, um at one point I came up with an idea [. . .] It's um a doorbell, you know, doorbells—doorbells, um—

BRUNO: Ding-dong!

PHILIPPE: Yeah, that's it.

ALL: [*laugh*]

PHILIPPE: It's—I'd take the—the doorbell, um, hooked up on my back with the—the button, you know, in a pocket? And um, I'd come up to a table, and, I'd come up like this [*steps forward*].

PHILIPPE: Tu sais, même en table en table, euh à un moment j'avais imaginé un truc [. . .] C'est euh une sonnette, tu sais, les sonnettes—les sonnettes, euh—

BRUNO: Ding-dong!

PHILIPPE: Oui, c'est ça.

ALL: [*laugh*]

PHILIPPE: C'est—Je prenais la—la sonnette, euh, attachée dans mon dos avec le—le bouton, tu sais, dans une poche? Et euh, j'arrivais à la table, et j'arrivais comme ça [*steps forward*].

GRAHAM: Oh, yeah!

PHILIPPE: [*mimes*] I'd take the—
a comb . . . You know, I'd make
myself all pretty . . . And then
I'd push the doorbell. Ding-
dong! [*smiles*] "Can I come in?"
[*laughs*]

GRAHAM: Oh, that's good!

PHILIPPE: But really so that
the—the people understand that,
I'm approaching them, but not
trying to—to make fun of them
with some kind of magical um
pranks that—to show that I'm
superior. But really, to show them
that, I mean to say that it's really
all in good humor. What I'm
doing is nothing, you know, it's
magic, it's—

GRAHAM: Ah, ouais!

PHILIPPE: [*mimes*] Je prenais
le—un peigne . . . Tu sais, je me
faisais tout beau . . . Et puis
j'appuyais sur la sonnette.
Ding-dong! [*smiles*] "Je peux
rentrer?" [*laughs*]

GRAHAM: Ah, ça c'est bon!

PHILIPPE: Mais vraiment pour
que les—les gens comprennent
que, j'arrive, mais pas en essayant
de—de me moquer d'eux avec
des espèces de farces euh
magiques qui—pour montrer que
je suis supérieur. Mais vraiment,
pour leur montrer que, je veux
dire que c'est vraiment du second
degré. Ce que je fais c'est rien,
quoi, c'est de la magie, c'est—

Persuading spectators to play along is the principal goal of the clever
icebreaker Philippe imagines. Miming the approach to someone's front
door, Philippe marks a threshold in both time and space. By ringing a
doorbell, he acknowledges that he is approaching the guests' intimate,
private space and interrupting their ongoing conversation. At the same
time, he makes an ostentatious show of deference, presenting himself
in a position in which one is normally embarrassed to be seen—in an
imagined backstage, in a state of self-involvement, nervously reading his
appearance for an important meeting. He enacts the stereotypical image
of someone who has stage fright, dramatizing his vulnerability at the
moment of contact with new spectators, and making his esteem for them
palpable.

After Philippe described this idea, Bruno placed the challenges facing
table-hoppers in a broader cultural perspective. In the following excerpt,
he contrasts the attitude of typical French spectators to the use of artifice
in special effects films and in magic.

BRUNO: It's true that the biggest problem we have in magic, is avoiding that [*punches his hand*]—that—that conflict, that kind of combat that the public generally expects and that's "[*angrily*] Grrrr, it's just a trick!" When they watch a um *Star Wars* film or this or that, they know very well that it's special effects, still they let themselves get into it for the most part—

PHILIPPE: "[*ironically*] It's not—It's not blood, it's ketchup!" [*laughs*]

BRUNO: Sure, you can say that sometimes in a horror film, et cetera, but even the person who lets himself get into it, he—You're not going to criticize a film for using special effects. Because you've gotten into it. Whereas someone'll say to a magician, "[*contemptuously*] Oh yeah, but you're—you, it's just a trick, um it's—" Because we haven't succeeded in getting him in . . . in the mood—into the universe that we want to create, or the persona, or the fantasy, or the—

GRAHAM: Is that something to blame magicians for . . . or is it more a lack of sophistication . . . on the part of spectators?

PHILIPPE: Both, both, actually.

BRUNO: Although strangely enough in Anglophone culture it gets through, um—

BRUNO: C'est vrai que la plus grosse difficulté qu'on a au niveau magie, c'est d'éviter ce [*punches his hand*]—ce—ce contact, cette espèce de combat que le public l'attend en général et qui est de "[*angrily*] Grrrr, y a un truc!" Quand ils regardent un film euh de *Star Wars* ou ceci cela, ils savent très bien que c'est du trucage, pourtant ils se laissent aller largement—

PHILIPPE: "[*ironically*] C'est pas—C'est pas du sang c'est du ketchup!" [*laughs*]

BRUNO: Bon, ça on peut le dire quelquefois dans un film d'horreur, et cetera, mais même celui qui se laisse aller, il—On va pas reprocher à un film qu'il y a un trucage. Parce qu'on est rentré dedans. Alors qu'un magicien on va lui dire, "[*contemptuously*] Ah oui, mais vous êtes—vous, c'est un trucage, euh c'est—" Parce qu'on a pas réussi à le faire rentrer dans . . . dans le milieu—dans l'univers qu'on veut créer, ou le personnage, ou le délire, ou le—

GRAHAM: C'est quelque chose à reprocher aux magiciens . . . ou c'est plutôt un manque de culture . . . parmi les spectateurs?

PHILIPPE: Les deux, les deux, en fait.

BRUNO: Alors bizarrement dans la culture anglo-saxonne ça se passe, euh—

PHILIPPE: like a letter in the mail.

BRUNO: Yeah.

GRAHAM: [*laughs*]

PHILIPPE: comme une lettre à la poste.

BRUNO: Ouais.

GRAHAM: [*laughs*]

Bruno asserts that the French public is suspicious of magical effects but not special effects used in science fiction or horror films. Even when the magician strives to create an imaginative presentation (involving aspects he identifies as "mood," "universe," "persona," and "fantasy"), it is not always easy to persuade spectators to "get into it," suspending disbelief as they would when watching a film. Bruno and Philippe agree that Anglophone spectators are much more willing to play along, and provide examples to support this claim as the transcript continues.

To say that filmgoers suspend disbelief of course does not mean that they mistake cinematic fictions for reality, but rather that they engage imaginatively with fictional worlds constructed through cinematic artifice. While magicians may aspire to induce this kind of imaginative engagement, Bruno acknowledges that their artifice has a different cultural status than filmmakers'. In a word, Western audiences typically expect that the subject matter of modern magic performances is artifice itself, displayed in the form of tricks. These expectations can be difficult to overcome for magicians like Bruno and Philippe, who want to do more than puzzle spectators with baffling tricks, and who also want to avoid whatever resentment of "being tricked" that spectators may feel—the attitude Bruno, pounding his fist, portrays as violent and irrational. Philippe's idea of using pantomime as a way of approaching spectators while table-hopping suggests one possible means of establishing a fictional world in which spectators more freely suspend disbelief.

While magicians may have to ostentatiously lower themselves to seduce recalcitrant spectators, their unusual position as entertainers gives them tremendous leeway to transgress social conventions. Within the play frame that they seek to co-construct with spectators, table-hoppers paradoxically occupy an interactionally powerful and potentially subversive position. Table-hopping creates a liminal breach, occasioning extraordinary events in everyday social spaces. Like trickster figures, table-hoppers can violate everyday taboos, making ostentatious sexual advances toward spectators or playfully ridiculing people in positions of authority. In a lecture on presentation at a Paris magic club, the Franco-German magician and pickpocket Romaric said, "We often get hired to perform for special occasions, thus formal social settings where everything is arranged *just-so*. And if the magician is *just-so*, that's nice, everyone's happy. But personally, I like to use magic to push things as far as I can, to make people cut loose." As an example, he said he likes to secretly steal a watch from one spectator and slip it into another's pocket, engineering a potentially volatile situation to exploit for the sake of fun. Nemo, who was seated next to me, voiced his agreement. "At events like that, we're in a position to break down social barriers by joking with people's boss, or with a family patriarch. It creates a transgression and it mixes things up. Paradoxically, we provide both a subversive element and social cohesion. It's our job, but it's also very pleasurable to play with!"

The kinds of transgressions that magicians engage in often involve violating sexual taboos. From flagrantly flirting to placing a selected card into a female volunteer's bra, male magicians often direct sexual play and innuendo toward female spectators. But many routinely direct sexual play toward other men. Outré sexual play of all sorts reflects magic's roots in the sexually permissive and experimental culture of the cabaret. Within the liminal moment of performing, magicians can flout sexual taboo and disclose sexual tension. For instance, in his show with Bruno, Philippe assumes the persona of a priapic mentalist, making advances toward men and women alike. In the grand finale, he customarily engages in several minutes of over-the-top homosexual play with a male volunteer. He told me that he deliberately crafted the routine to send a gay-friendly message, and is thrilled by enthusiastic responses from gay audience members and volunteers. Still, despite his best intentions, it is hard to know how well this message gets across. While spectators give themselves license to laugh, they could interpret his performance of homosexuality as a parody that ultimately upholds heterosexual norms. As with any text or performance, meaning is always indeterminate.

CONCLUSION

Conventions of gendered self-display in magic may be slow to change, but they are changing. Paradoxically, the continuing association of the genre with the expression of idealized heterosexual masculinity and femininity makes it particularly amenable to performances that critique gender norms. I end this chapter with an especially suggestive—and enjoyable—example. Several years ago, I attended a performance at the Lido, the grand Parisian cabaret on the Champs Élysées, featuring Parisian magician Otto Wessely. Striding onto the stage, Otto looked the consummate gentleman. Wearing a dapper tuxedo with a carnation in his lapel, he blew a kiss to the crowd. His partner Christa, smiling radiantly in a flowing evening gown, joined him to complete the tableau of a master magician and his lovely assistant. Christa handed Otto a long white rope, as the audience eyed him expectantly. Suddenly a woman's voice filled the theater: "Here we go again with another trick. Good god, what torture." I quickly realized it was Christa herself. Looking pretty by Otto's side as he worked his magic, her prerecorded thoughts were being publicly broadcast for all to hear. "I really shouldn't be on my feet like this with these varicose veins," she thought, shifting uncomfortably on her heels. "But I have to be here for forty-three minutes listening to this shitty music and passing him the pair of scissors. Talk about ecstasy!"

Otto, meanwhile, continued with his trick, taking the scissors from Christa and cutting the rope in two. Then, with a magical flourish, he put the two pieces back together again. "God, I'm sick of ropes!" Christa thought, as she extended her arms in "TA-DA" fashion, beaming at the magician's feat. "To cut them and then—*what a miracle*—restore them. No one gives a fuck! That's what I keep telling him. No one gives a fuck about a restored rope!" By this point, the audience was in stitches. Otto impishly tied the rope around his neck. "All these ropes must turn him on," Christa thought, still smiling vacantly. Otto pulled the rope through his neck, and triumphantly held it out toward the audience, winking coquettishly. "Are my eyes playing tricks on me? I'm starting to wonder if the old fart isn't a bit of a fag!"

Performing iconic rope tricks in elegant evening attire, accompanied by an (ostensibly) adoring female assistant, Otto seemed to incarnate the accustomed image of a modern magician. Yet Christa's voiced-over commentary entirely subverted his attitude of technical prowess and sexual magnetism. What's more, it undermined the gendered division of labor deeply entrenched in modern magic. "Traditional stage magic divides its performers into (male) capital and (female) labor," writes Francesca Coppa, "and exaggerates that distinction so that male magicians are defined by their role as possessors of restricted magical knowledge, whereas female assistants . . . are depicted within the magic act as hypnotized, asleep, unconscious, or mentally vacant." [56] Otto and Christa self-consciously upended these patterns of subjugation, exposing the gendered conditions of female labor. Here it is the male magician who performs mechanically, without a glimmer of self-consciousness, and the female assistant who reflects unflinchingly on her condition as exploited labor. By the end of their routine, Christa began to muse about changing to a career she framed as less exploitative than magic: prostitution. "At least it's *honest* work!"

While Otto and Christa's rope routine challenges some of the gender conventions of mainstream magic, it is also raucously funny. As a subgenre of magic, *comedy magic* generally flouts the preconceived notions spectators have about magic, portraying magicians as bunglers, nincompoops, or poseurs. It constitutes a reflexive, intertextually charged performance that presupposes familiarity with the standard conventions of "serious" magic presentation it satirizes. In this particular routine, the source of comedy is the feminine voice of the magician's female assistant offering metacommentary on the masculine role of the male magician. This performance reminds us that categories like "masculine" and "feminine" do not exist objectively, but are constantly negotiated and performed. Otto and Christa call attention to the way magic performance has been culturally constructed as a system of signs orienting to heterosexual ideals of gendered subjectivity. By disrupting established patterns of gender performativity, they suggest that anxiety about *failed* masculinity may be a subtext for performances articulating magical trickery with imagery of male potency.

As a vocal participant in magicos' staging talk, Otto has championed what Anglophone gender studies scholars would call a "queering"[57] of magic.[58] Some years ago, after taking part in the Paris Gay Pride celebration, he wrote an editorial for *Magicus* magazine about gays in magic. "The sad truth is that we [magicians] have never fought for an idea. We have never mobilized for a cause. There is gay cinema, gay painting, gay literature, but gay magic doesn't exist."[59] Still, he continues in upper case, "QUEER MAGICIANS EXIST! BUT QUEER MAGIC EXISTS ONLY AS MUCH AS MAGICIANS CAN THINK ABOUT ANYTHING ELSE BEYOND THEIR PAYCHECKS."[60] Otto's call to arms implies that economic factors may compel magicians to minimize divergences from the conventional expectations of magic as a genre: bluntly put, magicians are paid to amaze and amuse, not to provide social commentary. Yet his performance with Christa at the Lido shows how magicians can go about, in the terms of Briggs and Bauman, "maximizing and highlighting . . . intertextual gaps" as a strategy of "resistance to the hegemonic structures associated with established genres" and as a means of "building authority through claims of individual creativity and innovation" more generally.[61]

By systematically destabilizing both heterosexual categories and their customary means of signification, Otto and Christa give some indication of what a queer magic might look like. They reflexively reconextualize magical clichés as *evidence* of themes of male potency and female subservience that I have suggested are implicit in conventional presentations of magic. In so doing, they offer an example of the subversive potential inherent within apparently conservative genres—not in spite of stubborn conventions, but precisely because of them. On a basic level, queer magic is yet another style of presentation among many (albeit one that seeks to disrupt the established system of presentational categories) and reflects the general conditions of creativity within magic. Every magic performance provokes conscious or unconscious comparisons with antecedents. Magicians assert creative agency through presentations that play with the constraints of convention, constantly reworking intertextual associations remapping the terrain of magic as a genre.

FOUR Business as Un-Usual

Early on a brisk Saturday in December, while most of Paris slept, Nemo and I wheeled a big wooden box that looked like a medieval torture device (which would soon prove very close to its actual function) from the storage room at a nonprofit organization where he taught kite making into the back of an idling van. In the driver's seat, his bleary-eyed assistant Jeanne rolled a morning cigarette. After stopping to pick up lighter fluid for a flaming magic wand and a big bag of Nemo's favorite pastries (*chouquettes*, irresistible sugar-rolled puffs of fried dough), we set off for the industrial city in northern France where Nemo and Jeanne were to perform at a municipal Christmas party that afternoon.

Along with the spring wedding season, Christmas is the make-it-or-break-it time of year for French magicians. In a good economy, they might hope to perform at office parties and community centers almost every day for several weeks, sometimes with multiple gigs on the same day. During an economic downturn like the one we were experiencing, the holidays can be a grim period. With only a handful of gigs lined up, Nemo was particularly tense. As we merged onto the highway, he got out a minidisc he had prepared for us to listen to while driving. When Jeanne's cassette deck wouldn't accept his adaptor, he began to vent. "I've never seen anything like this! I can't believe it! It's so stupid! I carefully selected things I wanted you to hear—crap!" With rising frustration, he tried again and again to make the adaptor work until, utterly defeated, he unleashed a final string of obscenities and went to sleep for the rest of the two-hour ride.

The booking agency hadn't provided adequate directions, and we lost half an hour of precious setup time driving around a deserted industrial complex looking for the community center where the performance was to take place. We eventually arrived to find a gaping banquet hall ill equipped for a magic show. There was no stage, no backstage, and—to make matters worse—a looming DJ booth and sound system for a backdrop. The accommodating staff scrambled to improvise a makeshift backstage area by throwing a piece of black fabric over a coat rack.

With these arrangements in place, Nemo began to settle into what was obviously a well-established routine. From a suitcase, he placed the materials for different tricks on two long buffet tables, arrayed in the order he planned to use them. With the loving touch of a craftsman handling his tools, he inspected each trick one by one, and then put them in the weathered doctor's satchel he would bring with him onstage. "I start with the last trick and work my way to the beginning so everything is in order," he explained. The routine seemed to have a calming effect, and I tried not to interrupt. I could tell that he was mentally readying himself for the stage. Just as he finished, the event planner charged imperiously into the room, yelling on a cell phone and sending his staff scurrying in confusion. "We hired you for an hour, but we only want forty-five minutes," he snapped at Nemo.

"But I've planned a one-hour show just for the occasion," Nemo responded, a bit stunned.

"Then cut it."

Nemo resignedly took out his program for the show, which had been timed down to the second in order to sync the onstage action with the prerecorded music that Jeanne would cue offstage. "I have to cut fifteen minutes," he muttered, half to me, half to himself. "The thing about Christmas parties is that there are older people and children. If I do too many things that require more advanced comprehension, the little kids will tune out." He wanted to keep as many effects with bright colors in the show as possible, as well as routines featuring children as volunteers, which adults always enjoy. He decided to cut out a rope trick and a trick with silks scarves since he would still have effects with similar types of props in the show. Penciling changes to Jeanne's program and to the small "cheat sheet" he kept in his satchel, Nemo unpacked and repacked his tricks. After arraying the larger props on stage, pacing out the marks with Jeanne, checking the music and microphone, and quickly changing into a smart black suit, he was ready.

Once the show started, the magic flowed effortlessly from Nemo's fingertips. He ran through a tasteful, family-friendly repertoire of classic tricks, from the Gypsy Thread (a torn-and-restored cord effect) to the Twentieth-Century Silks (an effect in which a vanished handkerchief appears tied between two previously knotted scarves, which he presented as a "love story" between two children chosen from the audience). When he began to tie colorful balloon sculptures, exultant children mobbed the front of the room. For the grand finale, Nemo and Jeanne wheeled the mysterious wooden box we had moved that morning to the center of the stage. As medieval-sounding prog rock began to play, he coaxed Jeanne on stage, "hypnotizing" her with a wave of the hand. After closing her inside the box, he inserted two large, crisscrossing metal tubes, and then eight wooden batons at wild angles. He spun the box 360 degrees, making it perfectly clear that no one inside could escape multiple impalements. Still, Jeanne's hand popped out, waving at the crowd. "Should I let her out?" Nemo asked, parodying a gladiator in the coliseum. Deferring to the cheering audience, he removed the metal tubes and the wooden dowels, and Jeanne sprang out of the box. Hand in hand, they bowed and ran behind the coat rack curtain.

After a quick glass of champagne, we loaded in and raced back to Paris. Earlier that day, Nemo had received a call from a Pigalle cabaret asking him to perform two fifteen-minute turns that evening. (By that point, I had learned that cabaret magicians are always on call. They might get a request to perform with only a few hours' notice, and if they refuse too many times, the cabarets will stop calling altogether.) Unfortunately, we got stuck in traffic. I rolled cigarette after cigarette for Jeanne as Nemo grew increasingly flustered. Realizing we would never make it to the cabaret in time for his 7:30 turn, he looked forlornly out the window. "C'est ça la vie d'artiste," he said sardonically, repeating a favorite phrase. *Such is an artist's life.* "And what a life it is," I reflected in my fieldnotes later that night. "You *aren't* an artist; you have to fight to be one every day."

While an elite stratum of magicians can count on powerful agents and exclusive relationships with upscale clients to ensure a steady stream of work, the less established young professionals like Nemo with whom I spent most of my time were constantly hustling to get gigs. In addition to worrying about finding employment, they also deal with the day-to-day details of staging a magic show, working as their own agents, managers, publicists, scriptwriters, directors, creative consultants, stagehands, soundmen, technicians, makeup artists, and costume designers. I saw that their gigs often involved unforeseeable difficulties and stressful interactions with capricious clients whom they had no choice but to accommodate. Few people who watched them performing with the illusion of effortlessness could have realized the challenges or demands these professionals contended with behind the scenes.

In this chapter, I describe how professional magicians in France today conduct "business as un-usual," striving to earn a regular living by displaying their out-of-the-ordinary talents. Over the course of the twentieth century, the cultural landscape of popular entertainments has shifted dramatically. New forms of mass mediation and sociability have radically changed the marketplace, and tastes have naturally evolved. Magicians have adapted, and continue to adapt. Unlike members of some professions, magicians have no stable institutions to guarantee their livelihoods; they must continuously strive to assert their status as professionals and to recruit audiences for their entertainments.

Most of the professional and semiprofessional magicians in this study specialize in close-up magic and perform primarily as table-hoppers (Figure 12). Like Nemo, many also have a full stage show that they

Figure 12.   Spectators react to table-hopper David Stone's transformation of
a regular-size coin into a jumbo coin. Photo by the author.

perform whenever they can, with or without grand illusions; some also
have separate shows for children and adults (this kind of flexibility is
good business, but it also has creative incentives). As professionals, they
think differently about magic than the ranks of amateurs from which
they themselves emerged. In the following section, I examine important
divergences in the criteria that amateur and professional magicians apply to magic performance. I subsequently discuss the changing market
for professional magic performance in France from the nineteenth century to the present day, and consider the ways magicians adapt themselves to current working conditions. In the final section, I analyze magicians' staging talk concerning interactions with clients as evidence of
both their cultural aspirations and acute awareness of the co-constructed
nature of their status as professionals.

"A FEW PROFESSIONALS LOST IN
A SEA OF AMATEURS"

It is important to keep in mind that the magic community is diverse, with members defining success in different ways. Some crave superstar status; others are content to earn a respectable living doing what they love. Some want recognition from peers; others cultivate talents they share with virtually no one: "I'm the king of the mirror," one amateur joked. Magicos aspire to different things depending on whether they practice magic vocationally or avocationally. While professionals generally maintain an amicable rapport with amateurs, the way they talk "could possibly lead one to conclude that amateur-professional relations in magic are fundamentally hostile."[1] For instance, a reclusive professional confessed to me that he avoids magic clubs because he does not like being around amateurs and semiprofessionals: "I see in their eyes that they don't have any ambition. Week after week, they're always there, doing the same tricks for each other. They're at a magic meeting, but it might as well be a support group for rectal disorders."

One evening, I attended a talent show sponsored by one of the local magic clubs with Philippe and Loïc, both professionals. After we left, Philippe mused, "It's rather beautiful to see people coming together . . ." I couldn't tell if it was a setup, but Loïc broke in as if on cue, ". . . to destroy an art." This zinger reflects the common perception among professionals that amateurs perform substandard magic. Another young semiprofessional who had been following the progress of my research remarked, "Sometimes your approach bothers me. I've spent years trying to get out of the club scene that diminishes magic to its lowest common denominator, to connect with people who have an enlightened view of the art. And here you've met some of the most interesting magicians there are but you're spending all your time with club magicians [*magiciens de club*]. It really irks me!"

Such critical remarks belie inherent ambiguities in the amateur-professional distinction. The status of amateur or professional magician is as relative as it is transitory: all professionals start out—and many end up—practicing magic as amateurs and members of clubs. Furthermore, nominal amateurs who work paying gigs from time to time constitute a large and protean pool of semiprofessionals. Amateurs represent the most loyal fan base for professional magicians, not to mention a vast market for the gimmicks and instructional materials some professionals sell, and the paid instruction they offer. As many professionals are quick to point out, some of the most technically expert magicians and productive inventors are in fact amateurs like Christian Girard, who can indulge their passion for magic without worrying much about financial gain.

For professional magicians today, the club scene is virtually synonymous with amateurism, but this was not always the case. The growing popularity of magic as an avocational pursuit over the course of the twentieth century went hand in hand with the transformation of magic clubs into focal points for the amateur practice of magic, with groups that began as professional organizations gradually welcoming an increasing proportion of amateurs into their ranks. The FFAP, France's premier magic organization, is a perfect example. Founded in 1903 as a trade union by scarcely two dozen mostly Parisian professionals, the Association Syndicale des Artistes Prestidigitateurs (Syndical Association of Prestidigitatory Artists, or ASAP) only gradually evolved into a club for primarily amateur enthusiasts, with branches in nearly fifty cities. In the process, it relaxed once highly selective membership criteria, becoming increasingly open to amateurs and even novices.

"The object of this Union," the ASAP's initial charter read, "is to bring together Prestidigitators in order to defend their corporate interests, and contribute to developing friendly relationships among its members."[2] It created an emergency assistance fund to help professionals in financial distress, and issued union cards to assure employers and innkeepers of its members' good credentials. In response to an early critic of the ASAP's exclusivity, one founding member reaffirmed the association's commitment to professional concerns: "we are organized neither to spread the art of Prestidigitation nor to train students, but to further our professional aims."[3]

This evolution of the ASAP from an exclusive, predominantly professional, metropolitan club into an inclusive, amateur, and geographically decentralized federation was gradual, but not always consensual. By 1928, when the organization's membership had swelled to 120, its founding president, Agosta-Meynier, not only resigned his position but also terminated his membership, furious about the ascendancy of amateurs within club ranks. "Those who are today running the union office," he wrote bitterly, "all have another primary profession, being incapable of earning a living from the trade of prestidigitator. I contend that they will never accomplish anything useful and cannot but compromise, through ignorance, the interests of the very individuals they should be defending."[4]

With Agosta-Meynier's departure, it was an amateur, medical doctor Jules Dhotel, who assumed the presidency. His influence would shape the destiny of the organization in the decades to come. Although an amateur, Dhotel passionately defended a highly selective membership policy. In an editorial entitled "No, Not Everyone!" Dhotel wrote, "If it is in the interest of our Association to see its membership multiply, it would be perilous to pursue quantity at the expense of quality. I have in mind all those who are insufficient in knowledge. . . . We don't want just anybody and we don't want to see joining our ranks waves of amateurs or neophytes whose only interest in the Association stems from a desire to satisfy their curiosity."[5]

Dhotel was thrice president of the ASAP between 1941 and 1963, but the tides were against his selective vision. In 1945, the "syndical association" (i.e., union) was reconfigured as simply an "association," the Association Française des Artistes Prestidigitateurs (French Association of Prestidigitatory Artists, or AFAP). Its new charter read, "The goal of the [AFAP] . . . is to bring together prestidigitators, professional and amateur alike, along with other similar associations, to create friendly relationships between all adepts of the art of magic, to increase appreciation of this art, to grow it, and, if necessary, to defend it against abusive divulgation."[6] At the time, there were 400 members spread through ten chapters.

The turbulent 1960s brought a major watershed. Although he was no longer president of the association, Dhotel's death in 1967 marked a symbolic transition: a year later, student revolts would paralyze France, and the AFAP, under new leadership, embarked on a two-pronged project of "democratization" aimed to increase the influence of members in the provinces and to open the doors to younger members. In an editorial entitled "A Democratic Association," Maurice Gauthron reflected on these initiatives: "Things have changed a lot in the past forty years. . . . [These transformations] constitute simply the stone our generation adds to the edifice built by the previous generation, and which will serve the next. . . . The young have a debt of gratitude to pay their elders, who should, in exchange, seek to understand changing points of view."[7]

The ascendency of amateurs within the AFAP has continued in recent years. When the association's charter was revised in 1994, its preamble read, "The AFAP . . . is a friendly and confraternal association . . . with an essentially artistic and cultural mission."[8] A number of new goals were enumerated, including preserving the heritage of magic in France, fighting against charlatanism, and protecting magicians' intellectual property. In a reversal, the AFAP would now claim as a principal objective "the training and cultivation of magical artists through classes, meetings, lectures, exhibitions, conventions, and publications. The Association is particularly committed to encouraging the artistic efforts of the young." In 2005, as a part of its ongoing decentralization, the once Paris-centric association officially became a federation of its regional clubs, the Fédération Française des Artistes Prestidigitateurs (French Federation of Prestidigitatory Artists, or FFAP), retaining the same objectives articulated in the 1994 charter. There are now over 1,500 members.

At least since the founding of the first magic clubs, professional magicians have decried what they see as amateurs' obsession with techniques, and lack of attention to presenting magic effectively. A century ago, professional magician Édouard Raynaly proposed the following comedic definition for the term *amateur*:

> Friend of professional [magicians], and often their principal patron. . . .
> From a technical point of view, the amateur is, in general, quite sharp.
> His passion for Magic readily attaches itself to the most minor detail,
> which he is ever prepared to dissect, discuss, compare, analyze, etc.,
> with a faith, a passion, a patience that can, in certain cases, verge on
> sacerdotal severity.

When two amateurs meet, they never let merriment taint the blessed occasion. Colloquy is, for them, an infinite, incomparable joy. They exchange arcane wisdom, judiciously evaluating the value, skill, or ingenuity of a particular pass, change, or sleight, in whose secret beauty they revel.

Their technical expertise should therefore come as no surprise. It follows that they should be magnificent performers, exuding consummate artistry every time they do a trick. Sadly, they never do any.[9]

A strikingly similar characterization of amateurs as fixated on technique emerged during a conversation I had with professional magician Abdul Alafrez in 2005. "The magic scene is a few professionals lost in a sea of amateurs," Abdul told me. "Magic is so overwhelmingly amateur that all the criteria for judgment are amateur criteria. For example, amateurs don't give a damn about presentation or aesthetics; it's not their problem. They concentrate on the accumulation of tricks. They've always got to be learning new tricks." The distinction Abdul posits between amateur and professional criteria for judgment is crucial for understanding not only how magicians with different career paths relate to each other, but also the nature of the work professionals do.

As amateurs, many close-up magicians admire sophisticated sleight-of-hand artistry and seek to learn tricks that showcase their virtuosity. When they become professionals, they are faced with the realization that simple, even self-working tricks that they once might have scoffed at can, in fact, have a greater impact on the lay public than the kind of intricate tricks that impress other magicians. Furthermore, when performing an effect that can be produced using a variety of methods, amateurs might opt for difficult sleight-of-hand where professionals would choose a technically easier method, freeing themselves to concentrate on the other demands of table-hopping. Finally, while an amateur might boast of knowing hundreds of tricks, a professional can build a career on four or five tricks, performed, sometimes dozens of times, night after night.

The pull between amateur and professional criteria in magic parallels Howard Becker's famous description of the cultural predicament facing jazz musicians in 1940s Chicago.[10] While the musicians in that study esteemed avant-garde jazz and considered themselves artists, they could only make a living by playing low-prestige dance music for "squares." Similarly, magicos distinguish between *magie pour magicien* (magic for magicians) and *magie commerciale* (commercial magic). Like avant-garde jazz, magic for magicians is difficult to grasp for the uninitiated, demands discriminating taste from an audience, and showcases the performer's virtuosity. And like dance music, commercial magic has a widespread appeal, is intensely enjoyable for lay audiences, and does not necessarily demand much technical skill from the performer. Unlike the musicians in Becker's study, however, professional magicos generally do not resent performing commercial magic. In fact, they use the term *commercial* without a hint of pejoration, to praise effects, presentations, and performances that are particularly effective in the conditions of professional work. Instead, they treat "magic for magicians" as a pejorative term, referring to highly technical tricks designed to impress other magicians as *la branlette* (jerking off) and the amateurs who do them as *branleurs* (jerk-offs). In contrast, professionals might call an amateur who approaches magic with professional standards an *amateur éclairé* (enlightened amateur).

Some professionals have one set of material they perform among peers and another altogether for professional settings. For instance, one evening at the Illegal, I met Mickaël Stuzinger, one of the foremost young close-up magicians in France. I had seen him perform mind-boggling card routines at packed conferences around Paris, stringing together intricate sequences of effects for thirty minutes or more. I mentioned that I would be interested in seeing him work professionally. He told me that he had a weekly gig at a swanky Champs-Elysées restaurant, but that it was "nothing interesting, just table-hopping," in other words, not worth my time. At first I took this as false modesty, but I later realized that he meant it in earnest: for close-up virtuosi, performances for laymen are not an accurate reflection of the kind of technical skill valued among magicians.

Magicos do, on occasion, perform more complicated material for lay audiences. For instance, if a table-hopper establishes an especially good rapport with a particular group of spectators, he or she might be invited back to their table for a drink later in the evening. At that moment, with an assurance of the spectators' undivided attention, it is possible to perform less commercial effects, such as intricate card routines requiring a surface to work on. Loïc told me he sometimes employs a deliciously perverse ploy in moments like this. If spectators ask him questions about how he learned magic (as they often do), he tells them, "There are magic clubs where we get together and show each other tricks—really complicated stuff, not like what I've been doing tonight." When the spectators inevitably ask to see a sample of this "magic for magicians," he performs a simple, automatic trick known to almost every beginning magician. "It's all in the presentation," he assured me.

FROM THE STAGE TO THE SUPERMARKET

Magicos credit Jean-Eugène Robert-Houdin, the "Founding Father of Modern Magic," with elevating magic "from the street to the stage." Robert-Houdin represented the apogee of what a magician of his day could hope to achieve. In sharp contrast to the marketplace buskers and fairground mountebanks he describes in his memoirs,[11] Robert-Houdin had an eponymous boulevard theater in Paris decorated in the style of the most elegant bourgeois salons of the day. Dressed in fashionable eveningwear, he engaged spectators in worldly conversation while demonstrating sophisticated automata of his own invention. In the century and a half following Robert-Houdin's retirement, the marketplace for popular entertainment has radically evolved. Changing with the times, professional magicians have assimilated new tastes and adapted to new venues of performance. Depending on their perspective, they may view these cultural changes in terms of either growth or decay, expanding opportunities or declining traditions. In this section, I consider salient shifts in professional magic over the past century and the reactions they have occasioned among magicos.

Magicians sometimes refer to the period from roughly 1880 to 1920 as a kind of "Golden Age" during which large numbers of high-stature magicians crisscrossed the globe competing to bring the latest discovery to new audiences.[12] During the same period, many lesser known French magicians earned livings performing on street corners, in private salons, in cafés, seasonally at vacation resorts, and by providing light entertainment at parties and banquets organized by civic institutions and community groups.[13] This same period witnessed a rising vogue for a form of entertainment known as "music hall," a British import featuring variety artists (magicians, singers, acrobats, jugglers, etc.) performing short turns referred to as "numbers" because of the ordinal sequence in which they appeared onstage. "Today's spectators are not of a nature to revel for two hours in the wonders of the skillful, but nevertheless selfsame, performer," wrote a Parisian professional in 1905.[14] "They find the demands on their attention excessive and, faced with other choices, find the taste of variety more and more appealing." The music hall format required artists accustomed to performing long shows illustrating a wide range of talents and featuring polite banter with spectators to develop a new kind of routine: short, punchy, and nonverbal.[15]

Many of the most successful music hall magicians had specialty acts featuring dexterous manipulations of a signature kind of object: billiard balls, playing cards, coins, or cigarettes. And many of them came from abroad. For French magicians, the deluge of foreign performers and novel styles that came with the advent of music hall seemed to threaten an established tradition of French magic. An editorial in the first issue of the *Journal de la Prestidigitation* posed the question, "Will the entertaining magic conceived by the ingenious mechanician [Robert-Houdin] be swept aside by the manual virtuosity of the Germans and Americans, at present so popular? Or will it regain its place of pride and royal scepter among worldly amusements?" [16] Just before the outbreak of World War I, another professional magician wrote an editorial condemning the increasing popularity of manipulation acts widely perceived as an import from the United States: "I deplore the invasion of French prestidigitation by American manipulations that are nothing more than acrobatic jugglery—for a fleeting moment delightful and surprising to the spectator, but soon enough tedious. . . . French prestidigitators! My colleagues, let us remain therefore French, and hold strongly to the genre in which

our predecessors excelled: manual agility augmented with verbal subtlety, refined wit, and lively repartee."[17]

It is easy to imagine that the advent of cinema would have had disas-
trous consequences for magicians, but (in France at least) the reality was
more complicated. Magician Georges Méliès was among the first to exhibit film in Paris, incorporating it seamlessly into his magic show.[18]
While cinema would ultimately change the way audiences consumed
popular culture, state policies sought to ensure that it would not compete directly with live entertainments. In 2003, I was lucky enough to
hear retired magician Maurice Saltano recount the experience of turning pro in the period immediately following World War II. He described
how he got his start performing during intermissions between double
features in the movie theaters of his native Grenoble, benefiting from a
law that encouraged cinemas to hire live performers. "There was lots of
unemployment among live entertainers," Saltano explained. "This law
gave movie theaters that booked live performers a tax break; those that
didn't had to pay an extra tax. It worked great. One agency had 50 theaters around Grenoble, which gave me enough work for a year. They
didn't pay anything, but you could make a fair amount of money selling
horoscopes or other trinkets."

In the eyes of Saltano, it was the emergence of the modern record
industry—not cinema—that would devastate live magic in the mid-
twentieth century. He explained that he gradually progressed from home-
town cinemas to more lucrative contracts: first, movie theaters in Paris,
then long-term music hall engagements and touring revues. He recalled
the period as a kind of idyll. But in the early 1960s, the cultural economy
of popular entertainment suddenly began to change. Touring France
with rock and rollers Les Chaussettes Noirs, then Bill Haley, Saltano
encountered auditoriums full of crazed teenagers. "We had to fight with
the audience. It was horrible. That was the period of broken seats and
screaming crowds. The MCs couldn't introduce the acts. It wasn't a show
anymore [ce n'était plus du spectacle]. I saw artists leave the stage in tears."
In 1962, Saltano's wife gave birth to a son, and he retired from the stage.
"Frankly, it was just a pretext. I was soured on the profession." Other
magicos similarly attested that, by promoting concerts by individual

recording stars, the record industry undermined the kind of all-evening music hall reviews in which magicians and other variety artists shared the bill with singers.

For much of the twentieth century, another venue offered enticing opportunities for magicians to ply their craft: the cabaret. Provincial cabarets throughout France were often little more than glorified brothels adorned with stage shows,[19] but Paris was the cabaret capital of the world. In its heyday, the Parisian cabaret circuit was like an oil boom, and the magicians who plied its stages hardworking roughnecks. Those who knew the salad days of the 1970s boast of performing eighteen or twenty shows a day in the cabarets of Pigalle and Montparnasse. It was grueling work, and the audiences were unforgiving. But the bohemian lifestyle immortalized in Pierre Brahma's autobiography *La Malle des Indes* held a tremendous allure.[20] Drunken and rowdy cabaret audiences are often impatient with "visual acts" that interrupt the steady flow of exotic dancers. Cabaret performers embrace a style of presentation they call *rentre dedans* (roughly, "in your face"), with lots of attitude and a profusion of bawdy humor. Those I spoke with had little patience for artistic pretension; fiery cabaret magician Stephane Gali presented himself to me as a *paysan de la magie*—a peasant of magic.

In France today, Jean Merlin is the standard against which other cabaret magicians are judged. When I contacted him, he graciously invited me to meet him around midnight in front of a Pigalle cabaret. Tourists and revelers flooded the small side street. Drug dealers positioned in dark doorways conversed in their silent language of winks and nods. In front of an adjoining kebab house, a pack of teenagers was hassling passersby. Suddenly, Merlin appeared, all belly and mustache, elbowing his way through the motley crowd. With his brown three-piece pinstripe suit, trademark fedora, worn leather valise, and intelligent eyes, the boyish sexagenarian could have been an old-fashioned country barrister hurrying to court just as plausibly as a Parisian magician late for a cabaret gig. "Sorry," he panted, shaking my hand. "Just finished up another one around the corner. You ready?" I nodded, and he yanked me by the arm inside. Onstage, bare-breasted nubile maidens rhythmically cavorted to the sound of blistering synthesizer music, suspended in the giant web of a menacing mechanical spider with glowing red eyes. Merlin pointed to an empty seat near the rear of the smoky room, and disappeared backstage. Two minutes later, the MC announced him: "World famous showman, Mr. Jean Merlin!"

I was surprised that, in a twenty-minute turn, Merlin only performed two routines, spending most of his time engaged in rollicking repartee with the audience. He began as if he would do a card trick, then veered into a five-minute comedic tangent about how awful card tricks are. He eventually made it back to the trick, asking a female volunteer to join him onstage. The woman—who appeared a bit tipsy—picked a card, but after putting it back in the deck, immediately confessed she had forgotten it. "Even an eight-year-old kid knows that when you take a card you're supposed to look at it!" Merlin said with mock indignation, clearly savoring the ticklish situation. "It's like a woman, when you 'take' her, you need to look at her.[21] You have a role to play!" he told the volunteer. "It's like a movie." To drive the analogy home, he picked several more volunteers to play-act the roles of movie director, cameraman, and clapboard operator. What had begun as a simple card trick was spiraling into a hysterical imbroglio with five people onstage. After several abortive "takes," the director yelled, "Action," the clapboard clapped, the camera began rolling, and the volunteer selected a card, which she returned to the deck. Merlin melodramatically turned the cards over, revealing that fifty-one were facedown and one—the spectator's selection—was face-up in the middle of the deck. "You had one chance in two, and you blew it!" he laughed.

Over beers later that night, Merlin equated performing in a cabaret with bullfighting. "The bullfighter never knows what the bull is going to be like until it's released into the ring. The magician never knows what the audience is going to be like until he's up on the stage." Clearly, Merlin flourished when improvising comedic scenes with whatever raw material the boisterous setting of the cabaret offered up. "You can keep your big theaters and TV shows—screw 'em. The place for me is in the ring, right here." He gazed wistfully out the window at the tawdry, tumultuous Pigalle street scene. "Twenty years ago there were nearly a hundred cabarets in Paris where a magician could work, most of them here in Pigalle. Now there are only six . . . and counting."

While opportunities to perform in cabarets may be dwindling, table-hopping and strolling genres—ambulatory close-up magic performed for individual tables or groups of people at a restaurant, banquet, or reception—have been a dynamic growth sector in recent decades (see Figure 13). Table-hoppers operate under difficult conditions: their spectators may be inattentive, they have to contend with background noise and wait staff jostling them, the lighting is bad, they must spend hours on their feet, and often they have no surface to use in performing. Their tricks should be "visual," as magicos put it: eye-catching and easy for audiences to grasp. Because they perform for only four or five minutes per group, their tricks should also be easily portable and have a quick "reset time"—that is, the magician should finish at one table ready almost instantaneously to perform at the next. A typical table-hopping routine therefore might consist of a card trick, a bill change (the transformation of a borrowed banknote into a much larger denomination and back again), and perhaps an effect with sponge balls, coins, or scrunchies.

Magicians today also find work at trade shows and other corporate events, doing tricks that feature a client's product or brand. In 2002, professional magician Damien Bertrand cofounded the advertising agency Joseph to capitalize on this emerging market by hiring small armies of magicians to fan out across France promoting consumer goods. The success of their business model provoked sustained debate among magicos, many of whom worried that Joseph campaigns threatened to drastically devalue magic, financially and culturally.[22]

For its advertising campaigns, Joseph employs world-class magicians to script short magic routines that prominently feature a client's products: chocolate, shampoo, mobile phones, and so on. The company then hires scores of overwhelmingly amateur magicians to perform these routines in grocery stores, shopping malls, or commercial outlets. Recruits receive an instructional video featuring the celebrity *auteur* and whatever props may be necessary for the routines. In 2005, Joseph paid 100 euros for an eight-hour workday—three times less than a professional magician would minimally expect to earn *in an hour*. Their busi-

Figure 13. Table-hopper Marie-Odile
Langloÿs, wearing her signature tophat,
performs a torn-and-restored cigarette paper
routine. Photo by Antoine Mériaux.

ness model, which depended on a seemingly inexhaustible supply of
amateurs, was ingenious. For beginners, Joseph campaigns offered an
enticing prospect for gaining what seemed like professional experience.
One amateur magician who was on the verge of turning pro had already
done five Joseph campaigns when he told me, "It's not about money, but
honing professional skills. You do the same tricks, with the same patter,
all day long, hour after hour, and it allows you to really concentrate on
your presentation."

Most professional magicians quickly came to regard the agency with
open hostility because of its derisory rates.[23] "It's humiliating to work

for such a small amount. I would never do it," one told me. Others complained that Joseph campaigns cheapened magic as an art form. For instance, in an angry aside, a magician lecturing in June 2005 pronounced himself against "an unnamed agency that gives three tricks to any nincompoop who walks through the door." He gave several reasons for his hostility toward Joseph: "First, the kids that do their campaigns say, 'Well, it's a great experience.' To that I say, go give charitable performances in a hospital or a prison. That's an *experience* too and one that doesn't sabotage the professional pay scale! To those who say Joseph's campaigns don't compete with professionals, I say magic is the cherry on top of the cake. It's not the cake; it's not the icing; it's not the whipped cream. And sticking it all over the goddamn place degrades it pretty badly. Third, to those who say that it allows you to learn magic, I say it's like McDonald's: the kid who gets his first job there quickly figures out, 'Hey, this is bullshit. I'm not going to waste my time learning how to do this crap.' And that attitude sticks with them for good."

The controversy about Joseph was largely fueled by online debate in VirtualMagie.com forums. The "Joseph" thread, which began on the evening January 26, 2003, became the longest in the website's history three days later, with almost 100 postings.[24] The thread remained active for over two years, swelling to over 350 posts (it was surpassed in size in 2005 by a thread concerning techniques for customizing the images on playing cards, which elicited nearly 800 posts in a year). The first poster innocently asked, "Has anybody heard of Joseph?" Over the next two days, information trickled in from informed sources. Late on the second day came the opening salvo from critics: "Throngs of clones on an assembly line performing tricks on command for slave wages? That's far from my idea of a career in the arts." Christian Girard was the next to write in: "Keep taking 100 Euros per gig, and sooner or later someone will find a way to pay you even less. We're at the heart of a major problem facing the 'profession' of magic, and you need to close ranks or wages are going to be pulled further down."

The next day, amid calls to "wait and see," defense positions began to emerge. "These may be engagements for 100 Euros . . . but they don't have anything to do with traditional magic performances," one defender wrote. Another sarcastically remarked, "When I consider that some people work eight hours a day, sometimes even growing tired in the process . . . to earn 6.83 euros an hour [then the minimum wage], I think they've got to be crazy!!! To them I say: become magicians, damn it!" The debate continued to rage. Finally, on January 30, the cofounder of Joseph posted the company's promotional statement on the discussion board. It explained their business model with a cool, sententious logic: "**Joseph** positions magic as a new media at the service of brands. We associate a 'magical emotion' with a product so that consumers purchase it. This form of communication in settings of sale or consumption is called Operational Marketing. **Joseph** is an agency of Operational Marketing that uses magic as a **communicational support**. This concept is already well developed in the United States. . . . Such communicative magic is utterly different from entertainment magic." This explanation assuaged some concerns, but aggravated others. Someone wrote, "I don't think this is what Magic needs today—especially not today. It's going to erode magic's image even further, distancing the discipline from the notion of Art and relegating it even more irrevocably to the status of a sub-art. . . . Where are the Nobility and Seriousness of Magic? Nowhere . . . except maybe between two aisles of food or some DVDs."

After several months, personal testimonies began to appear on the thread. "Josephians," as they began to call themselves, recounted their experiences, commiserated, and shared helpful hints. Critics seemed silenced until Loïc—a notorious provocateur—rekindled the debate. In October 2005, he wrote, "Why not just start a special 'Joseph' chat-room? When I read the posts from some magicians who work for the agency, I feel like they're members of some club. . . . P.S. I have some magico-marketing ideas for maximizing the impact of FUCA dragées [a kind of candy]. Who can I talk to?" One of the more vocal Josephians responded, "Are you jealous?" This was a perfect taunt for Loïc, who reacted with characteristic élan:

Yes, I admit it.
  I too would like to sing the praises of such leading brands as Nestle, Bosh, or Pepsi.

I would like to stride down the supermarket aisles, and watch carts stop in their tracks because I'm doing tricks for the nice women buying hygienic napkins. Between tricks, I dream of helping that elderly woman who can't reach a special can of green beans that reminds her of childhood, and who asks for my help because I'm "such a big boy."

All that under magnificent fluorescent lights, with an impressive voice announcing my performances (not without failing to mention that, because it's the Wild Week of Toilet Paper, there's a special offer on two-ply).

Sometimes even I dream.

Sadly, I'm not there (yet), I'm just a beginner, but I sometimes I have the opportunity to practice in places where "magicians with six months of magic (but a fancy magic website) who can do nice little card tricks" haven't already unloaded their two-bit trickery.

One day, maybe. . . . We'll see each other there, and we'll kiss each other on the cheeks, because we're "Artists."

As amply illustrated by Loïc's brilliantly crafted post (which predictably ensured weeks of continued controversy), magicos are drawn to participate in VM forums not only to exchange information and debate issues, but also for the sheer pleasure of verbal playfulness. Loïc satirizes Joseph campaigns, suggesting that no self-respecting artist would perform in a place where hygienic napkins and toilet paper are sold. He construes the supermarket as an inappropriate, even demeaning, setting for magic—a precipitous decline from the cultural heights to which Robert-Houdin had taken the art in the nineteenth century.

Debates over Joseph cast the cultural predicament of French professional magicians into stark relief. In the terms of Robert Stebbins, few magicos today work as "entertainment attractions" who perform in theatrical settings with paying audiences;[25] most are "service entertainers" hired by clients, if not to promote products, then to provide what the French call *animation*—that is, enlivening diversions in spaces of organized sociability. For most, this would not be a source of concern, were market pressures not pushing magic toward what seems to be a slippery slope of cheapness. In the next section, I discuss how professional magicians reconcile a self-image as professionals with the realities of their working conditions as they strive to construct remunerative—and meaningful—careers.

GETTING THE JOB DONE

A variety of paths lead from amateur to professional magician. Some amateurs bide their time, waiting for an opportune moment to turn pro, while circumstances thrust others unexpectedly into professional careers. Jan Madd told me that, when his father lost a small business supplying American servicemen in the years following World War II, he was the only one in his family able to quickly earn much-needed cash. At the age of twelve, he became a busker, performing in the streets of his native Cherbourg, gradually working his way up to casinos on the coast of Brittany, where he earned so little that he had to make a daily choice between food and lodging. "It was fantastic," the regal Madd recalled wistfully, as we sipped champagne aboard the sumptuous riverboat theater he now owns, moored in the shadow of the Notre Dame cathedral. "I slept on the beach for two weeks straight." More recently, I knew several amateurs who turned pro when the Internet bubble burst and they lost their jobs in the computer industry.

While I did not explore the issue systematically, my informal observations suggest that, as amateurs weigh their prospects for social mobility, class can have an important, if not decisive, impact on decisions about turning pro. In a moment of candor, one highly successful young professional told me, "I loved magic when I started. Now I like it well enough because it's my job. What matters is that it gave me the opportunity to get out of the working class. It was a pretext for me to escape a shitty background." By contrast, an amateur from an upper-class background who chose a career in magic would likely risk downward mobility. When I asked one passionate middle-aged amateur—who also happened to hold a prestigious professorship at a major Parisian university—if he had once considered turning pro, he laughed. "I was too well educated."

Regardless of how they become professionals, magicos who hope to succeed as entertainers must set aside any attachment to magic for magicians and embrace commercial magic. Becker relates that, between the extremes of intransigent artist and resigned entertainer, some jazz musicians espoused what he calls a craftsmanly orientation: "One way of adjusting to the realities of the job without sacrificing self-respect is to adopt the orientation of the craftsman. The musician who does this no longer concerns himself with the *kind* of music he plays. Instead he is interested only in whether it is played *correctly*, in whether he has the skills necessary to do the job the way it ought to be done."[26] Professional magicians, particularly table-hoppers, subscribe to this craftsmanly orientation, almost as a rule.

Often, one magician favorably describes another by stating simply, "*Il bosse bien*" (roughly, he gets the job done). This kind of terse proletarianism is the exclusive province of professional magicians, and reflects a tacit consensus about the craftsmanly orientation toward work. Of course, saying that someone "gets the job done" is not the same thing as praising the artistic merits of his or her work. After watching an ascending star of the magic world perform several routines at a magic club, a friend whispered to me, "*Il bosse bien, je l'avoue* [he gets the job done, I admit it]." I knew this friend did not particularly admire the performer's work, and I took his begrudging praise as an indication that magicos recognize and accept that their own criteria do not always correspond to the expectations of clients and audiences at large.

The nature of work in magic is almost exclusively "entrepreneurial."[27] Many professional magicians lament not "knowing how to market themselves" (*savoir se vendre*). In this context, their biggest allies are also, paradoxically, their potential competitors. Professional relationships between magicians are characterized by a delicate balance between egoism and altruism. In Paris, with its high concentration of talent, competition for work can be fierce, but opportunities for cooperation abound. Magicos rely on each other's connections to ensure a steady stream of work. These equivocal professional circumstances, in which fellow magicians are both troublesome competitors and indispensable allies, shape the relationships between magicians, who individually calculate to maximize both short-term profit and long-term security.

There are several different circumstances in which one magician might help another find work. When an employer requests two or more magicians for a large function, a magicos can contact friends or associates, but a calculus is still involved: one wants to bring in the best talent possible without risking being outshone. If magicians cannot keep a gig, they can arrange for replacements, upholding their end of the contract and perpetuating a potentially lucrative relationship with the employer. Similarly, magicians offered gigs that they cannot accept (as often happens during the busy holiday season) might suggest colleagues. However, a performer must be cautious about furnishing replacements. One magician explained his reluctance to get stand-ins for his weekly Sunday brunch engagement at an upscale restaurant: "I used to call a replacement if I couldn't work. I don't do that anymore. If the guy is worse than you [*si le mec bosse moins bien que toi*], people won't tell their friends to come. If the guy is better than you [*si le mec bosse mieux que toi*], the boss will say to himself, 'Why isn't *he* working for me instead?' No, no, no. I won't call a replacement anymore."

When one magician gets a gig for another, it is with the tacit expectation of return favors. Stories of disappointment and betrayal abound, but the risk of sharing work has concrete payoffs, often resulting in the crystallization of long-lasting informal partnerships based on trust and reciprocity.[28] Bruno made the generally unstated principles undergirding these relationships explicit to me: "I have a list in my head of people that I would get gigs for, but it has to flow in both directions. Philippe [then his partner] is always my first priority. If someone else gets me a gig, he goes to the top of the list. If I get someone a gig, and he doesn't reciprocate, after a while he goes to the bottom of my list. There are guys who, out of fear, jealousy, or whatever, *never* get work for anybody else. I got [a particular magician] two gigs, and he never found me work. He's the kind of guy who would tell an employer, 'No, I can't work,' and cancel a gig rather than offering his contract to a friend. Then there are guys that screw up your contracts. [Another magician] screwed up three contracts for me. Three times, he told me he would work and then didn't show. And for a long time, I stopped trying to help him."

In their staging talk, magicos revel in telling stories about their work experiences, but secrecy regarding employment opportunities can dampen their loquacity. During the course of an interview, one professional table-hopper shocked my delicate ears with stories about his work in some of the most lavish—and decadent—of Mediterranean resorts, where he claimed Arabian sheiks and Russian mobsters delighted in dousing topless party girls with hundreds of thousands of dollars' worth of champagne. "See this watch?" he said, rolling up his sleeve to reveal an enormous silver Rolex. "This was a tip. 3,500 euros. Where I work, a meal for four costs 10,000 euros. A bottle of wine costs 1,500 euros. And there are guys who buy 100 bottles of champagne just to spray on each other. Down there, conspicuous consumption is the rule, and I'm part of that. They pick me up for work in a helicopter, for Chrissakes!" I had no idea that close-up magicians could make the kind of money he was describing. "Are there other people that have those kinds of gigs?" I asked. "There must be at least one or two, but I wouldn't know. When you get that kind of gig, *you shut your fucking trap!*" He prodded my arm with a menacing forefinger for emphasis. "You don't want *anybody* moving in on your turf."

Themes of corporate solidarity become especially apparent in conversations about the pay scale for magicians. In 2005, going rates for competent young professionals were around 400 euros for a table-hopping gig, 300–500 euros for a stage show, 200–400 euros for a children's party, and 50 euros for a ten-minute cabaret turn. A more established professional could charge at least twice as much, and everyone's rates double in peak seasons, especially around the winter holidays. Magicos use the French idiom *casser les prix*, which literally means "to bust prices," to describe magicians who perform for substandard rates, underselling colleagues and breaking corporate ranks. They also use the phrase *brader la magie*, which effectively means "to liquidate magic," in describing performers who accept work for substandard pay.

In the eyes of many professionals, the scourge of price busting is directly connected to amateurs seeking to perform professionally. Because of the low frequency of work, magic is compensated by high rates of pay,[29] making this a particularly attractive market to amateurs salaried in another field. Magic is an expensive hobby, and amateurs who perform occasional paying gigs may reinvest their earnings in equipment, sometimes in the hopes of one day going pro. Prestige comes with performing in professional settings, and many amateurs are eager to work either for a token fee or for symbolic gratification alone. Professionals worry not only about the basic quality of amateurs' presentation, but also that performers who do not depend on magic to make a living compete unfairly with those who do. Nemo told me that when he got his first cabaret gig as a budding semiprofessional, a professional magician also on the bill buttonholed him backstage, asking menacingly, "So, you're gobbling up other people's work?" Of course, professionals who live off magic are sometimes forced to lower their fees in order to work. Some argue that they would rather work than not, at any price. Others counter that once you lower your fees, it becomes hard to raise them again because employers will expect you to work for the same rates. Considering low pay a symbolic affront, some refuse it on principle.

INTERMITTENCE DU SPECTACLE

To my knowledge, France is the only country that widely subsidizes professional magicians. Called *intermittence du spectacle* (or *intermittence* for short), these subsidies come in the form of unemployment benefits available to all qualifying workers in the performing arts and audiovisual sector.[30] To people outside France, it may seem illogical that working performers and audiovisual technicians would receive unemployment benefits, unless one takes into account the peculiarities of the French welfare state. The *intermittence* program is designed to compensate for the intermittent nature of the predominantly freelance form that employment takes in performing arts and the audiovisual sector, allowing beneficiaries—known collectively as *intermittents*—to maintain a stable monthly income regardless of the irregular flow of gigs. While I don't have any exact figures regarding the effect of the program on careers in magic, many professionals cited it as the key factor enabling them to turn pro and to remain in the industry despite economic ups and downs.[31]

When I began my research in 2003, a magician could qualify for one year's worth of supplementary income after documenting 507 hours of work in a twelve-month period. Magicos use a variety of terms to denote gigs (*spectacle, gala, prestation, presta,* and *contract*), but when *intermittence* benefits are concerned, they refer to a performance as a *cachet*—literally, an official stamp. Regardless of the length of the performance, each *cachet* is the legal equivalent of twelve hours of work; thus, forty-three *cachets* a year (or about four gigs a month) was enough to secure *intermittence* benefits for the following year. After protracted controversy, the system was amended in 2003 order to make benefits more restrictive. At the time of writing, each *cachet* is still worth twelve hours, but an artist needs 507 hours of work in a ten- instead of twelve-month period to qualify for only eight months of benefits.

The practical challenges of mastering the complex system of *intermittence* and securing benefits made it a minor obsession for many professional magicians. Dealing with sometimes uninformed or unsympathetic staff at the unemployment office is a regular and often frustrating ritual. Magicos use the quaint verb *cachetonner* to describe the practice of accumulating sufficient cachets to qualify for *intermittence*. For many, every year is a *course aux cachets* (race for *cachets*)—a mad scramble after the forty-three requisite gigs, rendered all the more harrowing because unemployment benefits are based on the average value of each *cachet* a performer submitted the previous year, between a minimum and maximum level of funding. I knew at least one professional who worked for Joseph in order to reach his forty-three *cachets*, even though accepting those low-paying gigs would considerably reduce his overall benefits.

I documented a wide variety of stratagems that can be used to obtain and maximize *intermittence* benefits, but I won't describe them in any detail here. Such practices seem to be commonplace among *intermittents* of all stripes and stations, as investigators widely documented during debates leading up to the *intermittence* reforms of 2003.[32] Reflecting on this moment, one sociologist of the arts wrote, "Rarely has an entire sector of activity delivered . . . as many reports of such specificity about its daily dealings with rules, its myriad forms of strategic play, and its constant use of tactics for optimizing unemployment insurance."[33] Misrepresenting one's professional activities to the unemployment office may sound scandalous, but in a profoundly unstable professional sector, it may also be a realistic strategy for survival. I never met a magicos out to make a killing from the *intermittence* program, and many described it as an indispensable part of having a career in magic. For people struggling to support themselves and their families through a creative pursuit they care about passionately, *intermittence* often means the difference between making ends meet and being forced to give up magic altogether—especially in the decisive early stages of a career.[34] It is a financial lifeline that they must grasp and hold at all costs.

Some magicians decry their colleagues' obsession with the scramble for *cachets* and self-satisfaction with the comfortable status of being *intermittents*. "In the cinema circuit, with matinee and evening shows four times a week, we had ten gigs a week," Maurice Saltano said, reflecting on his experiences in the postwar era. "With other work, that added up to fifty gigs a month! It meant that you got your chops young [*on s'est rodé très jeune*]. Today, it's crazy—you've got so-called *intermittents* who don't even do fifty gigs a year! The profession isn't what it used to be." Mimosa, an unrepentant agitator, sparked a minor scandal in 1992 when he published an article in one of France's leading magic magazines exposing principles of subterfuge used by *intermittents* to obtain and maximize benefits.[35] "I had just quit my job as an engineer," he explained to me in an email, "where, after six years of school, I made 12,000 francs a month for twelve hours of work a day. . . . I saw magicians driving luxury cars making three times more than me working only four days a month—it didn't make any sense!" Once he figured out for himself how professionals cheated the unemployment system, he considered it a "civic duty" to let the world know, and give "other beginning professionals the same opportunities" as their craftier seniors. "For YEARS there were people who wanted to beat me up," he reflected with a hint of morbid pride.

The *intermittence* program has affected not only the way magicians work but also the way that they think about the work that they do. For magicians, receiving *intermittence* benefits has become a de facto badge of professionalization, as it has in other performing arts.[36] One semiprofessional argued to me that professional peers should recognize him as "a real magician" because he "files his paperwork with the unemployment office" just like they do (but without reaching a sufficient number of *cachets* to be an *intermittent*).[37] Moreover, because the status of *intermittent* establishes an equivalency between magicians and artists in more prestigious sectors (such as dance, music, and theater) who receive the same benefits, it reaffirms the cultural value of a magician's labor—an issue I explore in the next chapter.

I have shown that, in building their careers, magicos rely on collegial relations with other professionals and, in most cases, financial support from the state. A craftsmanly orientation toward magic allows them to resolve the potential incompatibility between their cultural aspirations and the sometimes harsh realities of their work as service entertainers. In the final part of this chapter, I consider limitations of this craftsmanly outlook, examining complaints about clients who fail to accord magicians the respect they feel to be their due.

"PEOPLE NEED TO KNOW YOU'RE AN ARTIST"

Like members of every community, magicos swap stories. Taking pleasure in hearing and pride in telling stories about the ups and downs of their work, they use narrative to interpret experience, establish relationships, and configure selves.[38] I often listened with rapt attention as they vaunted triumphal performances or decried the treachery of other magicians. Social occasions frequently gave rise to storytelling sessions in which magicos would try to upstage each other with increasingly outlandish tales, riffing off particular themes or motifs.

For instance, a conversation one evening at the Illegal turned into a long storytelling session about problem spectators (spectateurs chiants) when Sébastien Mossière described an encounter with what he called "a table of old Trotskyists. One of them coldly shook my hand, and said condescendingly, 'We saw what you did at the other table, and it was very nice.' I turned around and walked away without saying a word. When someone treats me like a dog, I respond like a dog." On another occasion, I listened to Jean-Luc Bertrand and Guilhem Julia swap stories about the most harrowing moments in their table-hopping careers. Guilhem told us about the time he filled a glass of water with live goldfish, produced out of thin air, only to have a drunken spectator gulp it down, fish and all. Amateur magician Patrick Rivet had a string of outrageous misadventures to recount. I often requested personal favorites by title, such as "The Handcuffs," about the time Patrick, practicing an escape trick alone at home, cuffed his hands behind his back and had to seek help at the nearest police precinct—where he was temporarily detained.

As Heather Levi found with Mexican professional wrestlers, I sometimes suspected magicos of embellishing upon the truth for the sake of effect.[39] Overall, this community of consummate showmen seems to tolerate—and even expect—a degree of artistic license in storytelling, as long as narratives conform to shared understandings of how the world works. Richard Bauman found that Texas dog traders take similar liberties in the telling of what he calls the "hound and hunting" story: "whatever its referential and rhetorical functions, it constitutes a form of verbal art. . . . The aesthetic considerations of artistic performance may demand the embellishment or manipulation—if not the sacrifice—of the literal truth in the interests of greater dynamic tension, formal elegance, surprise value, contrast, or other elements that contribute to excellence in performance."[40]

The stories that magicos tell each other are imbued with sincere sentiments and firm moral perspectives. Elinor Ochs argues that moral stance is "central to narratives of personal experience," allowing storytellers to "articulate a temporal and causal sequence of events in relation to principles of goodness. . . . Moral stance and tellability are intertwined, in that a highly tellable incident often involves a violation of moral standards or canons of behavior."[41] In this section, I consider a series of stories that focus on the morally sensitive issue of interactions with employers. Like encounters with spectators during the course of performance, interactions with clients objectify public perceptions of magicians and their work. Sometimes magicos form ongoing working relationships and even friendships with clients; but problematic encounters with employers can trigger lingering feelings of anger and resentment. In addressing such problems, the narratives I consider here constitute an indictment of unsatisfactory treatment and convey a set of expectations about how magicians *ought* to be treated.

The stories I have selected for analysis all occurred during the course of a long interview conducted with Peter Din in 2005, when he was president of the largest magic club in Paris. Having seen his children's show

Le Magicien voyageur several times, I was in awe of Peter's ability to connect with young audiences. Offstage, the weary-eyed forty-four-year-old was one of the most outspoken voices in French magic, both on and offline. We had been talking for almost three hours when he steered the conversation to the increasing economic hardships facing professional magicians. "Do you think the public recognizes the true value of magic?" I asked him with dewy indignation. Peter's response caught me flat-footed. "Of course the public recognizes the true value of magic. Its value is zero, and the public knows it." He paused for effect, and then launched into a long, unblinking description of a world in which magicians and the work they do are accorded little value, in the making of which magicians themselves are largely complicit. "Someone once said that for any dirty, piss-stained wall, you can always find a magician to perform in front of it. Magicians are willing to perform whenever, wherever, and whatever with no demands and no compunctions. And so they end up working at the supermarket down the street."

Peter viewed the social dignity of magicians and the cultural valuation of magic as covariant in the marketplace of service entertainment. On the one hand, as increasing numbers of amateurs aspire to join the ranks of professional magicians, pressures from a competitive market impose growing indignities. On the other, magicians' willingness to demean themselves for work seems to further diminish the cultural value of magic in the public eye, exacerbating market pressures. He described this disheartening situation as a "race to the bottom."

In the ensuing minutes, Peter substantiated his argument with a series of problem client narratives—anecdotal vignettes addressing personal confrontations with professional indignities. Below, I examine three representative segments of narrative, selected from a profusion of stories. While these narratives are exceptional in both their attention to detail and their cumulative effect, they resemble storytelling practices that make up a significant part of magicos' staging talk more generally. Such narratives, addressing problematic service encounters, offer storytellers and listeners an opportunity to reaffirm shared values as they critically examine moral problems.

For Peter, the public's undervaluation of magic and disrespect for the work of magicians can become apparent from the moment potential employers first establish contact via telephone. In the first example I consider, he typifies problematic phone calls from clients and demonstrates one way of dealing with them.

PETER: When people call you they don't say, "Hello, Mister Peter Din? I would like you to come and put on *your* show." They call up, "[*brusquely*] Hello, how much is a little number?" . . . Me, that's what I hear on the telephone, "How much is a *little* number?"

PETER: Quand les gens t'appellent ils disent pas, "Bonjour, Monsieur Peter Din? J'aimerais que vous veniez présenter *votre* numéro." On t'appelle, "[*brusquely*] Bonjour, c'est combien pour un p'tit numéro?" . . . Moi c'est ce que j'entends au téléphone, "C'est combien pour un *p'tit* numéro?"

GRAHAM: Really?

GRAHAM: Ah bon?

PETER: Well, often I laugh and I say, "Well, excuse me, but I don't do a little number . . ." "[*brusquely*] Yes—No—But well—that's not what I meant to say, um—Um, how much do you take for the evening?" I say, "But what kind of event? Which act do you want?" People, when you say that to them they say, "[*brusquely*] Oh really? Because—" For them, it's—They buy it—they buy a magician like they buy um a cake for the end of a meal, you know.

PETER: Alors, souvent je rigole et je dis, "Ben, excusez-moi, mais je fais pas de petit numéro . . ." "[*brusquely*] Oui—Non—Mais enfin—c'est pas ce que je voulais dire, euh—Euh, vous prenez combien pour la soirée?" J'dis, "Mais quelle type de soirée? Quel spectacle vous voulez?" Les gens, quand tu leur dis ça ils disent, "[*brusquely*] Ah bon? Parce que—" Pour eux, c'est—Ils achètent ça—ils achètent un magicien comme ils achèteraient euh un gâteau pour la fin de repas, quoi.

GRAHAM: Mhm.

GRAHAM: Mhm.

PETER: And it has to be as cheap as possible.

PETER: Et il faut que ça coûte le moins cher possible.

In this strip of talk, Peter highlights points of contention in conversations with prospective employers, using hypothetical reported speech to dramatize the collision of opposing perspectives on magic's value and the magician's status. He portrays himself, by turns, as victim of and victor over clients' stereotypical disrespect, ignorance, and stinginess.

Scholars have noted that speakers often use reported speech to provide evidence supporting assessments and accounts,[42] relying on quoted voices to stake out a range of moral positions and elicit moral feedback from their listeners.[43] In this example, Peter vividly recreates problematic scenes of confrontation, dramatizing conflicting viewpoints by embedding dialogues between himself and others within his narration of past events. He demonstrates what a respectful caller would say, contrasting it with what he claims many actually say. While a respectful caller would address Peter by name and ask him to put on his show, the problem client—clearly uninterested in the distinctive qualities of Peter's own creative work—asks brusquely for the price of "a *little* show." Peter says that he customarily responds to such affronts by asserting that he doesn't do "a little show," indicating that he has highly specialized services to offer depending on a client's individual needs. He portrays this assertion of professionalism—and with it, cultural value—as catching clients off-guard. Using constructed dialogue, he carefully crafts his portrayal of these encounters to disclose divergent assumptions about magic's value and magicians' status.

Struggles over status don't end once the magician lands a gig but can continue in the workplace. One of the recurring motifs in Peter's stories was the symbolic importance of a dressing room. He inveighed against not only employers who expect magicians to get dressed in the bathroom, but also the magicians who assent: "As long as they let him do his tricks, a magician will change clothes in the shitter [*les chiottes*]!" he exclaimed in disbelief. In the following example, he recounts how he contends with employers who fail to provide a dressing room:

PETER: Personally, in my contracts—I can show you, I have contracts where it's written, "I refuse to dress in the bathroom."

GRAHAM: Really?

PETER: Mhm. Because I have to write it. Because one time I showed up for a job, I asked

PETER: Moi, dans mes contrats—Je peux te faire voir, j'ai des contrats ou y'a marqué, "Je refuse de me changer dans les toilettes."

GRAHAM: Ah bon?

PETER: Mhm. Parce que je suis obligé de le marquer. Parce qu'une fois je suis arrivé sur une affaire,

where I was supposed to get dressed. They say, "You get dressed in the bathroom." So I say, "But no, I can't." "Um, last week the other magician agreed." I say, "Well me, I don't agree." And so they thought that I was quite unpleasant.

j'ai demandé où je me changeais. On dit, "Vous vous changez dans les toilettes." Alors je dis, "Mais non, je peux pas." "Euh, la semaine dernière l'autre magicien a accepté." Je dis, "Ben moi, j'accepte pas." Alors on a considéré que j'étais très désagréable.

As in the previous example, Peter constructs a dialogue that emphasizes a client's dismissive stance ("You get dressed in the bathroom") and his own insistence on maintaining professional standards ("But no, I can't"). Again, he presents the client reacting in confusion to his apparent intransigence. He told me about a gig he played with other entertainers, where the employer provided dressing rooms, appointed with refreshments, for singers and actors but not for magicians. "No one bothers to plan ahead for magicians," he sighed. "Everyone else had bottles of water. The magicians didn't even get drinks." A background in the theater makes Peter particularly sensitive to subtle and not-so-subtle differences in treatment he is accorded as an actor and as a magician. He makes a practice of confronting clients who fail to provide him with a dressing room or a meal, or who otherwise treat him condescendingly. As a prominent figure in the French magic community, he encourages other magicians to do the same.

As the previous example suggests, each encounter between a magician and the public sets precedents for future interactions ("Um, last week the other magician agreed"). In the following example, Peter constructs a conversation between himself and several colleagues on a worksite to show that magicians do not customarily demand the respect Peter believes they are due as artists, nor even the common courtesy they deserve as human beings.

PETER: You know, yesterday I worked for [. . .] Foundation. If I were alone, I would have left. Because I showed up—they made

PETER: Tu vois, hier j'ai travaillé pour la Fondation [. . .]. J'aurais été tout seul, je serais parti. Parce que je suis arrivé—on m'a fait

me come at six o'clock at night, and didn't pay any attention to me until nine o'clock . . . So I was waiting, sitting on a chair from six o'clock until nine o'clock—

GRAHAM: Whew.

PETER: And every time I asked a question, "Yes yes we'll get to you, yes yes yes" like, "you're bothering me." So—I wasn't all alone—It wasn't me who was—Had I been all alone I would have left. "Well listen I won't bother you for a minute more. I'm leaving. There's no reason for me to stay, you don't need me. So long." But you see, there were four—there were three other magicians with me. They didn't make a peep. They looked at me saying, "But, how? Um . . . Oh no! We can't do that, ummm—" It seems normal to them.

GRAHAM: Mhm.

PETER: They get treated badly, but it seems normal to them.

venir à six heures du soir, et on s'est pas occupé de moi avant neuf heures . . . Alors j'ai attendu, assis sur une chaise de six heures à neuf heures—

GRAHAM: Ouf.

PETER: Et chaque fois que je posais une question, "Oui oui on va s'occuper de vous, oui oui oui" du style, "vous me dérangez." Donc—J'étais pas tout seul—C'est pas moi qui étais—J'aurais été tout seul je serais parti. "Ben écoutez je vais pas vous déranger plus longtemps. Je m'en vais. C'est pas la peine que je reste, vous avez pas besoin de moi. Au revoir." Mais tu vois, y'avait quatre—y'avait trois autres magiciens avec moi. Ils ont rien dit. Ils m'ont regardé en disant, "Mais, comment? Euh . . . Ah non! On peut pas faire ça, euhhh—" Ça leur paraît normal.

GRAHAM: Mhm.

PETER: On les traite mal, mais ça leur paraît normal.

Peter describes a situation in which an employer for a charity benefit made a group of magicians sit waiting for hours without offering them anything to eat or drink. He claims he would have responded to the situation by leaving the job with his dignity intact ("Well listen I won't bother you for a minute more"), and complains about the cowed demeanor of the magicians he was working with, which he also portrays through reported speech ("But, how? Um . . . Oh no! We can't do that, ummm").

These three examples typify the importance of encounters with clients as a theme in magicians' staging talk. In their role as entrepreneurial entertainers in a shifting cultural landscape, magicos identify signs of respect and strive to achieve them. Through co-constructed encounters with clients, they endeavor to establish and sustain a sense of professional dignity. As Peter's stories make clear, incidental features of work—an employer's tone on the telephone; the provision of a dressing room, food, and drinks; and the expression of care or concern more generally—can take on tremendous personal significance: they betoken whether or not the magician's self-image as a legitimate professional is being endorsed or declined. Goffman explains that "when an individual projects a definition of the situation and thereby makes an implicit or explicit claim to be a person of a particular kind, he automatically exerts a moral demand upon the others, obliging them to value and treat him in the manner that persons of his kind have a right to expect."[44] For magicians who view themselves as legitimate professionals and serious artists, the failure of clients to treat them in a culturally befitting manner is not just a practical oversight. It is a moral affront. Telling stories about such incidents, Peter uses narrative to construct accounts of problematic situations, making his sense of indignation palpable and providing evidence to justify his stance.

I want to signal how differently Peter frames the dynamics of interacting with clients behind the scenes from the way he describes interacting with spectators in the front stage of a performance. In the previous chapter, Peter said that performing magic as a table-hopper is a "game" in which he does not hesitate to ridicule himself for the sake of entertainment. The narratives I consider here suggest a far different attitude toward encounters with employers, in which the magician is *out of character* and has a sense of personal and professional dignity to uphold.

Peter summarized his perspective to me in the following terms: "If I became an artist, it wasn't to have the status of a cleaning woman. With all due respect to cleaning women, of course, if I wanted that status, I would have chosen to be a cleaning woman. I became an artist. And you don't just become an artist by accident. You become an artist because you like the applause, because you like the glittery lights. . . . I have an image to uphold. It's a performance too! When I'm in front of clients, I'm an artist. I don't mean you have to have a chip on your shoulder or be unpleasant, but let's just say that people need to know you're an artist.

You're not just Mr. So-and-So [*Monsieur Tout le Monde*]. And often, when they understand who you are, people are very nice to you. They play along." While he may seem exigent, Peter makes it clear that the tokens of esteem he expects from clients are not only necessary to uphold his own self-image as an artist but also a complement to his self-presentation as a professional in contexts of entertainment service encounters, ensuring that people recognize the tremendous pride he takes in his work. As he explains, this is also part of the "performance."

CONCLUSION

In 2006, David Stone released *The Real Secrets of Magic*, an instructional video on the craft of table-hopping magic, which the magic world greeted with thunderous acclaim.[45] The film featured a number of comedic vignettes in which David, table-hopping in a fancy restaurant, squares off with parodically obnoxious problem spectators: he slaps someone who tries to explain a trick, head-butts a person who interrupts a routine, and bites off a heckler's tongue. When a spectator inanely asks, "Can you make my wife disappear?" David has her bound, gagged, and carted off. Similarly, when a spectator smugly says, "I saw it coming," after David produces a bottle of wine from thin air, the elegantly dressed magician smashes the bottle over the spectator's head and shoots another member of the party. "Did you see that coming?" he pants ferociously. I participated in parts of this project as a script coach for English language sections of the DVD, and saw firsthand the painstaking care that David and director Jean-Luc Bertrand lavished on the special effects, stunts, and trick camera work that went into scenes like these. Some of the actors playing spectators were themselves magicians, and delighted in the chance to caricature the kinds of people who antagonize them professionally.

I asked David and Jean-Luc if they felt these vignettes were an expression of anger. "For us, it's not anger," David said emphatically. "It's a way of releasing the stress that builds up when you're an artist. When you've worked for ten years, busting your ass in restaurants where people tell you to piss off before you can even open your mouth, after a while, you need to get it off your chest." Jean-Luc agreed. "As much as I like working in restaurants, you internalize all these frustrations. All of the things that the hecklers say in the film are things I've heard myself. They came back to me while we were filming." For David and Jean-Luc, these violent vignettes are playful exorcisms of the resentment that professional close-up artists can come to feel toward discourteous spectators, but that cannot normally be expressed. Magicians around the world could identify with their imagery of retribution: in 2006, a short film showcasing these vignettes (subtitled in English) won first prize at an international magic film festival held in Las Vegas.

David and Jean-Luc inserted their film into magicians' ongoing conversations about interactions with two salient categories of nonmagicians: clients and spectators. Their parodic representation of encounters with problem spectators addresses, in the imaginative idiom of a fictional film, situations that magicians deal with all the time and that constitute a central concern in their staging talk. Drawing on their own experiences, the magicians involved in making the film collaboratively scripted and improvised a collection of constructed dialogues that dramatize the kinds of challenges they face while performing close-up magic professionally. They brought the roles of these problem spectators to life, much as Peter did when he narrated a series of encounters with problem clients to me.

I hope this chapter does not give the mistaken impression that French laypeople dislike magic. That is certainly not the case. My experience is that most of them enjoy it immensely and that many hold magicians in a kind of awe. But in the eyes of performers, problematic encounters have a way of standing out, both because they are emotionally unpleasant and because they seem indicative of larger patterns of disvaluation in which doing magic is not considered a particularly respectable career choice by standards of either social utility or cultural merit. Problematic encounters strike a raw nerve, even for very successful magicians like those I describe here.

As entertainers, close-up magicians enter into face-to-face interactions with spectators; as entrepreneurs, they are also generally responsible for interacting directly with clients. In both situations, they must carefully control their reactions, even when confronted with discourtesy. While magic is an offbeat profession, they are self-conscious about its value and about their status as professionals, just like people involved in more mundane lines of work. It is easy for laypeople to write magic off as a frivolity, particularly when they fail to appreciate the passion and intelligence these professional tricksters invest in their trade. Efforts to promote high professional standards and to resist trends of degradation reflect the conviction that magic is a meaningful mode of self-expression and a significant form of expertise. Yet, unlike practitioners of more highly esteemed professions, magicos are conscious of the need to demonstrate the worth of their work and convey their cultural aspirations even as they go about business as un-usual.

FIVE Conjuring Culture

Around the beginning of the twentieth century, a small pamphlet began to circulate among Parisian magicians. It was entitled "Eulogy to the Sublime Art of Prestidigitation" and signed "Ferraris Folletto, A Fanatic of Prestidigitation, the Queen of the Arts." The author proclaimed, "As beauty, nothing . . . compares [to prestidigitation], and as art, it is everything that is truly superior. . . . No other art . . . could rival prestidigitation. . . . It alone merits the appellation Queen of the Arts."[1] An Italian immigrant with a thick accent and an expansive personality, Folletto performed for several years at the Théâtre Robert-Houdin, and was a well-known figure around the cabarets of Montmartre. His contemporary Raynaly wrote this of him: "He attaches to his experiments a comically capital importance. For him, secrets of state and the mysteries of Antiquity are nothing but laughing matters compared to the experiments he presents in exhibiting his noble talent. Do not tell him that there is an art superior to Prestidigitation. To prove the contrary, he will spew so much verbal spaghetti that you won't know where to put your hands."[2]

The grandiloquent Folletto may have been an object of good-natured jibes from contemporary magicians, but time has brought him some measure of vindication: today it is not uncommon to hear French magicians earnestly tout magic as the "Queen of the Arts." But while Folletto's formula has acquired talismanic status within the magic world, few nonmagicians in France today would place magic on the same level as artistic forms like painting, literature, or music—much less in a sovereign position above them. As demonstrated in the previous chapter, magicians face difficult professional prospects, and struggle to assert the cultural status of magic and their social status as performers in day-to-day working conditions. Among amateurs, I encountered prominent scientists and academics at magic meetings who cautiously hid their hobby from colleagues for fear of ridicule. Someone who has worked successfully in magic for several decades told me that his own brother, a philosophy professor, still scoffs at his career choice in front of their family. Yet the abiding conviction that magic deserves greater cultural legitimacy resounds in the circulation of a well-worn phrase like "Queen of the Arts."

Magic's status in respect to other genres of expressive culture was a frequent topic of conversation during my research. It was often complicated by semantics. For instance, early in my fieldwork, I accompanied Zeev Gourarier, a curator from France's national folklore museum, to a meeting with Georges Proust, the founding director of the Musée de la Magie. Building on the success of a recent exhibition on the circus,[3] Gourarier was hoping to curate a show on magic and was seeking Proust's help. Proust gave us a tour of his small jewel of a museum.[4] Situated in a cavernous seventeenth-century basement, its hidden alcoves brimmed with automata, antique magic sets, large stage illusions, and colorful posters heralding the wonders of a bygone era, like the girl-with-a-spider-body sideshow attraction. Over lunch, the two curators joked and commiserated about the challenges of persuading public sector funding agencies to take popular culture seriously. At one point, Proust asked pointedly, "Do you think magic is an art?" Gourarier looked embarrassed. "That depends on how you define art," he parried.

Indeed, the term "art" has multiple meanings. Insofar as it can denote any skilled cultural practice, we can say that there is an "art of magic" in the same sense there is an "art of boxing" or an "art of cooking." But it can also refer more restrictively to the exclusive class of expressive practices (e.g., painting, sculpture, music, literature, and dance) associated with creative genius, contemplative modes of appreciation, and transcendent aesthetic value—that is "fine art," "high art," or "Art" with a capital A.[5] Clearly, Proust had this latter meaning in mind, and Gourarier's evasion was answer enough for him. "You see?" he said to me, as if I had just learned an important lesson. Throughout this book, I have described magic as an "art" in the general sense of a skilled cultural practice. In this chapter, I turn to the more specialized meaning of "art" as the paramount category of high cultural distinction. Historically, magic has not been considered an art in this sense. In this chapter, I ask, along with a number of French magicians, if it ever could be.

Overcoming magic's peripheral status in respect to the distinguishing categories of high culture involves a number of challenges. Its close association with the exhibition of manual skill rather than the expression of ideational content is a particular problem. Hegel, for instance, distinguishes between "conjuring tricks" that rely on clever technique and true works of art, which put expressive technique in the service of transcendent truths.[6] Because the allure of magic performance is so closely connected with the "fascination of secrecy"[7] and the desire it engenders, it can be difficult for magicians to construe what they do as something other than just trickery. Why, even Folletto in his more candid moments was known to refer to prestidigitation less flatteringly as "the art of fucking with people without seeming like you are."[8] Furthermore, since the category of art is constructed as the contemplative alternative to merely pleasurable entertainment and purely functional craft,[9] the cultural legacy of magic as a popular entertainment constitutes a symbolic liability.

Scholars have widely noted the prevalent role of taste in marking class boundaries in French society from the Ancien Régime to the present day.

From consumers' everyday preferences in food, clothes, and music, to the internal organization of museums and other large cultural institutions, hierarchies of taste pervade French life.[10] In a setting where symbolic oppositions between high and low culture are so significant in the expression of social status, many magicians are acutely aware of the way they are publicly perceived in respect to the categories of art and entertainment. In this chapter, I examine ways some have sought to conjure different understandings of magic by creating more favorable associations with the high cultural conception of art. In particular, I focus on how they strive to distinguish themselves as artists through strategic engagements with the state's cultural apparatus.

To be clear, not all magicos look favorably on such projects. Certainly some believe that efforts to make magic more art-like are, at best, unrealistic. "We're not there for people to have a *cultural* reaction to what we do," Jean-Marc Gaheri, a professional table-hopper, told me. "People just want to relax. We're there to make them laugh. If we start to do *dramatic* magic, they run away. We need to stop these head games [*prises de tête*]. Head games are so typically French. We're not at the Comédie Française to judge our magician!" After years of table-hopping, Philippe came to a similar conclusion. "As far as table-hopping goes, at this point I've essentially put an 'X' through anything artistic," he said. "I try to make people have fun, nothing more." Still, he remains optimistic about the possibilities for more creative forms of expression through stage magic rather than close-up. "Everything artistic, I save for the stage." Clearly, not all performance settings are amenable to culturally refashioning magic. The magicians in this chapter are particularly interested in circulating magic beyond accustomed venues and cultivating ties within novel institutional configurations.

Magicians, like all performers, are cultural producers. According to Fred Myers, "A focus on the political economy and the social relationships of producing culture, rather than the critical analysis of representations, not only allows for recognition of the possibility of agency (within limits) on the part of the various participants but also engages the rather complex intersections and reorganizations of interest that are inevitably involved in any production of culture."[11] In this chapter,

I focus on individuals who have engaged in particularly self-conscious projects of cultural production—projects that reveal opportunities and challenges for extending magic as a signifying practice into arenas other than entertainment. In different ways, these projects involve efforts to change the terms in which people habitually talk about magic, and my discussion consequently emphasizes the circulation of discourses about art and culture.

In the following section, I examine the legacy of France's most famous magician, Jean-Eugène Robert-Houdin (1805–1871). In a national setting where history is an overwhelmingly important source of cultural legitimacy,[12] invoking the legacy of Robert-Houdin is a way for magicians to distinguish magic as a national cultural tradition. At the same time, Robert-Houdin serves contemporary magicians as a conceptual reference point for situating magic in a broader cultural landscape, as a model for their own continued self-fashioning, and as a basis for community building. That the historical figure of Robert-Houdin is particularly amenable to these kinds of projects is not coincidental; he too was an acutely self-aware cultural producer who strategically crafted his image to conform with contemporary criteria of social distinction.

THE FAMILY ROMANCE OF MODERN MAGIC

"I hold Robert-Houdin personally responsible for all the crap that passes for magic today!" Raphaël Navarro proclaimed, looking me straight in the eye as he unleashed ultimate blasphemy. Imagine a jazz soloist blaming Louis Armstrong for the decline of improvised music or an anthropologist laying responsibility for decadence in ethnographic methods at Malinowski's tent flaps. I had before me what appeared to be just such an apostasy. Magicians around the world have long revered Robert-Houdin as the "Father of Modern Magic," a spiritual paternity reaffirmed twenty years after his death by the adoring young American magician Ehrich Weiss's choice of the Italianized stage name "Houdini." Among magicians in his native France, Robert-Houdin generally still inspires something verging on religious awe.

With his oversized earth-toned sweater, thick beard, and sandy hair pulled back into a long ponytail, Raphaël could have easily been an iconoclastic student reflexively scoffing at a symbol of establishment culture. Yet the reality was more complicated. It was the spring of 2005, and we were meeting to discuss the promising steps he was taking toward realizing a dream dear to several generations of French magicians: creating a state-sponsored national magic conservatory. At a mere twenty-three years old, Raphaël was already a founding co-director, along with Clément Debailleul, of the acclaimed performing arts ensemble Cie 14:20, whose avant-garde productions incorporating magic, juggling, dance, and pantomime had garnered generous national and regional funding. With an intellectual's fluent erudition, Raphaël had emerged, somewhat meteorically, as one of the savviest culture brokers in the French magic world. So why attack magic's greatest cultural hero—and a native son at that? "I know what I'm saying is a bit incendiary," he admitted. "It's just that magic today is not an art, it's just not artistic. And it's not artistic because Robert-Houdin's vision of magic wasn't artistic."

Raphaël was holding a distorting mirror up to the past as I, and practically every magician everywhere, saw it—leaving key features generally intact but inverting and rearranging them. The result was an almost unrecognizable vision of magic history with Robert-Houdin cast as arch-malefactor rather than messiah. According to French magicians' catechism, Robert-Houdin gave magic its "deed of distinction" (*lettres de noblesse*), transforming a crass fairground amusement into a refined art form, and, in the process, making France "the birthplace of modern magic" (*le berceau de la magie moderne*). These phrases frequently recur in conversations about Robert-Houdin, constituting a tacit party line that I, for one, had been happy enough to toe. Even Raphaël agreed that Robert-Houdin reinvented magic in a form more palatable to nineteenth-century bourgeois taste, purifying it of associations with the popular, carnivalesque, occult, and criminal; he simply considered the resulting product commercially safe but ultimately vacuous entertainment—not high art.

Raphaël's assessment, while debatable, raises a substantial question: how have articulations of class and culture shaped the expressive idiom of modern, Western magic, and why does Robert-Houdin's image of the magician as an elegant upper-class gentleman in sober evening attire still retain so much resonance today? Elsewhere I have argued that, in part, Robert-Houdin's successful achievement of cultural respectability as a magician is connected with a particular approach to performing not only class but also gender and race.[13] Enacting an ideal of white, bourgeois, male subjectivity, Robert-Houdin established himself as magic's archetypal father figure, an achievement that has made him an object of both patriarchal adoration and patricidal repudiation.

In his 1858 memoir, *Confidences d'un prestidigitateur* (*A Conjurer's Confessions*), Robert-Houdin amplifies an image of himself as a principled man of science and good taste, who singlehandedly reforms magic into a respectable bourgeois entertainment by purging it of problematic associations with low culture, the criminal demimonde, and backward superstition.[14] Depicting predecessors as "mystifiers" guilty of deluding the public, he likewise decries the intellectual shortcomings of spectators prone to delusion. He plots relationships of correspondence between modes of apprehending magic and spectators' social stations, with the male monarch, Louis-Philippe, typifying an appropriate attitude of playful, self-reflexive detachment, and members of the working class, women, and African colonial subjects embodying naïve, uncritical perspectives. In this rhetorical framework, a mission on behalf of the French Army to disenchant popular religious practices in colonial Algeria serves not only to burnish the author's reputation as a national hero but also to buttress his distinction between modern magic—a harmless mode of entertainment amenable to bourgeois sensibilities—and primitive charlatanism linked with superstitious fanaticism.[15] Writing his memoirs was part of a broader strategy of staking out his own professional status and establishing illusionism as a legitimate form of expertise, compatible with a scientific worldview and opposed to unscientific forms of knowledge.

The period of my fieldwork coincided with the 2005 bicentenary of Robert-Houdin's birth, and throughout France magicians were celebrating his cultural progenitorship. Streets were renamed in his honor; the presence of his elderly great-grandson, André Keime Robert-Houdin, at one such ceremony I attended in the industrial city of St-Etienne made the occasion particularly moving. The magic museum in Robert-Houdin's native Blois hosted a series of lectures and a contest inviting magicians to dream up a twenty-first-century performance by Robert-Houdin. Proust's Musée de la Magie undertook extensive renovations in preparation for an exhibit of Robert-Houdin artifacts featuring some superbly restored automata. The metropole also played host to an unprecedented European convention of magic collectors, with a particular focus on magic before Robert-Houdin. "How could we fully appreciate the Master and the advances he brought to the Art of Magic," the convocational statement questioned rhetorically, "if we didn't have information about the repertoires of the magicians who preceded and who followed him?"[16] Most of the over 100 participants, many from as far away as Australia and the United States, made a daylong pilgrimage to Robert-Houdin's gravesite and former residence, The Priory.

On November 26, 2005, the FFAP organized a state-sanctioned National Magic Day, encouraging its 1,500 members to give charitable performances throughout the country to "help raise awareness of the Art of Magic [*sensibiliser le public à l'art de la magie*]," as one of the event's organizers told me. In preparation, they printed thousands of jaunty J'♥ *la magie!* stickers and the informative pamphlet "Who Was Robert-Houdin?" Lamenting the too-frequent confusion between the nineteenth-century French conjurer and his twentieth-century American namesake, the pamphleteers minced no words: "Robert-Houdin developed a new conception of magic performance and for that . . . every magician owes him a debt of gratitude. He remains a worldwide point of reference, perhaps *the* point of reference. . . . Robert-Houdin laid the foundations of today's magic through his creativity, his modernity, his conception of performance and staging, and with his pioneering tricks and routines."[17] Such statements, characteristic of these commemorations, simultaneously reaffirm the universality of magic as an international tradition, while insinuating a nationalistic claim about France's unique historical role in its development. Indeed, Robert-Houdin's contribution to global magic culture is, in France, a source of national pride—one that has gained rather than lost in appeal as other countries, particularly the United States, have asserted leadership within the field.

History may prove 2005's most enduring tribute to Robert-Houdin to be a literary event: the much-anticipated publication of the final install-ment of a multivolume biography by Christian Fechner, a French movie mogul and magician of tremendous distinction.[18] Fechner contended that "Robert-Houdin elaborated the golden rules of magic, untouched by time, and recognized by every great artist ever since."[19] This conception of magic, Fechner wrote, can be summed up in two words, *naturalism* and *modernity*, and expresses itself in "elegance of presentation, purism, and the absence of any obviously specialized props."[20] Fechner had long demonstrated his fidelity to Robert-Houdin's magical vision through collection, scholarship, and performative emulation. In 1979, his applica-tion of what he considered Robert-Houdin's "timeless" principles earned him two of magic's most prestigious awards: the World Championship in Stage Illusion and the World Championship in Invention (both conferred at the triennial congress of the International Federation of Magic Societ-ies, or FISM). Fechner's painstaking biographical research is a monument to one man's unflagging passion and another's undying allure.

Most French magicians agree that Robert-Houdin's career marked a major cultural watershed, a generative moment in which magic assumed its present-day form. Still, most would also agree that in the twenty-first century, few people in France consider magic a high art and magicians artists, regardless of what Robert-Houdin may have accomplished. Did, as Raphaël argued, Robert-Houdin's success establish a stifling prece-dent that has hindered the emergence of an artistic avant-garde in magic? Or has neglect of the timeless principles Robert-Houdin enumerated and enacted led, as Christian Fechner implied, to the genre's gradual decline into cultural irrelevance?

To answer these questions, we must return to the autobiographical text in which Robert-Houdin staked out his intertwining claims to origi-nality and respectability—the rhetorical bedrock on which he built his reputation. In the *Confessions*, Robert-Houdin connects his individual reputation to the status of magic as a medium whose foundation in sci-ence, similarity to fine arts, and amenability to urbane, bourgeois sensi-bilities he consistently emphasizes. Regardless of his accomplishments as a performer, as a writer Robert-Houdin sensitized future magicians to connections between the cultural legitimacy of magic and their social status as performers. By articulating this nexus of status and value, Robert-Houdin assured his longevity as an iconic cultural progenitor.

The influence of Robert-Houdin's literary efforts is manifest in the testimonials of readers like Bernard Bilis, a jovial middle-aged card virtuoso, beloved of French television audiences for his regular appearances on the popular Saturday-night program *Le Plus Grand Cabaret du Monde*: "It was one of my brother's high school friends who showed me my first magic tricks and gave me a copy of Robert-Houdin's memoirs when I was around ten. . . . The book gave me the will to continue down that path [into the world of magic]; it showed me the inherent nobility of our art; it taught me that one needs perseverance, hard work, and passion."[21] Likewise, magic historians generally agree on the importance of Robert-Houdin's literary achievements in cementing his enduring legacy. Surveying gushing contemporary reviews of the English language translation, one cultural historian affirms that "what these opinions documented most of all was Robert-Houdin's virtuosity as a maker of powerful new literary images."[22]

Perhaps no episode has reaffirmed the impact of the *Confessions* better than the publication of Harry Houdini's *Unmasking of Robert Houdin* in 1908. In a gesture of supreme narcissism, Houdini—who had once been so impressed by the *Confessions* that he adopted its author's very name—set out to demolish his own youthful idol. In essence, he argued that Robert-Houdin "was not a master magician, but a clever purloiner and adapter of the tricks invented and used by his predecessors and contemporaries."[23] Described by biographer Kenneth Silverman as both "parricidal" and "regicidal,"[24] the publication ultimately did more to tarnish Houdini's reputation than to refute Robert-Houdin's claims to originality and distinction—especially in France, where magicians rallied to defend their spiritual progenitor against aspersions cast by an American parvenu.[25] Houdini had failed to understand the difference between a *first practitioner* and a *founding father*.[26] While magicians before Robert-Houdin might have performed similar tricks or adopted similar conventions of presentation, no other had succeeded, as he did, in establishing himself as what Jim Steinmeyer quite simply calls "the important transitional figure" in magic.[27] Why?

I believe that Robert-Houdin's continuing centrality in the collective imaginary of the international magic community hinges not only on the staying power of the *Confessions* as a literary broadcast of its author's reputation, but also on the usefulness of that reputation to subsequent generations of magicians. Howard Becker explains that "art worlds, in a variety of interwoven activities, routinely make and unmake reputations—of works, artists, schools, genres, and media. . . . They use reputations, once made, to organize other activities." [28] Promoting public recognition of Robert-Houdin's legacy has been a means for French magicians to legitimize the medium through a process one sociologist of art describes as the "transfer of the title and merit of past artists and creators onto their contemporary heirs." [29] Meanwhile, other magicians, also despairing of magic's lack of cultural legitimacy, have found him a tempting scapegoat.

While a vocal majority of magicos still upholds Robert-Houdin's paternal image as a source of vocational pride, not everyone is happy about his continuing influence. The more I encountered complaints about Robert-Houdin's unhealthy influence, I began to realize that his iconic status has made him the focus of what Freud called a "family romance"—an Oedipal whirlpool of admiration and resentment perhaps befitting the profoundly androcentric culture of magic.[30] While Raphaël offers an especially vocal example, I encountered a number of magicians who lamented what they saw as the slavish emulation of the founding father's imago. French magic historian Fanch Guillemin is one of the few to air such views in print. In a recent article, he acknowledges Robert-Houdin's ambivalent importance as the "very image of the magician in coat and tails. He made this outfit emblematic of the profession, so much that some modern magicians, converts to the religion, couldn't 'defrock' themselves without fearing sacrilege. It's no different than an earlier generation of magicians who thought it necessary to wear astrological robes and pointed hats as guarantees of their magical powers." [31]

Hervé, a factory worker's son and self-described sixties radical, expressed disgust with the nineteenth-century magician's bourgeois sensibilities and lack of social conscience: "When the revolution broke out in 1848 did he care? No! He left for England so he could keep making money!" Hervé called Robert-Houdin a "spoiled brat" (*fils de papa*) who succeeded not because of any unique talent, but because of his bourgeois boarding school education and, more importantly, the social connections he calculatingly made with people of money and influence, such as his father-in-law. So repulsed was he with the figure of Robert-Houdin that Hervé even forgave Houdini his parricidal screed: "Sure Houdini was an egocentric jerk, but in his case, it's excusable. He grew up dirt poor, never got an education—he was a self-made man. He had an excuse for being insecure."

Whatever contemporary magicos say about him, Robert-Houdin remains a decisive point of reference. As a performer and author, he brought new cultural legitimacy to magic as a respectable bourgeois entertainment, shoring up the particular class, gender, and racial identity of the modern magician. The legitimacy he gained individually nevertheless proved limited in terms of the absolute cultural distinction it has conferred on magic as a whole. The gulf in prestige between the fine arts and magic has been a lingering source of concern for magicians in France, and, not surprisingly, they have turned to modern magic's founding father for explanation.[32] In both celebrating and repudiating his legacy, they reiterate his seminal formulation of the problem of magic's legitimacy, and reactivate the sense of cultural anxiety he bequeathed to his vocation.

THE ENCHANTED STATE

The cultural and discursive strategies that magicos use to verbally assimilate magic to the realm of high culture are not just symbolic gestures. Because of the singular role of the French state as a patron of the arts, implicit cultural rankings can have serious consequences for cultural producers. Compared to the relatively minimal involvement of the American government in financing cultural production, in France the state is a paramount cultural patron and, hence, arbiter of taste.[33] State postures simultaneously reflect and affect the role of magic (and other expressive forms) in French cultural life. This, in turn, has a direct impact on the lives and livelihoods of practicing magicians, in terms of the prestige they enjoy and the creative and professional opportunities open to them. The French state's capacity to bestow legitimacy on expressive practices gives it an almost fetishistic quality for those seeking to harness its cultural enchantments.[34]

No one was more aware of the enchantments of the state than magician Jacques Delord. From 1981 to 1995, he crisscrossed the globe as a French cultural ambassador for the Alliance Française, performing and giving magic workshops at universities, schools, and French cultural centers, and making occasional appearances at embassies or on local television stations. On peregrinations that took him to dozens of countries, from Cambodia to Togo and Saudi Arabia, Delord considered himself the purveyor of a distinctively French tradition in magic that includes not only Robert-Houdin but also other luminaries of legerdemain such as Georges Méliès and Buatier de Kolta. This tradition Delord regarded as a vital part of France's cultural heritage.

I met Delord for lunch in a cozy café near Place de la Nation, where he was on a first-name basis with everyone from the Italian owner to the African dishwasher. As we spoke, he tugged absentmindedly at the zipper of his fleece coat, his blue eyes sparkling. "What is *French* magic?" I asked. At first, Delord's answer disconcerted me. "It's a length of rope, a newspaper, banknotes, silks, eggs—simple objects." Clearly, he was not describing a characteristically French repertoire, for magicians everywhere use these same simple objects. "And," he continued, "it depends on the hands, the hands, the hands." He lingered thoughtfully over the words, raising his palms in an ambiguous gesture, both illustrative and supplicant. "As few gimmicks as possible. As little effect as possible—as little *visual* effect." I realized that Delord was describing what he saw as a characteristically French style typified by minimalism and aesthetic purity. To this he juxtaposed an ascendant "American" style involving loud music, dazzling lights, and garish costumes. "All these excesses only alienate the magician from the magic."

Some of Delord's hosts found his vision of "French magic" initially disconcerting. He told me, for instance, about a mid-1980s engagement in San Luis Potosi, Mexico. "It was at a big university. The director of the

Alliance Française met me on the tarmac. I had two pieces of luggage: a big trunk and a little satchel. I said, 'Here are my bags.' The director looked panicked. 'But what about your props—the show?' he whimpered. 'The show's in the little one!' I said, cheerily. The director was horrified. 'But the theater is sold out—a huge theater!—for two shows. One and a half hours each. The mayor is coming, the president of the university, five TV stations. . . .' He almost put me back on the plane. But I explained to him, 'When French singers come, they sing French songs. When French magicians come, they do French magic.' And that's what I gave them, pure French magic, the magic of Robert-Houdin. It was a triumph!"

For most magicians, magic begins as an adolescent obsession. Delord, by contrast, discovered it only in early adulthood, after receiving classical training as an actor. His background in the theater shaped his approach to the new expressive medium. "As an actor, I immediately used magic as a further means of dramatic expression. Not trick after trick but, like theater, a means of evoking timeless human problems." In a regular column in *Magicus* magazine, Delord often wrote about literature, music, and the theater. He complained that magicians care too much about "magic culture" but lack "general culture," or what we would call cultural literacy. "Magicians are obsessed with the trick, and with the pursuit of the trick," he told me. "You've got people coming into magic without any general culture. They can barely speak French. Their patter is crude, their language inarticulate, their jokes more or less shameful. They don't know how to present themselves onstage, nor do they have any sense of the theater. Their performances are inevitably vulgar. Which is why I always tell magicians, go to the theater, go to museums, listen to serious music—develop some taste!"

Delord made his début in the early 1960s in the literary cabarets of Saint-Germain—the epicenter of postwar bohemian chic. In his trademark routine—immortalized by François Truffaut in the 1968 film *Baisers volés (Stolen Kisses)*—Delord stands on an empty stage, illuminated by a single beam of light.[35] Grinning, he pulls a white rope back and forth, hypnotically, between his agile hands, making it wriggle electrically with life. Then he begins to recite a story:

'Twas a sailor, at journey's end
an old sailor, sorcerer, storyteller of the prow
ageless, timeless, he seems now
like some figure from a myth.

As he speaks, he ties a square knot in the middle of the rope. He pulls it taut, and grips it in his fist. When his hand comes away, there is a red scarf imprisoned in the knot. He pulls it forth, and waves it playfully in the air.

The children still went to see him
summer evenings on the harbor slope
at play, with his rope
depicting exotic tales.

Instantaneously, the rope changes from white to red. As the story unfolds, Delord produces ropes of several different colors. Like an Odyssian trickster, he ties knots, *one-two-three*, in a gold rope, only to have them suddenly vanish and reappear across the stage, *one-two-three*, on a blue rope. Then back again. Other magicians might approach an effect like the Teleportation of Knots as sufficiently entertaining in its own right; Delord wove it seamlessly into an enchanting tale, constructing a poetic tableau redolent of the Old English "Seafarer." When performing this routine before audiences numbering in the thousands, Delord would have the rear curtain opened to reveal the stage's vast expanse—to accentuate his existential vulnerability, he explained to me. Magicians who had worked alongside him told me that standing ovations were the norm (see Figure 14).

By the time I met him in 2004, Delord had personally achieved many hallmarks of cultural distinction (not least of which was his work with Truffaut). Although he had traveled the world as an embodiment of French culture, he sadly perceived French magic—his magic—as beleaguered and unjustly neglected at home. "It was in France that a magician gave magic its deed of distinction. France is the source of magic's great revitalization. France took magic from the street and put it on the stage," he told me, invoking the celebrated legacy of Robert-Houdin.

Figure 14.   Jacques Delord performs a rope routine. Photo by Zakary Belamy.

What may sound like a chauvinistic boast was, in fact, a lament for what Delord considered a nation's stinging betrayal. "France created a splendid theater for magic, Robert-Houdin's Théâtre des Soirées Fantastiques, in the Palais Royal—which now houses the very Ministry of Culture. And, paradoxically, if you were to walk into the Ministry of Culture right now and say, 'I'd like to organize a magic festival'—*hah*! They'll laugh you right out the door. They won't even look at the proposal. *That*'s distinctively French too."

And so it is. No democratic country has made culture and the arts more unconditionally an affair of state than France.[36] In 1959, President Charles de Gaulle gave the cultural power of the state new institutional prominence by creating a Ministry of Culture.[37] As the first head of this new ministry, novelist André Malraux set out to propagate high culture through an agenda of, in his words, "making the major works of humanity, and first and foremost of France, accessible to as many French people as possible; of ensuring that our heritage has as vast an audience as possible, and of encouraging the creation of works of art and the mind that enrich it."[38] Subsequent ministers would seek to transform the Malraucian paradigm, expanding state support to popular forms of cultural expression—from rural folkways such as gardening to urban graffiti and hip hop. Today, funding from the Ministry of Culture has become both a vital factor in stimulating interest in once marginal domains of cultural production and a potent token of official recognition for cultural producers in those domains.[39] If Delord characterized the ministry's failure to support magic as "typically French," so too was his expectation that it should.

In the next sections, I examine some ways magic has entered into the ambit of French cultural policy. First, I will consider a surprising moment when the Ministry of Culture embraced Robert-Houdin's legacy as a constitutive element of the nation's cultural heritage, with mixed results. Then I discuss Raphaël Navarro's efforts to create an institutional framework, using state resources, that would encourage avant-garde cultural production in magic. As a whole, the efforts of French magicians to harness the enchanting power of the state, whether they ultimately succeed or fail, reveal much about shifting ideas of culture at a moment of accelerated change.

MAGIC AS CULTURAL HERITAGE

Perhaps the most prominent success in national cultural policy toward magic was also almost its most notorious disappointment. Opened in 1998, the Maison de la Magie, a large regional museum devoted to modern magic in its founding father's native Blois, was an outgrowth of the Ministry of Culture's move toward embracing more popular forms of national cultural heritage during the presidency of socialist François Mitterrand. Ultimately, the assimilation of magic to the official categories and national organs of high culture proved fragile; as the political climate changed, the Ministry of Culture withdrew its support, leaving the fledgling museum at the mercy of the free market. As I learned about the Maison, I felt something like a detective trying to piece together a vaguely conspiratorial sequence of events fraught with frustration. "I hope you find out what *really* happened," a person once intimately involved with the project told me (I couldn't tell if he did not actually know or simply didn't want to tell me).

The saga began with a serendipitous coincidence. In 1989, Jack Lang, Mitterrand's minister of culture, also became the mayor of Blois.[40] (It is common for French politicians to hold multiple political posts, an arrangement called *cumul des mandats* that lends itself to pork barreling.) The most influential head of the Ministry of Culture since Malraux himself, the flamboyant Lang built his political reputation promoting an agenda of cultural decentralization characterized by a broadly inclusive vision of expressive culture. In a famous 1982 speech, he stated programmatically, "There must be no hierarchy separating 'minor arts' and 'major arts,' 'noble arts' and 'vulgar arts.' All are forms of art and culture."[41] Decentralization also meant directing ministerial energies to projects benefiting not only Paris but provincial France as well. Lang quietly promoted the then-controversial idea that the cultural sector should be envisioned as an engine for economic growth, particularly in provincial areas.[42]

When the magicians Gérard Majax and Georges Proust, at the time organizers of an annual magic festival in Blois, broached the possibility of creating a national magic museum there, Lang recognized an opportunity to spur tourism in his provincial mayoralty—which already owned a handsome collection of Robert-Houdin artifacts donated by the conjurer's descendants. Lang assured ministerial support for an ambitious project that, reportedly, would ultimately jeopardize his political fortune: the Centre National des Arts de la Magie et de l'Illusion (National Center of the Arts of Magic and Illusion).

Project planners envisioned an international institution that would combine the functions of a museum, conservatory, theater, and research institute—all devoted to illusionism. The Ministry of Culture allocated just over 46 million francs in start-up funds, and the city of Blois, at the cost of millions more, purchased a mansion directly across from the historic chateau to house the new institution. Lang named sculptor Jean-Marc Ferrari chair of the project's planning committee. A visual artist,

Ferrari saw magic as only one arena among many for thinking about illusion as a philosophical and artistic problem. In a prospectus prepared during the early planning phase, the Ferrari-led team outlined an ambitious project that, "in homage to Robert-Houdin . . . will be dedicated to promoting the florescence and renewal of the arts of magic and illusion." It described the center as a "site of education and awakening" where magic would "reveal the relativity of the visible world . . . and raise questions about the nature of reality . . . stirring both emotion and the desire for knowledge."[43]

A research institute called the Academy of Secrets was to be the crowning jewel of the Ferrari plan. Its inaugural members, mainly philosophers, historians, and literary scholars from prestigious Parisian universities, would convene to "explore the techniques of illusion-production in the history of our civilization and elucidate their role in different fields of knowledge-production: the search for truth in philosophy and the construction of an image of reality in the history of science."[44] The academy embodied the planning committee's aim to enhance the cultural image of magic by associating it with traditional mainstays of cultural capital: philosophy, the fine arts, and the hard sciences (Robert-Houdin himself would have no doubt approved). This agenda was reflected in an exhibit organized at the Château de Blois, sponsored by the Ministry of Culture, and under the stewardship of Ferrari and an Association de Préfiguration de la Maison de la Magie (Association for Planning the Maison de la Magie). Entitled "La Belle Magie: Artifices, illusion, raison" (Beautiful Magic: Artifice, Illusion, Reason), the exhibit focused on the foundations of science in the natural magic of Renaissance alchemists and astrologers, with little mention of prestidigitation.[45]

For their part, French magicians saw the creation of a National Magic Center as a harbinger of magic's long-awaited cultural redemption. Georges Proust, who would shortly open the private Musée de la Magie in Paris, was an indefatigable champion of the Blois project. He later told an interviewer, "What I wanted was to make magic an officially recognized part of France's national cultural patrimony. . . . No one [at the Ministry of Culture] understood what I was talking about. All the officials I met with thought that magic was just gags and practical jokes—nothing serious. . . . So for me, when the Ministry of Culture took charge of creating the magic museum [in Blois], it was an important indicator that my dream of seeing magic incorporated into the official realm of high culture might come true. That the Ministry of Culture was interested in the project was for me a consecration."[46]

The planning committee invited Jacques Delord to oversee development of the center's educational programs, on the strength of his visionary children's television program, *Les Ateliers du magicien*, and an inspired series of tie-in books. In 1991, he drafted a seventy-five-page tract entitled "The Teaching of Magic and Illusion as Gestural and Verbal Poetry" outlining, in terms sometimes mystical, a project for using magic to awaken the innate creative faculty and universal sense of wonder that he feared consumer society and mass culture dulled.[47] He envisioned a pedagogical agenda that began with the design of the exhibits, extended through magic and poetry workshops for children and adults, and culminated in a conservatory program for training professional magicians. Like Proust, he was jubilant about the project.

Unfortunately, the cost of renovating the mansion—the entire building was lifted so that space for a 400-seat theater could be excavated beneath it—consumed most of the project budget. In 1993, with national elections approaching, France's premier newspaper *Le Monde* ran a short piece on the project in the "Arts" section entitled "Une Maison d'illusion pour M. Jack Lang" (A House of Illusion for Mr. Jack Lang). After a seemingly enthusiastic description of the project, the article ended with a sucker punch: "Construction, which began last fall, is proceeding well. . . . The initial investment . . . is entirely covered by the Ministry of Culture . . . which is thus extending (an important first!) its prerogative to the celebration of ectoplasm. This generosity will certainly be appreciated by the Ministry's traditional beneficiaries at a time when the budget is facing drastic reductions. . . . Even Mr. Lang's worshipers and the proponents of his brand of cultural pluralism think the magician of the rue de Valois [the location of the Ministry of Culture] has finally overdone it, especially on the eve of legislative elections."[48] The attack was not only on Lang but also on magic itself. Through an anachronistic reference to "ectoplasm," a substance that nineteenth-century spirit mediums were purported to materialize when entranced, the journalist denied magic's pretense to a place among the fine arts, associating it instead with charlatanism, superstition, and the occult. But, a decade later, it was another phrase that remained lodged in Delord's memory. "When *Le Monde* called Lang the 'magician of the rue de Valois' that effectively ended the project," Delord opined. "Lang saw that, and he wanted out. He dropped us like a hot potato."[49]

Although he remained mayor of Blois, in 1993, Lang was replaced as minister of culture. National sources of funding dried up, rendering the ambitious Ferrari plan effectively obsolete. Although construction had finished, the center sat empty, without an operating budget. Then movie producer and magic enthusiast Christian Fechner not only volunteered portions of his extraordinary magic collection, but also offered to finance and oversee the design of the center's exhibitions. Meanwhile, French amusement park giant Astérix contracted with the municipality to manage day-to-day operations of an institution no one still called the Centre National des Arts de la Magie et de l'Illusion, but simply the Maison de la Magie. The extreme rarity of this kind of public-private partnership in France (as opposed to the United States) suggests that this was a last-ditch attempt to salvage the project.

Though a far different institution than the Ferrari team had envisioned, the Maison that opened in 1998 seemed poised for success. Large crowds gathered in front of the stately mansion to watch six roaring, smoke-bellowing, animatronic dragons that emerged from its shuttered windows every half hour, and attendance was brisk. Unfortunately, Astérix approached the Maison like an amusement park, gambling on the appeal of live entertainment rather than the historical collection that was the institution's real strength. The galleries were understaffed, and employees instructed not to discuss the exhibits with guests. Furious, Fechner withdrew his priceless collection and his support for the museum. In failing to foreground the historical importance of Robert-Houdin, Astérix not only alienated the Maison's greatest ally but also made a grave commercial miscalculation: though the management, to its credit, brought in some of the best magicians in the world to perform, few people proved willing to travel to Blois for a magic show. Having lost millions, the company defaulted on its payments to the city. In 2000, the municipality assumed full control of the Maison.

Attendance continued to drop. Journalists widely proclaimed the failure of what locals had come to call the "Maison de la Gabegie" (*gabegie* connotes an expensive boondoggle). Then, just in time for the 2002 season, the Bureau of Cultural Affairs in Blois hired Céline Noulin as its director of cultural action and communication. A native of Blois and born on the Rue Robert-Houdin, Noulin had just completed a master's thesis on the Maison de la Magie for an advanced degree in cultural administration. In her new position, she would face challenges that were far from academic. When we met in her office several years later, the buoyant Noulin had much to be proud of: within a year, the negative articles had stopped (she had thick binders of newspaper clippings to prove it). Indeed attendance was so high that the entire Loire Valley was poised to launch a magic-themed advertising campaign to promote tourism in the region.

The success is a testament to the close cooperation between Noulin and the Maison's small but devoted staff. When I first visited the Maison on a brisk February day in 2005, I found them happily preparing to reopen after the winter off-season. Arnaud Dalaine, the resident magician, walked me through the galleries. "There are basically four of us," he explained. "And we do mostly everything ourselves." Dominique, nominally the museum's tour guide, was rearranging an exhibit of Robert-Houdin's workshop. "Do you want to see the Pendulum?" he asked, motioning me toward an open case containing one of Robert-Houdin's priceless creations, a functional clock made entirely of crystal with no visible mechanical components. In previous years, Dominique had organized special exhibits of magic in the work of Jean Cocteau, and then on his literary hero Sherlock Holmes.

In the cavernous theater, Benoît, nominally the coordinator of educational outreach, was building sets with Gilles, an actor originally hired to appear in the Maison's magic productions. The stage was strewn with cardboard boxes, scaffolding, paint canisters, and power tools. "And when it's done, it going to look even worse!" Arnaud laughed. The setting for the magic show was an enchanted construction site, where a pair of bungling hardhats would experiment with magical powers. Each staff member was learning both parts; when the Maison reopened, they would perform the twenty-minute show every hour in rotating pairs. "We hardly have any money," Benoît said. "We can recycle some illusions from previous years, like the levitation, and the rest we build ourselves. Everything is held together with bubble gum and rubber bands. But we're essentially free to do whatever we want with the show, the exhibits, and the educational programming. It's great!"

In the few years since the city had taken charge of the Maison, the unlikely team of museographers had not only redesigned the exhibition spaces, filling the gaps left when Fechner withdrew his collection, but also developed an effective educational outreach program, and, with help from director James Hodges, staged a new magic show every year. With Gérard Majax's "Hallucionoscope," a room in which visitors use special glasses to traverse an oneiric landscape, providing an added attraction, the Maison remains one of the biggest tourist draws in the region.

Particularly in a place like France where they are so often beholden to national political agendas, the life cycles of cultural institutions such as museums offer valuable insights into shifting ideas about culture—regional and national, indigenous and foreign, popular and elite.[50] The Maison was initially conceived at a moment when progressive currents in cultural policy and an interest in regional cultural patrimony made magic seem like an attractive object of state intervention. In the end, magic's questionable cultural status made support from the Ministry of Culture difficult to sustain, but, thanks to the resourcefulness and imagination of its staff and the commitment of local authorities, the Maison appears to have found a viable cultural niche. As a project of culture making, the Maison has consistently drawn on discourses of heritage as a source of legitimacy. In the next section, I explore the relevance of another conceptual framework—one based on modernist aesthetic thought—to strategies for promoting the cultural status of magic in the French national context.

MAGIC AS FINE ART

Critical theorists describe the emergence of modern art as a cultural institution in terms of "autonomization," or the emancipation of cultural production from the practical concerns of everyday life.[51] Historically, this process has involved an evolution in the status of European art makers from the Renaissance onward. As they came to work with relative independence from the heteronomous (i.e., externally originating) demands of powerful patrons such as the Church or the royal court, once anonymous artisans like painters or musicians became culture heroes celebrated for individual genius, whose creative practices could have purely aesthetic justifications. This "art for art's sake" ideal coevolved with new modes of aesthetic appreciation; institutions like museums and concert halls developed to promote the contemplation of artwork as an end-in-itself. In the modern West, autonomy of production and consumption ultimately came to be viewed as the very essence of high art.

Indeed, when French magicians talk about elevating magic to the status of a high art, autonomization is clearly a large part of what they have in mind. As a form of entertainment, magic is conspicuously shaped by the heteronomous demands of the cultural marketplace. Whether performing for crowds in cabarets, providing service entertainment at social events, or shilling consumer goods, magicians are compelled to satisfy clients' demands and gratify popular taste. They can ill afford creative risks. Whatever an autonomous magic might be, it would at the very least give magicians the opportunity to create performance works free from immediate market pressures, and to have those works evaluated as a serious form of creative expression.

For many magicians, the *intermittence* program I describe in the previous chapter serves as a kind of cultural patronage that promotes some degree of autonomization by subsidizing artistic production and valorizing magic as an art form. However, that may never have been the program's intention. *Intermittence* originally arose from the idea that certain kinds of work are fraught with unique difficulties, which should be mitigated through the support of the welfare state. It is important to differentiate here between the state's roles as a patron of cultural production and as a protector of cultural producers, though on the surface these may seem the same thing. Arts patronage, generally administered through the Ministry of Culture, is ultimately concerned with the product of artistic labor, the artwork itself; the welfare state, by contrast, intervenes on behalf of the cultural producer as a citizen—the arts worker him or herself.

The Popular Front government created an embryonic version of the *intermittence* program in 1936 specifically for film technicians. As a measure of indirect protectionism for the French film industry, this legislation intended to guarantee a living wage to film crews in the dry periods between shoots. In 1969, these benefits were extended to all workers in performance-related professions able to demonstrate an annual minimum of working hours.[52] Achieving the status of *intermittents* proved highly desirable: at the time I began my research in 2003, there were around 100,000 people receiving unemployment benefits as *intermittents*—over ten times more than twenty years earlier.[53] By that point, the program faced a deficit of 828 million euros, and its annual benefits—around a billion euros—far surpassed the Ministry of Culture's entire annual budget for the performing arts.[54] Because these benefits came in a form of unemployment insurance rather than an officially allocated cultural subsidy, huge budgetary shortfalls raised difficult questions: "Is *intermittence* there to alleviate structural instabilities in a particular sector of the economy," legal experts asked, "or rather to sponsor artistic creativity?"[55]

In 2003, as politicians debated sweeping reforms, *intermittents* took to the streets in high-profile protests culminating in the cancellation of the Avignon Theatre Festival.[56] As a representative of the FFAP, Peter Din was invited to speak with a member of parliament working on *intermittence* reform. "The guy didn't even realize that magic was a profession," Peter later told me. "He was astonished. He asked me if someone could actually earn a living doing tricks!" That summer, although I knew a number of magicians who attended rallies and protests, few actually went on strike; canceling Avignon was one thing, but refusing to perform at a wedding reception would have done little to raise public sympathy for the *intermittents'* cause. Peter, who was working on a cruise ship at the time, opted to make a public statement before his performances, which he posted on VirtualMagie.com as a model for other magicos: "Ladies and gentlemen, this evening, a group of musicians and myself are going to perform for you. We're lucky, because tomorrow it might not be possible for us to share our work with you under normal conditions. Culture depends on a decent standard of living for artists, and tomorrow that may cease to exist. So let's make the most of this evening together."

Despite his vocal advocacy, Peter confessed to deep ambivalence about the program. "The problem is that I'm both a militant supporter and vocal critic of *intermittence*," he told me. "On the one hand, it's a superb program that enables many artists to live from their vocation. I'm one of them. Since the age of twenty-one, I've paid every month to have the right to be an artist, and now *intermittence* allows me to devote my time to magic without worrying if I'm going to be able to pay my bills. If it weren't for *intermittence*, I never would have become a magician. But there's a flipside to the coin. Now you've got lots of people living off *intermittence* who forget why they're getting that money in the first place. It's not a gift. They're supposed to devote the time *intermittence* gives them to artistic creation. And if they're not working on their art, they're basically stealing the money." Here, Peter emphasizes the perspective, pervasive among magicians, that the program's intent is to compensate performing artists for the time they spend between paying gigs creating new works.

While designed to provide unemployment insurance for workers in the predominantly freelance sector of cinema and the performing arts, *intermittence* has come to be widely recognized by its recipients and aspirants as a form of cultural patronage.[57] *Intermittence* not only serves as a token of cultural legitimacy, placing magicians in the same professional category as symphonic musicians, ballet dancers, and opera singers. It also compensates them for what one sociologist, in a study of French jazz musicians, calls "the invisible part of artistic work."[58] For magicians as for jazz musicians, *intermittence* is quite simply not an unemployment benefit, but payment for time spent productively between performances "maintaining or improving the mastery of one's craft" and "developing new performances."[59] In this sense, magicos overwhelmingly construe *intermittence* in ways that maximally emphasize the most art-like feature of their work—the creative process itself.

The political positions that magicians generally have taken in respect to what they perceive as the cultural subsidies provided by *intermittence* reflect the conviction that they, with other artists, have a special role to play in national life and that the state should accord them special rights and protections. This reflects a broader context in which "a national discourse on culture, influenced but not wholly directed by the Ministry of Culture," heavily impacts cultural producers' "understandings of citizenship." [60] Thus, *intermittence* not only has contributed to the economic viability of professional careers in magic, but also has provided a conceptual framework that has allowed magicians to articulate their relationship to other performing artists and to the nation as a whole in a way that is socially and culturally validating.

TOWARD A NEW MAGIC?

In the eyes of many, *intermittence* is an equalizing force in French cultural policy. Since any performer who works a sufficient number of hours in the arena of performance qualifies for benefits, the program seems to encourage production that reflects a real public demand, rather than the aesthetic or political priorities associated with funding from the Ministry of Culture.[61] Nevertheless, it should be clear from earlier comments by Jacques Delord and Georges Proust that, as a potential source of support, the Ministry of Culture remains unrivaled in prestige.

It is precisely from that ministry that Raphaël has sought funding for his magic conservatory. He hopes that such funding will one day liberate magic from what he sees as the tyranny of the marketplace and usher in an avant-garde paradigm that he refers to as "new magic." In 2005, he summed up the present situation grimly: "Magicians are stuck doing light entertainment, and I don't even mean aesthetically, just economically. They can work in cabarets or restaurants, maybe weddings, corporate gigs. But it's all the private sector, the free market. And in the free market, you can't afford to do things that don't work, or things that might disturb people. The advantage of state funding is that you *can* do things that don't work, that don't have mass appeal, that don't satisfy the public's immediate thirst for entertainment. Plus state funding gives you time to create. A magician who has to make a living grinding out birthday parties and bar mitzvahs can't spend three years crafting a serious work of art. And even if they did, where would they perform it? Who would be the audience?"

The model for the changes that Raphaël envisions is the circus—a once moribund folk tradition that, through a series of surprising transformations over the course of recent decades, has become one of the most vibrant sectors of artistic production in contemporary France.[62] The almost meteoric transformation of the circus into a form of high art is a useful counterpoint for understanding the cultural status of magic, and French magicians themselves speak of it in envious tones. By 1970, competition from newer forms of entertainment had driven the circus to the brink of seemingly irreversible decline. Yet several factors contributed to an unexpected turnaround often described as nothing short of a renaissance. First, a consensus emerged about the importance of preserving the traditional circus as a form of living cultural patrimony. In 1978, President Giscard d'Estaing himself transferred supervision of the circus from the Ministry of Agriculture to the Ministry of Culture. Around the same time, avant-garde theater groups around the world were starting to experiment with the circus idiom, using juggling, acrobatics, and clowning as novel modes of artistic expression. The best-known example of this "new circus" movement, as it came to be known, is probably a Canadian one—Cirque du Soleil—but the movement took firm root in France as well.

Also under Jack Lang, the new circus emerged as a darling of the Ministry of Culture, which, in 1985, helped establish a national institute of circus arts, the Centre National des Arts du Cirque (CNAC) and, within it, a national circus academy, the École Supérieure des Arts du Cirque (ESAC). These institutions have considerably reshaped the circus as a cultural practice. In the traditional circus, performance skills were handed down from parent to child through participatory apprenticeship; most of the early performers in the new circus were autodidacts. Graduates of the ESAC program are, by contrast, conservatory-trained virtuosi, proficient in a variety of different expressive disciplines and endowed with a rich critical vocabulary.[63] Journalistic critiques and academic studies set a new precedent for interpreting circus performances hermeneutically, and performers have come to speak of their work in ways that highlight ideational content rather than physical prowess,[64] evidence that criticism is not *"external* to the production of significance in (or through) art." [65] Raphaël hoped to see the same pattern of discursive elaboration develop in magic. "That's why it's so important that you're taking the initiative to write about magic," he told me.

It is important to recall the potential of new critical discourses to impact reception more broadly. Just as being a magic performer is a culturally scripted role, so is being a spectator, and verbal responses to magic consistently employ a handful of predicable tropes. In France, I heard countless spectators proclaim that magic "makes them feel like a child again"; at least as many grumbled that it "drives them nuts." The recurrence of these stock responses points to an underlying contrast between rapt enchantment and skeptical disenchantment as readily available cultural attitudes toward magic, and magicos know them well. When I mentioned this to Raphaël he agreed that "everyone reacts to magic in those two ways," but complained that neither childlike awe nor petulant skepticism is an *aesthetic* response of attempting an interpretation. "Magicians have created a cult of the trick," he said. "Their only goal is to trick people," which leaves spectators either amazed or annoyed.

A direct beneficiary of the institutional changes that have elevated the cultural status of the circus, Raphaël and his company have received funding for works of new circus performance involving juggling and magic that they have staged at prestigious theaters around the country. He explained the emergence of the new circus in terms imbued with modernist aesthetic theory. "Before television, the circus was a way to bring the wonders of the world into the village. It was like, 'We're going to look at the world as it is and be fascinated by the men who jump so high, the women who have beards, a juggler who can keep so many balls up in the air, or the strongest man alive.' It was either an extreme of virtuosity or an extreme of curiosity, but that was it. Then suddenly, with the new circus, people started to use it as an artistic medium: to represent the world not as it is, but as it appears from the unique perspective of the individual artist." Raphaël considered it ironic that, by this standard, magic too had not become an art. "A magician can never represent reality as it is, only a fictive version of it!"

In his efforts to found a state-funded magic conservatory, Raphaël's connections in the world of new circus have enabled him to activate networks of influence leading, through the CNAC, to the Ministry of Culture. In discussing his project for a magic conservatory—what he calls the Centre de Recherche pour une Magie Nouvelle (Research Center for a New Magic)—with officials from the Ministry of Culture and the CNAC, Raphaël emphasizes the potential of magic to become a high art with widespread public appeal. "I tell them that through magic, we can create a contemporary art that is eminently popular. It's a way of selling the project. Today magic is in the same situation the circus was twenty years ago. Everyone thinks it's kitschy [*ringard*], and they're right. If I walked into the Ministry of Culture and told them I was a magician, they'd blow me off [*se foutre de ma gueule*]. But going through the new circus, I was able to get my foot in the door."

The first step toward realizing his dream of a conservatory has been to organize a program of advanced training in new magic at the CNAC, involving master classes with magicians, choreographers, and jugglers as well as presentations by philosophers, anthropologists, cognitive scientists, and historians. In 2007's inaugural cohort, half of the twelve participants were professional magicians, and the other half were creative professionals from fields such as jazz, dance, puppetry, and haute cuisine. If the new magic workshops successfully inspire new directions of cultural production in magic, Raphaël told me he would feel emboldened to seek more substantial support from the Ministry of Culture. "I want to prove that interesting things can come out of this, so that the Ministry recognizes that it's worth investing in magic. They're skeptical, but they're giving me a chance to prove that there really are magicians out there who want to do new things, and who just need to be given the means to do it."

As this book goes to press, more than five years after Raphaël first discussed his vision with me, it appears that his efforts have largely been rewarded with the increasing recognition of new magic as a genre. As an indicator of institutional stability, in 2010 the new magic course at the

CNAC recruited its fourth cohort of advanced students. "Detached from the restrictions of repertoire, new magic is not apprehended as a technique, but rather a language," the application form read.[66] "At the end of this training, students will master this language and enrich themselves with its potential for artistic composition based on disrupting reality and rendering the impossible." Meanwhile, "Vibrations," Cie 14:20's most recent production, has toured France and met with critical acclaim, serving as a de facto "proof of concept" for new magic. The combination of ambitious subject matter, cutting-edge illusionary techniques, and breathtaking choreography make it an extraordinary theatrical experience.

For instance, one of the show's four twenty-minute acts draws on research conducted in collaboration with Raphaël's girlfriend, a graduate student in anthropology, among the Lacandon Maya in Chiapas, Mexico. Describing the production, Raphaël explains that the Lacandon believe that every gesture people make leaves a trace in time, and that when one dies, it is necessary to retrace those gestures in order to reunite the alienated aspects of an inherently plural soul. In the sequence inspired by this understanding of Lacandon cosmology, a dancer moves acrobatically around the stage, leaving three-dimensional images of her body frozen in space (the technique used to produce these holographic sculptures represents a synthesis of space-age technology and canonical principles of modern magic). Gradually, the after-images, with the physical weightiness of real flesh and blood, begin to move independently, and to interact with the dancer and with each other. It quickly becomes impossible to distinguish between the original dancer and her magically generated doppelgangers. When the dancers eventually dematerialize, there is no one left on the stage. It is a hauntingly beautiful piece, and a disquieting meditation on identity, mortality, and time that easily transcends its sources.

Another important sign of legitimacy has been the uptake of "new magic" as a category among journalists and academics. In April 2010, the magazine of circus arts, *Stradda*, published a twenty-page feature on new magic, proclaiming "the emergence of a contemporary art."[67] Later that year, a long story in *Le Monde* described a "renaissance in new magic as an artistic movement," pointing to "some thirty troupes" in France embracing it as a genre and "expanding its aesthetic horizons." [68] Both reports singled out Cie 14:20 as the leader of this movement. In January 2011, France Culture, the national public radio station devoted to culture and the arts, broadcast interview segments with Raphaël and Clément on three consecutive days. [69] The pair make magnetic spokespeople for a nascent artistic movement: young, forcefully articulate, and irresistibly nice. They are currently coauthoring a new magic manifesto that promises to define the movement in years to come.

On January 21, I attended a daylong colloquium on new magic at the Maison des Sciences de l'Homme, a major social science institute just north of Paris. Co-organized by electronic music scholar Anne Sèdes and my friend Guilhem Julia, an award-winning magician and rising legal scholar, the workshop featured presentations by Cie 14:20 and drew an audience of some thirty scholars and graduate students. Over the course of the day, Raphaël and Clément described their creative approach as the preeminent exponents of new magic, and Guilhem spoke about his efforts to create a legal framework for protecting magicians' secrets by extending extant copyright protections for choreography to what he calls the "choreography of the invisible," that is, the hidden sleights magicians use to produce illusions. [70] While new magic's emerging cultural legitimacy and the protection of magicians' intellectual property may seem like distinct issues, Guilhem connected them brilliantly, arguing that "the recognition of an art as legitimate" can "oblige the law to recognize it" and lead to its "juridical consecration" as a domain of legally protected intellectual property. (This argument recalls the connection Foucault draws between the rise of the Romantic cult of the author and the advent of "a system of ownership for texts" with "strict rules concerning author's rights, author-publisher relations, [and] rights of reproduction.") [71]

For their part, magicos have expressed some disagreement about the significance of new magic as a cultural development. In the midst of a particularly heated debate on VirtualMagie.com, Loïc wrote (with his usual flair): "It seems like [the proponents of new magic] want to make magic into a kind of contemporary art (for me, adding 'contemporary'

means 'now no one will understand anything'). Kind of like super aggravating contemporary dance where, noting the consternation on your face,
aficionados reassure you on the way out, 'Well, of course you have to
understand the codes.' Or like painters of monochromatic canvasses. . . .
Things that thrill the kinds of pretentious people who only feel alive
when they can rhapsodize over a painted old bread crust, convinced they
have discerned the complexity of the artist's intention. It scares me a bit, I
confess." [72] Writing in an obviously satirical vein, Loïc nevertheless points
to a critical difference between modern magic, conceived essentially as
playful entertainment, and new magic, conceived as serious art. As these
two models of cultural production are increasingly recognized as distinctive genres by people within the magic world, it will be fascinating to
observe how they will coexist and, perhaps, interact in the years to come.

CONCLUSION

Magicus magazine pounced on the hot topic new magic in the first issue
of 2011. "Does NEW MAGIC Get Your Whites Whiter?" the cover story
asked, parodying the ad copy for the latest laundry detergent.[73] On the
first page, editor Didier Puech gave a sobering assessment: "Besides the
label, new magic offers nothing new. . . . And it's quite aggravating to
see some of our colleagues—no doubt blinded by their idealization of
youth—extolling its virtues without reservation. Instead of reviewing
the historical facts, citing notable magicians who have been blazing
trails for years, or offering an opposing point of view, *squat!*" [74] To prove
his point, Puech selected as the cover not a photograph of one of new
magic's rising stars, but rather an image of Abdul Alafrez, which he
dated to the 1970s. "This towering, talented fifty-something magician
has traveled the world (but not the magic world!) for more than thirty
years," Puech explained in his editorial. "In his work as a magician, he
has always drawn on the assets of circus, dance, music, visual arts,
clowning, etc. . . . The good Abdul has been doing 'new magic' . . . all
along without knowing it!"

An atypical professional whom I encountered through academic rather than magical channels, Abdul tends to eschew (as Puech implies) what he calls the "show business circuit." Although he takes table-hopping gigs just like everyone else ("I've got to survive," he said), by the time I met him in 2003, the lumbering fifty-year-old had accumulated a remarkable string of high-culture achievements: designing special effects for the national opera, performing magic at the prestigious Comédie Française, and staging collaborative performances with avant-garde musicians from American free-jazz trumpeter Don Cherry to the Ensemble Modern of Frankfurt. He is occasionally invited to participate in academic colloquia around Paris, including some organized by anthropologists (in an email, he described one such event as "Abdul in the land of anthropologists"). Setting aside vexed distinctions between new magic and modern magic, I would characterize Abdul as a—if not the—central figure in French magic's avant-garde (see Figure 15).

Sensitive ("I know my limits," he told me after walking out of a horror film) but with a keen eye for the absurd (in French, his Arabic-sounding stage name means "Strawberry-Flavored Abdul"), he was one of my most engaging interlocutors, judiciously unpacking my questions and laughing gleefully at my platitudes. When I told him I was conducting my research in France because it was the "birthplace of modern magic," he practically split a gut. Abdul is one of those who consider Robert-Houdin's transformation of magic into a respectable bourgeois entertainment inimical to the genre's artistic and expressive potential. In an interview for an issue of the journal *Critique* (in which I was also a participant), he explained, "If Robert-Houdin is so important it's . . . first and foremost because he conquered a new audience, resituating magic culturally. Sweeping away allusions to the Devil or the occult, the cape with stars and the pointy hats, the black robes and cabbalistic formulae, he invented an art of the salon, performed by someone dressed like his clients. It was by using quasi-scientific rhetoric and attracting a bourgeois audience that he gave magic its 'deed of distinction.' Not that pointy hats have been permanently mothballed—I, for one, remain quite attached to them."[75]

Likening himself to a Pre-Raphaëlite in painting, Abdul self-consciously draws on the supposedly naïve forms of magic Robert-Houdin pur-

Figure 15.   Avant-garde magician Abdul Alafrez. Photo by
Dominique Gérard.

ported to displace, costuming himself in ornate robes and masks, and
surrounding himself with otherworldly imagery. For instance, in a silent sequence of a 1998 ensemble work entitled "Les Escamoteurs" (The
Conjurers), he and Bertrand Crimet, dressed in hieratic regalia, perform
a series of feats that resemble esoteric rituals more than entertaining
tricks. When Abdul, skulking like a hunchbacked lab assistant, presents
him with platters heaped with a cottony material, Crimet consumes it by
the handful, then bellows smoke and fire from his mouth. (This is, in
fact, an effect commonly associated with circumpolar and Native North
American ritual experts in the ethnographic record.) They usher a third
illusionist, Carmelo Cacciato, dressed in street wear, onstage. When
Cacciato refuses to consume the cotton himself, Crimet plunges an arm

into his back and out his chest, grabs a huge handful of the material, and deposits it inside the unwilling initiate's belly. Then he and Abdul clothe Cacciato in a flowing yellow robe (perhaps the costume of an initiate?) and levitate him in the air. This sequence suggests how the three magicians move beyond the limits of spectacular entertainment, presenting effects drawn from the standard magical repertoire as a humorous—but also haunting—parody of sacramental rites.

Abdul credits his artistic success to keeping a safe distance from other magicians. "Like everybody," he told me, "I've been a member of magic clubs. I started out at age fourteen. I went to the AFAP [now FFAP]. I learned a lot, because, well, learn one must. And then, when I was around twenty, I realized I had problems to solve—not personal problems, I've still got those—but magical problems. And magicians couldn't help me—quite the opposite! For example, if I want to make a sugar cube vanish, that's a problem. The solution has two parts—what magicians call 'technique' and 'presentation'. For me, presentation is an eminently technical problem. In theater or dance, performers study it systematically. But magicians only approach it in the most rudimentary way. All they're really capable of discussing is technique as they understand it—that is to say, in terms of sleights." Abdul saw magicians' focalization on technique as a product of the way knowledge is socially organized within the magic world. "It has to do with how one learns magic. In the theater, there is a real pedagogy," he said. "People are trained within different philosophies or schools, but they acquire a shared aesthetic vocabulary that allows them to work together. In magic, pedagogy is nonexistent. Of course, you can always find people to explain tricks to you, but that's not equivalent to an education. Precisely because there's no real education in magic, magicians have to see each other all the time to keep learning."

As Abdul implied, the lack of a shared aesthetic vocabulary can inhibit magicians' ability to collaborate with cultural producers in other artistic arenas. For instance, I once accompanied a cabaret magician to an audition at an experimental theater near the Bastille. The theater director said that she was planning a "cabaret" performance, and wanted to feature a magician. However, when my friend enthusiastically performed his entirely authentic cabaret act, she recoiled from the bawdy humor (she was presumably looking for a suitably stagy portrayal, not straight-outta-Pigalle authenticity). "What does she think cabaret is?" he fumed afterward. This kind of miscommunication is not surprising given the infrequency of exchanges between magicians and counterparts in the fine arts. Perhaps the new magic program at the CNAC will eventually facilitate more collaborations of this sort; the new magic movement is partially an initiative to expand the horizons of modern magic by introducing new discursive practices into extant forms of staging talk. Although Abdul does not identify with the new magic moniker, he did give master classes—on the historical relationship of magic and theater, on working as a magician in theater, and on constructing grand illusions—during the first three years of the program.

"Opera is a high art about trivial matters," Abdul once told me. "And magic is a trivial art about matters of the highest importance." He was only half joking. In France and elsewhere, magic is generally produced and received as a genre of spectacular entertainment, performed in recreative settings for audiences who do not expect to engage in serious interpretive activity by performers who don't expect that they should. But it is also a genre that flirts with fundamental metaphysical questions about the nature of reality and truth: *What is real? What is merely illusion? How can we tell the difference? Why do these distinctions matter?* Many of the talented magicians in this book strive, in their own creative ways, to give their audiences profound experiences. This chapter has largely concerned several unique individuals involved in sustained efforts to broaden the cultural horizons of magic as a form of cultural production capable of addressing serious issues, largely through engagements with the cultural apparatus of the French state.

As a foreign observer in the world of French magic, I have often been struck by magicos' preoccupation with the category of art as the ultimate measure of cultural prestige, and in their faith in the state as the ultimate motor of cultural ratification. Both reflect a national setting far different from my native United States, where show business is arguably widely esteemed as a field of cultural production and the state plays only a minor role in fashioning taste. Of course, not all magicos are as concerned with issues of cultural distinction as the figures I discuss in this chapter. As a cultural ambassador, Jacques Delord was uniquely self-conscious about participating in a national tradition of magic, and few magicians are as steeped in the discourses of modernist aesthetics as Raphaël. But in their efforts to locate dimensions of the artistic within magic, these unique individuals clearly reflect the broader cultural landscape in which magic is positioned in contemporary France. Moreover, as French magic moves forward in the new millennium, individuals who challenge conventional wisdom about what and how it may mean have the potential to dramatically influence the directions in which this living tradition will continue to evolve.

EPILOGUE "Giving People a Gift"

From an anthropological perspective, the vibrancy of magic as a subculture attests to the unique importance of imaginative play in human life, and the richness of magic as a form of expertise (whose depth and variety I have only just hinted at) illustrates amazing human capacities for the cultivation of skill. Of course, we encounter countless systems of expert knowledge during the course of an average day, whether they are objectified in technologies or embodied in people. While expertise is often associated with seriousness and predictability, in magic it takes a decidedly mischievous form that serves to generate surprise and uncertainty. Magic nevertheless exemplifies the kinds of social processes that shape many, if not all, expert systems: interactions not only among experts themselves, but also between experts and novices, laypeople, and experts in other fields during which the value of a definitive set of skills is at stake.[1] In this sense, this book is a contribution to what Dominic Boyer has recently identified as the burgeoning "anthropology of experts and expertise."[2]

Due in part to constraints of secrecy and perhaps also to a pervasive ethos of individualism, magic is a staggeringly complex form of expertise that, like traditional crafts, flourishes as a self-regulating subculture rather than as part of an institutionalized discipline. To highlight dimensions of expertise in magic, I have focused on the behind-the-scenes occasions of craft sociability, with a special emphasis on staging talk—the array of verbal practices through which magicians constitute expertise as a discursive arena. In so doing, I have not meant to minimize the importance of moments when magicians present more-or-less finished illusionary works in public performance. As I complete this project, precious memories of such moments vie emphatically for my attention.

Mostly, these are not memories of celebrity magicians on expansive stages with truckloads of dangerous felines and glittery big-box illusions. They are memories of normal people doing extraordinary things in and to everyday situations. Against the backdrop of mundane expectations about what can and cannot happen in the course of ordinary waking life, magicians cleverly divert routine patterns of perception and interaction, delivering spectators to the thrilling brink of the rationally comprehensible. Often working with little more than a deck of cards or perhaps some loose change, they create ephemeral illusions that are hard to forget. They remind us that we do not, and cannot, know everything, but reassure us that not knowing can be a source of delirious pleasure.

The figure of the magician—that trickster who fiddles with the iron-clad rules that govern the cosmos—is an archetype associated with timeless themes. "The Magician's gift for miracle and for deception is manifold," writes one Jungian analyst.[3] "By directing our attention away from the golden coin, he can ensnare and befuddle us with his sleight of hand. . . . By making the objects on his table disappear, he can dramatize the simple truth that every object, every thing, is but an *appearance* of reality." Magical effects exert a kind of instinctual appeal that magicians themselves sometimes struggle to fathom. "I'm amazed by the hold the lost-and-found card has over people's imaginations," Abdul once told me. "There must be some biological basis for it in the reptilian brain. If I come right up to a table, have someone choose a card, lose it in the deck, and then find it, for me, it's done. I've proven I can do it. But I still get guys who want to choose *another* card, lose it, and have me find it *again*. It's mind-boggling!"

Despite their wide and enduring appeal, magicians are always products of specific times and places. Literary critic Roland Barthes, for instance, speculates that the surging popularity of modern magic in nineteenth-century Europe can be seen as a symbolic negation of harsh industrial working conditions, principally directed to audiences in large industrial cities. He writes that, like other variety artists, magicians who make material objects appear and disappear at will represent "the aesthetic form of work" or "human labor memorialized and sublimated," transformed into "a profound fantasy that erases all brutality from labor, leaving nothing but its purified essence."[4] Yet if the current vogue for close-up magic is any indication, in the postmodern, postindustrial world, it may be the magician's ability to incarnate labor rather than symbolically negate it that is most culturally resonant today. At this historical juncture, the expansion of a genre hinging on a performer's embodied dexterity and face-to-face human contact with individual spectators may complicate the art-entertainment dichotomy central to the last chapter, situating magic within an entirely different neo-artisanal regime of value.

These kinds of close-up performances may represent a cultural adaptation to the attitudes of audiences inured to mass-mediated spectacle. "It's one thing to see it on TV," I've often heard spectators tell close-up performers, "but when it's right in front of your eyes, it's a whole different story." Over thirty years ago, the president of the FFAP (then AFAP) wrote, "Magic has lost none of its appeal, and it's comforting to note . . . that even people who are unimpressed by the fabulous achievements of astronauts, conquerors of the moon, rediscover their faculty of amazement before a simple manipulation of cards, coins, or balls. People may be indifferent towards the extraordinary march of progress that makes everything seem to exceed the human scale, but the magician's millennia-old artifice can still awaken their natural curiosity."[5] The face-to-face

scale of close-up magic in particular allows performers to build interest and intrigue on a personal basis, engaging directly with spectator
reactions.

In this book, I have examined some of the ways contemporary French
close-up magicians cultivate the ability to enact a mastery of mystery in
situations that spectators co-construct. Becoming a magician is a complex and multifaceted process of personal transformation. Novices acquire technical skills and embodied dispositions while constituting
themselves as members of the community of magicos. Magic is a secretive subculture and a competitive business, but magicos constantly help
each other grow as entertainers and succeed as professionals by communicating what they have learned through a variety of channels. They
are passionate about their craft, infusing unending projects of enskillment with the excitement of discovery, the sheer satisfaction of acquiring new abilities, and the pleasures of collaborative practice.

The French magic scene is both a community of practice and a speech
community with distinctive forms of staging talk inseparable from other
dimensions of expertise. Language shapes magic in a variety of ways.
Whether conducted in person, in print, over the Internet, or on film, staging talk often takes the form of speech play and verbal art through which
magicos seek to entertain each other and display their wit. In ways that
are essential to the expert practice of magic, they use constructed dialogues to model the reactions of hypothetical spectators, whose mental
states they present as inner monologue. When telling stories, they use
reported speech to relive past encounters with spectators, clients, and
other magicians, thereby rendering other significant interactions available for assessment. Language also mediates the critical moments when
magicians exchange secrets, keying a shared affective stance and thereby
helping constitute transfers of knowledge as instances of social reproduction rather than gratuitous dispersal.

Magicos share corporate group interests, such as maintaining a standard valuation of secret knowledge, that members of the community are
expected to uphold. While they do not always agree about what constitutes a violation of community norms, indignant references to the exposure of secrets to laymen as *débinage* reinforce representations of secrets

as something sacred, just as gossip about intellectual property infractions sensitizes novices to the value of owning secrets and to the rights of their owners. Over time, participation in the production and circulation of secrets inculcates a secretive habitus attuned to the way value is produced through both giving and keeping, revealing and concealing. Exhibiting secrets to audiences in the context of performance similarly reaffirms the value of magicians' secrets, as spectators react to illusions with fascination and awe.

Magic is risky. Whenever they are put to use, the secrets on which illusions depend are also put in jeopardy of inadvertent exposure. Facing audiences that always already expect to be fooled, magicians must be especially crafty in the way they engineer illusions, using every means at their disposal to falsify potential solutions. Performing illusions, magicians also stake their reputations as masters of illusion—expert deceivers capable of outfoxing even the most watchful spectator. In modern magic, acts of exhibiting secrets and tricking people have been culturally associated with masculine themes of potency, inscribed in the metaphor of "screwing" that magicos sometimes use to describe their performances. As magic grows more diverse, male and female performers are challenging these associations and the stereotypical image of a modern magician as a white, heterosexual male more generally. Conventional correlations of magical signifiers and gendered meanings can even become a resource for articulating subversive critiques of prevailing gender norms, as we see in queer magic presentations.

Magic is also a risky career choice. As freelancers, magicos are at the mercy of a volatile cultural marketplace; as entrepreneurs, they must constantly promote themselves and seek out new opportunities to perform. The unique structure of the social welfare system in France makes it possible for them, along with all other performing artists who work on a freelance basis, to receive an unemployment benefit. This supplementary income provides them a relative measure of financial stability from month to month and year to year. Receiving *intermittence* benefits also has come to serve as an important marker of professional legitimacy and cultural distinction in a national setting where magic occupies a conspicuously inferior status vis-à-vis high arts. For better or worse, recent controversies about *intermittence* likewise ensure that French audiences are increasingly aware that professional magicians receive what amount to state subsidies, and performers sometimes speak with them about the topic.

Many magicos feel a sense of frustration with what they see as a persistent undervaluation of what they do by the French public at large, and in some cases even the people closest to them—friends, family, and colleagues. Proud participants in a storied tradition, they may use performances to inform audiences about the history of magic. Thus, Jan Madd projects images of the influential magicians—from Harry Houdini to Chung Ling Soo—whose effects he reinterprets onstage, and Dominique Duvivier relates stories about close-up pioneers like Albert Goshman as he performs. Others strive to burnish the image of magic by associating it, in ways that are distinctively French, with the prestige of national patrimony and the culturally legitimating, artistically liberating power of the state. These are ambitious, long-term projects, but the increasing recognition of new magic as a category of legitimate art may be a bellwether of change. In the meantime, magicos will continue to display their talents in surprising—and necessarily unforeseeable—ways.

Magicians mingle among us, literally embodying a complex craft that they are eager to share. Their practice changes the way they relate to the world around them. Constantly on the lookout for resources to augment their skill and opportunities to display it, they see realities most people take for granted as contingent and subject to strategic manipulation. The illusions they create depend on an acute sensitivity to the way others view the world. Paradoxically, practicing the art of deception can even bring them closer to the people they deceive, occasioning fleeting moments of intimacy and dialog. If they sometimes vent their frustrations about underappreciative publics, it is only because they place so much value on "sharing something" in interactions with the spectators who co-construct their tricks.

The images I have in my mind as I complete this book are of normal people reaching out to others with small but profound gestures of artistry, stirring imaginations and satisfying a basic human need for wonder. It is the image of country doctor and accomplished amateur magician Pierre Guédin fulfilling the dying wish of one of his cancer patients by performing in an empty hospital on a Sunday afternoon for no one but her.[6] Or the image of Loïc and fellow magician Ratcékou filling a dreary dive bar where we wandered in for a nightcap with exuberant glee as they improvised tricks with everyday objects for its working-class clientele of mostly African immigrants. (I will confess that when the diminutive Ratcékou—whose stubby fingers are improbably adroit, but whose stage name means "Blows-His-Shots"—performed an unannounced feat of pickpocketry, stealing an expensive-looking watch off the wrist of the bar's hulking, mustachioed owner, I feared the night might not end so well for us.) Or, finally, the image of Philippe stopping to talk with a pack of scruffy teenagers lurking in the shadows of the Chartres cathedral as he and I made our way home from a pub in the wee hours of the morning. "Name an animal!" he cheerily began, digging into his backpack.

"A dog," one of the youths mumbled suspiciously between world-weary puffs on a cigarette. Within minutes, Philippe had made not only a dog (a poodle, to be exact), but a veritable Noah's Ark of multicolored balloon animals for the astonished teenagers, as well as a flower (for the one girl present) and helmets adorned with disconcertingly realistic phalluses (for the boys, myself included). We lingered on, talking amicably about their experiences growing up in the idyllic town they called "boring" and about my life in a New York I described as "frenetic," seemingly worlds away. Disappearing back into the night, we could hear their youthful laughter echoing along the ancient cobblestone streets. "That's what magic is all about: giving people a gift," Philippe reflected. "They'll remember that forever."

"Me too," I whispered, my green boner helmet glistening in the moonlight.

Notes

1. PREFACE AND ACKNOWLEDGMENTS

1. Marsh (2008).

INTRODUCTION

1. Volkmann (1956).
2. Alciphron et al. (1949: 111).
3. Hamburger (1984).
4. Curry (1965: 15).
5. For background on Binet's study, see Lachapelle (2008). For a critique of recent psychological discussions of magic, see Lamont, Henderson, and Smith (2010).
6. Binet (1894: 916).
7. Marchand (2009: 25).
8. Cavanaugh (2007); Paxson (2006, 2010); Sennett (2008); Trubek (2008).

9. Bromberger and Chevallier (1999); Rogers (2002); Terrio (2000).

10. Berger and Luckmann (1967); Garfinkel (1984).

11. Sociologist Robert Prus explores similar themes through detailed interviews with American magicians (Prus and Sharper 1991).

12. Argenti (2002); Coy (1989); Dilley (1989); Herzfeld (2004).

13. Goffman (1969).

14. Melton and Wallace (2009).

15. Tamariz (1988).

16. Simmel (1950: 332).

17. Simmel (1950: 333).

18. Durkheim (1995); P. Johnson (2002); Luhrmann (1989a, 1989b).

19. Simmel (1950: 333).

20. Briggs and Bauman (1995: 578).

21. Yankah (1985: 149).

22. Keane (1997: 22).

23. Anthropologists working on ritual performances in other cultural settings have come to similar conclusions, e.g., Howe (2000) and E. Schieffelin (1996).

24. Cf. Kapchan (1996).

25. Hyde (1999: 7). For discussions of magicians as trickster figures, see Hansen (2001: 130–147) and Hass (2008: 22–23).

26. Cocteau (2003).

27. Lamont and Wiseman (1999: x–xi).

28. Lamont and Wiseman (1999: 31). In the jargon of everyday practice, magicians reserve the term *misdirection* for the momentary distraction of spectators' attention away from a *specific* action, not the overall guidance of attention toward the effect.

29. Nardi (1984: 29).

30. Gell (1998).

31. Boas (1930); G. Lewis (2002); P. Singer (1990).

32. Lévi-Strauss (1963); Taussig (2003).

33. Hallowell (1971); Merkur (1985). Cf. Morris (2000).

34. Luhrmann (1997: 298).

35. Luhrmann (1997: 299). Definitions of entertainment magic proliferate: for example, "the game of entertaining by tempting a particular audience to accept, temporarily, infractions of natural law" (Hay 1975: vii–viii); "creating, by misdirection of the senses, the mental impression of supernatural agency at work" (Maskelyne 1946: 110); and "a performing art that aims at playing on a spectator's sense of wonder, either by apparently doing what is actually impossible, or by actually doing what is apparently impossible, from the spectator's point of view" (Tigner 1989: 671).

36. The meaning of this kind of entertainment is culturally and historically variable. In India, entertainment magic is associated with the cosmological principle of *maya*, the world-as-illusion (Siegel 1991), just as in Western modernity, an empiricist epistemology and materialist ontology infuse magic (Schmidt 1998). In early twentieth-century China, Western magic was associated with modernity in another way, symbolizing cosmopolitanism and progress (Pang 2004).

37. Goldenweiser (1942: 212).

38. Swiss (2002: 274).

39. Beeman (2000: 104).

40. Caillois (2001: 23).

41. According to Shklovsky (1965: 12), "The purpose of art is to impart the sensation of things as they are perceived and not as they are known. The technique of art is to make objects 'unfamiliar,' . . . to increase the difficulty . . . of perception because the process of perception is an aesthetic end in itself."

42. Alzaris (2000: 26).

43. Pierre Brahma (2000) offers an evocative profile of Bébel.

44. Lamont and Wiseman (1999: 104–106).

45. Nelms (1969: 4–6).

46. Steinmeyer (2003: 141).

47. Robert-Houdin (1878: 29).

48. During (2002: 81).

49. Likewise, the fictional Greek bumpkin says of the Athenian conjurer, "I hope no creature like him ever gets on to my farm. No one would ever catch him; and he would steal everything in the house and make off with all the goods on the place" (Alciphron et al. 1949: 113). Magicians' potential for criminal mischief is a common theme in audience responses as well as works of literature, e.g., I. Singer (1968).

50. Mauss (2001: 40).

51. Jones (2008, 2010).

52. D. Boyer (2008: 40).

53. Carr (2010).

54. When describing French magicians' views and translating their talk, I follow the speech patterns of contemporary Anglophone magicians, using "layman" and "laymen" instead of the gender-neutral "layperson" and "laypeople."

55. Nelms (1969: 17).

56. Goffman (1959: 32–33).

57. In the jargon of American magicians, these fanciful displays of technical prowess are sometimes referred to as "late-night locations," which Whaley (2007: 524) defines as "impossible seeming card locations done during late-evening card sessions. Usually so boring to the laity because of the number of contrived restrictions that they are only appropriate for other, equally interested, cardmen."

58. Haring (2007); Kelty (2008).

59. McArthur (2009: 62).

60. Goffman (1967: 194–214).

61. Caillois (2001: 37–38).

62. Mimosa (2005: 72).

63. Stebbins (1984: 42).

64. Dunbar-Hester (2008); Fine (2002); Haring (2007).

65. Nardi (1988: 764).

66. Nardi (1988: 766).

67. Nardi (1988: 767).

68. Lave and Wenger (1991: 29).

69. Lave and Wenger (1991: 98).

70. Lave and Wenger (1991: 109).

71. Gumperz (1962).

72. On jargon in the magic subculture, see Fleischman (1949) and Whaley (2007: 7–32).

73. Goffman (1959: 175).

74. Goffman (1959: 175–176).

75. On speech play and verbal art, see Sherzer (2002).

76. Wacquant (2004: 100).

77. Jacoby and Ochs (1995: 175).

78. Tannen (1986: 312).

79. Carr (2010: 20).

80. For a concise background on linguistic anthropology, see Duranti (2003a).

81. Duranti (2006); Ochs (1979).

82. A comma (,) represents a brief pause with a continuing intonation; a period (.), a question mark (?), and an exclamation point (!) represent a full stop with, respectively, falling, rising, or emphatic intonation. A dash (—) represents a break in speech, such as a self-interruption or a false start. Ellipses (. . .) represent a significant pause. Quotation marks (" ") indicate reported speech or thought. Italics indicates emphatic stress. Repeated letters represent the lengthening of a sound; the more letters, the longer the sound (e.g., ummm). Nonverbal behavior or transcriber comments appear in italics inside square brackets ([*italics*]); ellipses within square brackets ([. . .]) indicate that a part of the transcript has been omitted.

83. Benjamin (1969).

84. On this distinction, see Stebbins (1984: 43).

85. To lay readers interested in magic theory, I recommend Alzaris (1999), Lamont and Wiseman (1999), and Swiss (2002).

1.   AN APPRENTICESHIP IN CUNNING

1.   Stone (2008: 145–146).
2.   Mauss (2006).
3.   Brahma (1979: 124).
4.   Harry Houdini developed this illusion, which he called "Metamorphosis," in the early 1890s (Silverman 1996: 12–13). Known as the *Malle des Indes* in French, it remains one of the staple effects of stage magic.
5.   On capoeira, see Downey (2005) and J. Lewis (1992); on improvisational music, Stoichita (2008); on computer hacking, Coleman (2009).
6.   See, respectively, Hyde (1999) and Herzfeld (2004).
7.   Detienne and Vernant (1978: 3).
8.   Homer (1996: 77).
9.   Darnton (1984: 64).
10.   Azouvi (2002).
11.   Malinowski (1984).
12.   On the history and practice of collecting in magic, see Voignier (2003).
13.   Durkheim (1995: 228).
14.   Caldès (1909).
15.   See Anderson (2006) and Warner (2002).
16.   On the history of the *Revue de la Prestidigitation*, see Voignier (1998).
17.   Puech (2005).
18.   Respectively, *Magicus* (2004, 2007, 2009).
19.   Cf. Jones and Schieffelin (2009b) on YouTube forums.
20.   Other Paris clubs I regularly attended include Les Amis de la Magie, founded by the now sadly deceased Belgian pickpocket Pierre Jacques; the Club Magique de Paris, an exclusive group of top magicians that met in the Musée de la Magie; and Les Pizzas Magicos, an informal monthly get-together in a pizzeria by the Musée Grévin. From time to time, I also took part in the meetings of magic clubs in provincial cities like Dijon and Angers.
21.   Simmel (1950: 363).
22.   R. Brown and Gilman (1960).
23.   Interestingly, I noticed that when demonstrating a trick at a magic club, a magician who picks another magician as a volunteer will sometimes switch to the formal mode of address, performatively using *vous* to create a fictionalized relationship of social distance for the sake of the performance—as if both parties weren't "in" on the trick.
24.   H. Boyer (1997).
25.   No one seems to know who first started using the term *magicos* to refer to a magician or magicians, but some speculate the usage was inspired by the

well-worn term *musicos*, which designates "ordinary" musicians as opposed to superstars (see Perrenoud 2007a).

26. Bryant (2005); Grasseni (2007); Marchand (2009).

27. Briggs (1986).

28. Hahn (2007); Sudnow (2001); Wacquant (2004).

29. Levi (2008: 27).

30. P. Johnson (2002).

31. I also took an introductory course through the FFAP designed to prepare pupils for the membership examination, and, for a period, classes at the magic bar Le Double Fond.

32. Alzaris (1999).

33. Singleton (1998: 3).

34. Tufte and Swiss (1997).

35. The thirteen principles are reproduced on the FFAP website at http://cmpcours.magie-ffap.com/load/cmp1_2/TestJSh2.pdf.

36. Macknik, King, et al. (2008: 871). See also Macknik, Martinez-Conde, and Blakeslee (2010).

37. Kuhn et al. (2008: 350).

38. Vygotsky (1981: 56–57). Also see Jones and Shweder (2003: 56).

39. Cf. Bateson (1958: 285).

40. Vygotsky (1981: 86).

41. Bakhtin (1981).

42. Goffman (1969).

43. Goffman (1974: 83).

44. Tomasello (2009: 21); Vasek (1986).

45. Goffman (1961); Mead (1967); Sacks (1980).

46. Tamariz (1987: 9).

47. Any resemblance to the practice of science is not accidental: the conventions of magic performance evolved in a self-conscious dialogue with practices of scientific demonstration. See Nadis (2005) and Stafford (1994).

48. Kelley (1980: 32).

49. For influential discussions of reported speech and thought, see Bakhtin (1984), Bauman (1986), Coulmas (1986), Goffman (1981), Holt and Clift (2007), and Voloshinov (1986).

50. G. Myers (1999).

51. B. Schieffelin (2008).

52. Duranti (2008).

53. C. Goodwin (2000); M. Goodwin and Goodwin (2000).

54. See, for instance, Din (2004) and Mimosa (2005: 29–61).

55. Kelley (1980: 33).

56. The referentially ambiguous French pronoun *on*, which appears inside of the quoted utterance in this example, can be used in the place of any other pronoun depending on the context (Le Bel 1991). Here, the contrast Nemo establishes between the pronouns "I" and "he" inside the quoted utterance indicates that the best gloss for *on* is "we." In subsequent examples, I also gloss *on* as "people" and the generic subject "one" (which also could be translated as a generic "you"), depending on contextual cues.

57. Note that Nemo designates the speaker of the hypothetical utterance with the pronoun *on* ("Somewhere one says to oneself"). Le Bel (1991: 109) argues that the use of the indefinite personal pronoun distances speakers from speech, rhetorically establishing an "objective" perspective on a situation, detached from a particular personal reference. This connection is suggestive given the kind of intersubjective perspective that Nemo creates through talk. Compare to the two following examples.

58. Marnette (2005: 50–54).

59. Clark and Gerrig (1990).

60. Ovid, *Metamorphoses* 10.252.

61. Marnette (2005: 63).

62. Compare with the use of quotative "be + like" among American teenagers (Jones and Schieffelin 2009a).

63. Lucy (1993: 9).

64. Levi (2008: 43) describes a very different pedagogical strategy in Mexican professional wrestling: systematically avoiding the discussion of audience perspectives helps maintain a focus on the sport-like dimensions of what could otherwise be viewed as staged entertainment.

65. Wood et al. (1976).

66. Ochs and Schieffelin (1984); Kulick and Schieffelin (2004).

67. Jacobs-Huey (2006); Mertz (2007).

68. Sacks (1984: 417).

69. The thread "Copier une routine: Mal ou bien" began on February 9, 2001. I accessed it on November 28, 2004, at http://virtualmagie.com/ubbthreads/show flat.php/Cat/0/Number/1561.

70. Monson (1996).

71. See Tufte and Swiss (1997); cf. Swiss (2002: 125–135).

72. On Dai Vernon, see K. Johnson (2005).

73. Castiglione (2003: 67).

74. Robert-Houdin (1878: 20).

75. Bell (2001); Duranti (2003b).

76. For many communities of practice, technologies of knowledge mediation constitute a pedagogical problem. Instructors in traditional Japanese dance

and music told ethnographer Tomie Hahn (2007: 142–143) that students who learn from recordings perform "like robots" without understanding or emotion, and boxing trainers cautioned Loïc Wacquant (2004: 100–102) that he could learn nothing of value from textbooks.

2. THE SOCIAL LIFE OF SECRET KNOWLEDGE

1. Scot (1972: 199).
2. Scot (1972: 180).
3. Scot (1972: 180).
4. Simmel (1950: 334).
5. Beidelman (1993).
6. Maskelyne (1946: 155).
7. Maskelyne (1946: 157).
8. These two examples are among the few that I could translate into English without losing the original wordplay.
9. In 2009, Girard released a new DVD, *Ultimate Scrunchy Magic, Vol. 1*. As this book goes to press, a second volume is in production.
10. Deafenbaugh (1989: 164).
11. Coleman (2009) and McAllister (1996), respectively.
12. Weiner (1985).
13. Strathern (2001: 8).
14. Strathern (2001: 9).
15. Strathern (2001: 10–11).
16. Barth (1975: 217).
17. Latour (1993).
18. Rhod (2000).
19. Steinmeyer (2003).
20. Cf. Rhod (1998: 11–12).
21. Latour (1987: 118).
22. Grac (1999); Julia (2009). Cf. Dougherty (2010).
23. Loshin (2010: 124).
24. Fauchart and von Hippel (2006: 4).
25. Oliar and Sprigman (2009).
26. Lave and Wenger (1991: 108).
27. Bourdieu (1977).
28. For example, Downey (2005), Herzfeld (2004), Kondo (1990), and Terrio (2000).
29. Meyerhoff (1978: 104).

30. On the development of magic shops in France, see Voignier (1994).
31. Thompson (1971).
32. Bourdieu (1977).
33. Simmel (1950: 333).
34. Blum (2007: 50).
35. P. Brown and Levinson (1987: 25).
36. Sifianou (1992: 188).
37. P. Brown and Levinson (1987: 145), and Holmes (1990: 197).
38. Sifianou (1992: 179).
39. Lakoff (2004: 47–51); cf. Holmes (1990). According to Beeching (2004: 71), *hein?* in the sentence-final position "clearly invites a positive answer from the interlocutor (which, however, does not necessarily have to be forthcoming) and is socially and interactionally motivated" In the above example, both instances of the tag question do provoke a positive response.
40. Beeching (2004: 73).
41. P. Brown and Levinson (1987: 49).
42. Sifianou (1992: 185).
43. P. Brown and Levinson (1987: 17).
44. Herzfeld (2004: 128–132).
45. Schegloff (2007: 81–84).
46. Levelt (1989: 460–461).
47. Ochs and Schieffelin (1989: 15).
48. Barth (1975: 219).
49. Bellman (1984).
50. Erikson (1966: 4).
51. B. Schieffelin (1990: 163–176).
52. Cf. Fine (1998).
53. Schegloff (2007: 59).
54. *Muggles* is the term for nonwizards in the *Harry Potter* series. In the French version of the books it is translated as *moldus*, a term magicos sometimes facetiously employ in reference to laymen.
55. The thread "Du secret entre magiciens?" began on December 12, 2002. I accessed it on February 26, 2005, at http://virtualmagie.com/ubbthreads/show flat.php/Cat/0/Number/19133.
56. Mauss (1990).
57. Mauss (1990: 11–14).
58. Cf. Munn (1986).
59. Loshin (2010: 129).
60. AFAP (2003: 228).
61. Rollat (1998).
62. *Grand Robert de la langue française*, 2nd ed., s.v. "débinage."

63. The earliest apparent use I have found comes in a 1902 editorial referring to professional divulgers as *débineurs* (Berry 1902: 5). In 1904, Raynaly published a long screed against exposure in which the term *débinage* does not appear (Raynaly 1904). Two years later, writing again about exposure, he now placed the term in quotation marks, apparently to qualify its use of an informal oral expression in a formal written register: "this famous question of *'débineurs'*, which I designate using the argotic expression because it is the most widely used, is still a pressing matter" (Raynaly 1906a: 114).

64. Blanche (1934: 31).
65. Vaillant (1998).
66. Dhotel (1930: 2).
67. Metayer (1962: 109).
68. Dhotel (1935: 1–3).
69. Raynaly (1904: 254).
70. Raynaly (1904: 255).
71. Raynaly (1906b: 123)
72. Gauthron (1955: 1).
73. Metayer (1976a: 129).
74. Merlin (1982: 128).
75. Nieman (2005).
76. Dore and McDermott (1982).
77. Mauss (1990: 46).
78. Eamon (1994: 113).
79. Eamon (1994: 90).
80. Simmel (1950: 333).
81. Cf. Hass (2008).

3 . POTENCY AND PERFORMANCE

1. In his memoirs, Robert-Houdin (1995: 100) defines *fioritures* (flourishes) as manipulations that "have no purpose other than dazzling the eye by showcasing extreme digital dexterity." He argues (through the mouthpiece of a fictional mentor) that flourishes have no place in magic performance because they convey that all the effects a magician performs are feats of dexterity as well.

2. Butler (1993: 22).
3. Butler (1993: 25).
4. Kulick and Schieffelin (2004: 355).
5. Kulick and Schieffelin (2004: 356–357).
6. During (2002: 108).
7. Coppa (2008: 94).

8. Beckman (2003).

9. Steinmeyer (2003: 141).

10. During (2002: 215).

11. Cook (2001); Durbach (2010); During (2002); Fahy (2006); Jones (2010); Lamont (2005); Stahl (2008); Steinmeyer (2005).

12. Cf. Dearborn (2008).

13. Bryant (2005: 224).

14. Goffman (1959: 75).

15. Lamont and Wiseman (1999: 2).

16. Goffman (1981).

17. Bauman and Briggs (1990: 73–74).

18. Jones and Shweder (2003: 55).

19. Bauman and Briggs (1990: 68).

20. Topas (n.d.).

21. For a collection of Zakary's photos, see Belamy (2004).

22. Consistent with this image, Goffman (1976: 135–138) found that, in a large corpus of advertisement imagery, women were more often depicted in states of detachment and reverie, while men displayed active involvement in the situation around them.

23. Bryant (2005: 232).

24. Buscatto (2007).

25. See Puech (1997).

26. Mimosa (2005: 20).

27. Fischer (1979: 35).

28. In a recent English language survey of 220 amateur and professional magicians, Peter Nardi (2010) identifies some notion of womb envy as one recurrent explanation of why there are so few female magicians. Generally speaking, views expressed by respondents in Nardi's presumably largely Anglophone sample closely parallel my own findings among French magicians.

29. Jones and Shweder (2003: 62).

30. Zempléni (1976: 324). Magicians also describe their onstage persona as a mask. For instance, David Stone (2005a: 157) writes, "It's much easier to go on stage with your face hidden behind a mask than to show up before the public dewy-eyed and wincing. My mask is my extravagance. In everyday life, I'm not at all like that. I don't like to be noticed, I'm rather mild-mannered, even annoyingly straight-laced."

31. Simmel (1950: 337).

32. Simmel (1950: 338).

33. Gell (1998: 71).

34. Mangan (2007: 1–18).

35. Burger (2009: 69).

36. SFP (2004).

37. Brahma (1998: 24).

38. Some have sought to apply magic's capacity to build confidence in thera-peutic settings. For instance, as a graduate student in psychology, Elisabeth Amato taught tricks to psychotic teenagers in the context of ongoing therapy. "The children were having problems becoming integrated subjects," she told me. "Having a secret to themselves, something they could do that even their parents couldn't understand, was a tremendous help to them in developing a sense of subjectivity."

39. Mann (1989).

40. Nardi (1988: 766).

41. Nardi (1988: 767).

42. Kotthoff (2006: 4).

43. Kotthoff (2006: 5).

44. This usage predated, and presumably inspired, Topas's theory of the three magical personae (killer, victim, and witness) cited above.

45. Mel'čuk (1994: 394).

46. Romaine (1999: 110).

47. Cohn (1987: 688).

48. Cohn (1987: 693).

49. Cassell (1998: 101).

50. Cassell (1998: 71).

51. Haydn (2000: 15).

52. Goffman (1967: 12).

53. Goffman (1967: 13).

54. Stone (2008: 240).

55. Bateson (1972: 179).

56. Coppa (2008: 86–87).

57. Butler (1993).

58. For more on Otto's life and career, see his recent autobiography (Wessely 2011).

59. Reprinted as Wessely (2010).

60. In this quote, I translate the French *pédé* as "queer."

61. Briggs and Bauman (1995: 585).

4. BUSINESS AS UN-USUAL

1. Stebbins (1984: 106).

2. AFAP (2003: 485).

3. Thiels (1905: 2).

4. AFAP (2003: 37).

5. Dhotel (1929: 1). It should be mentioned that Dr. Dhotel authored a classic introduction to the art of conjuring (Dhotel 1987). Further, he had a progressive, internationalist vision of magic: after World War II, he cofounded the International Federation of Magic Societies (FISM) and the first French chapter of the International Brotherhood of Magicians (IBM).

6. AFAP (2003: 486).

7. Gauthron (1968).

8. AFAP (2003: 489).

9. Raynaly (1909: 248).

10. Becker (1991).

11. See Jones (2008: 43–45).

12. On the notion of a "Golden Age" in magic, see Whaley (2007: 422–423).

13. Raynaly (1905a, 1905b, 1905c).

14. Raynaly (1905a: 11).

15. Raynaly (1905b).

16. d'Alcy (1905: 4).

17. Alber (1914).

18. Solomon (2010: 40–59).

19. Régil (2002).

20. Brahma (1998).

21. Here, Merlin punned on double meanings of the verb *tirer*—"to pull" and "to fuck."

22. French business and marketing publications reported favorably on Joseph (e.g., Briard 2003; Lavabre 2003).

23. For positive reactions from professional magicians, see Beretta (2005) and Stone (2005b).

24. The thread "Agence Joseph" began on January 1, 2003. I accessed it on January 19, 2006, at http://virtualmagie.com/ubbthreads/ubbthreads.php/topics/20959.

25. Stebbins (1984: 43).

26. Becker (1991: 112).

27. Stebbins (1984: 25).

28. This kind of strategizing assuredly obtains in all kinds of freelance work and has been widely documented in the entertainment industry. Becker (1991: 104), for instance, describes how "a network of informal, interlocking cliques allocates the jobs available at a given time" among Chicago jazzmen.

29. Menger (1999: 550).

30. For an overview, see Menger (2005) and Kenneybrew (2006).

31. In 2003, reliable estimates placed the number of magician-beneficiaries somewhere between 300 and 400.

32. See, e.g., Roigt and Klein (2002). Evidence also emerged that large employers such as television networks and production companies were hiring large

numbers of permanent workers on temporary contracts to reduce salary costs (Latarjet 2004).

33. Menger (2005: 140).

34. Cf. Perrenoud (2007b).

35. Mimosa (1992).

36. Menger (1997: 325–326).

37. Other researchers have suggested that the advent of *intermittence* dramatically changed patterns of socialization and sociability within artistic communities of practice. For instance, Coulangeon (1999a, 1999b) argues that unemployment benefits allow novice jazz musicians to circumvent much of the paid hackwork that was once a necessary rite of passage in the industry, and to thereby dissociate themselves from the older musicians who would have secured that work for them. Since magicians are not ensemble players, the same considerations do not seem to apply.

38. Ochs and Capps (2001); Mattingly (1998).

39. Levi (2008).

40. Bauman (1986: 21).

41. Ochs (2004: 284).

42. Bauman (1986); Holt (1996); Holt and Clift (2007).

43. Jones and Schieffelin (2009a).

44. Goffman (1959: 13).

45. Stone (2006). Also see Stone (2007).

5. CONJURING CULTURE

1. Folletto (1907: 265).

2. Cited in Caroly (1907: 257).

3. See Gourarier (2002).

4. See Musée de la Magie (2009).

5. See Kristeller (1990) and Shiner (2001).

6. Hegel (1975: 43).

7. Simmel (1950: 332).

8. Seldow (1959: 186).

9. Becker (1982).

10. On the sociology of taste in everyday French life, see Bourdieu (1984) and Reed-Danahay (1996). On hierarchies of value in French cultural institutions, see Born (1995), F. Myers (1998), and Price (2007).

11. F. Myers (2006: 506).

12. Rogers (2001).

13. Jones (2008).

14. In 1859, a year after its publication in French, Robert-Houdin's memoir appeared in British and American editions, translated by Lascelles Wraxall. Over the years, English language editions have employed a range of subtly tweaked titles (e.g., *Memoirs of Robert-Houdin: Ambassador, Author, and Conjurer*; and *Life of Robert-Houdin, the King of the Conjurers*). I refer to this work as simply the *Confessions*, and base my discussion on the authoritative edition edited by Christian Fechner (Robert-Houdin 1995).

15. Jones (2010).

16. Club des Magiciens Collectionneurs (2005: 5).

17. FFAP (2005).

18. Fechner (2002, 2005a).

19. Fechner (2005b: 14).

20. Fechner (2005b: 16).

21. Bilis (2005).

22. Cook (2001: 194).

23. Houdini (1908: 264).

24. Silverman (1996: 133–134).

25. Sardina (1950).

26. A distinction I owe to my colleague Hester Schadee.

27. Steinmeyer (2003: 144).

28. Becker (1982: 352).

29. Menger (1999: 570).

30. Freud (1959).

31. Guillemin (2002: 22).

32. While magicians in the English-speaking world may worry about cultural stigma (e.g., Swiss 2002: 3–12), in France these anxieties take a local and, I argue, particularly acute form because of a notoriously hierarchical system of the arts.

33. Looseley (1995, 1999); Ingram (2011).

34. Cf. Taussig (1997).

35. See Truffaut (2001).

36. Ahearne (2002: 1).

37. Lebovics (1999).

38. Quoted in Ahearne (2002: 8).

39. Terrio (2000: 211).

40. Lang served a total of ten years as minister of culture (1981–1986, 1988–1993). He served as mayor of Blois from 1989 to 2000.

41. Lang (2002: 117).

42. For more on the Lang ministry, see Loosely (1995, 1999) and Ingram (2011: 12–17).

43. Centre National des Arts de la Magie et de l'Illusion (n.d.)

44. Centre National des Arts de la Magie et de l'Illusion (n.d.)

45. See Blon (1993).

46. Proust (1997: 12).

47. Delord (1991).

48. Roux (1993).

49. Covering the grand opening several years later, *Le Monde* gleefully embellished upon its earlier send-up of Lang, reminding readers that the erstwhile minister of culture had been "labeled a *prince of illusion*, criticized in the corridors of his very ministry for . . . making public bids for rabbits hidden in bottomless hats" (Bugier 1998).

50. Born (1995); Price (2007).

51. My discussion relies on Bürger (1984: 35–46).

52. Menger (2005: 14).

53. Menger (2005: 15).

54. Benhamou (2004: 107–108).

55. Daugereilh and Martin (2000: 87). Insofar as freelance work now characterizes many sectors of the postindustrial economy, it has become increasingly difficult to justify *intermittence* in terms of the peculiar nature of employment in the performing arts (Menger 2002).

56. See Sinigaglia (2009).

57. Cf. Menger (1997: 325).

58. Coulangeon (1999b: 174).

59. Coulangeon (1999b: 174).

60. Ingram (2011: 194).

61. Padis (2004: 54).

62. See Cordier (2007), Guy (2001), and Wallon (2002).

63. See Fourmaux (2006) and Sizorn (2008).

64. Rosemberg (2004).

65. F. Myers (1994: 13).

66. Online prospectus available at http://www.cnac.fr/page.php?rec=364.

67. *Stradda* (2010). English version published electronically at http://www.circostrada.org/IMG/file/PUBLICATIONS/Dossiers%20Stradda/Stradda7e-npdf.pdf.

68. Boisseau (2010).

69. Navarro (2011a, 2011b); Debailleul (2011).

70. Julia (2009). For more on magic and law, see Corcos (2010).

71. Foucault (1984: 108).

72. The thread "La 'magie nouvelle' sort du chapeau dans Le Monde du 301210" began on January 1, 2011, when I posted a link to the article from *Le Monde*. I accessed it on January 24, 2011 at http://www.virtualmagie.com/ubbthreads/ubbthreads.php/topics/277076.

73. *Magicus* (2011).
74. Puech (2011).
75. Alafrez (2003: 545).

EPILOGUE

1. Abbott (1988) discusses these themes form the perspective of professions.
2. Boyer (2008: 39).
3. Nichols (1980: 46).
4. Barthes (1958: 177–178).
5. Metayer (1976b).
6. On performing magic in hospitals, see Dumont (2006).

Bibliography

Abbott, Andrew Delano. 1988. *The System of Professions: An Essay on the Division of Expert Labor*. Chicago: University of Chicago Press.

AFAP (Association Française des Artistes Prestidigitateurs). 2003. *100 ans d'histoire, 100 ans de magie*. Paris: Association Française des Artistes Prestidigitateurs.

Ahearne, Jeremy. 2002. "Introduction." In Jeremy Ahearne, ed. *French Cultural Policy Debates: A Reader*. New York: Routledge, 1–35.

Alafrez, Abdul. 2003. "Éloge des chapeaux pointus." Interview with Yves Hersant. *Critique* 673–674: 538–548.

Alber. 1914. Editorial. *Journal de la Prestidigitation* 39: 1.

Alciphron, Aelian, and Philostratus. 1949. *The Letters of Alciphron, Aelian, and Philostratus*. Cambridge, MA: Harvard University Press.

Alzaris, Stefan. 1999. *Illusionnisme et magie*. Paris: Flammarion.

———. 2000. "Illusionnisme, le miroir magique." *Singulier/Pluriel* 10: 26–33.

Anderson, Benedict. 2006. *Imagined Communities: Reflections on the Origin and Spread of Nationalism*. New York: Verso.

Argenti, Nicholas. 2002. "People of the Chisel: Apprenticeship, Youth, and Elites in Oku (Cameroon)." *American Ethnologist* 29(3): 497–533.

Azouvi, François. 2002. *Descartes et la France: Histoire d'une passion nationale.* Paris: Fayard.

Bakhtin, Mikhail. 1981. *The Dialogic Imagination.* Austin: University of Texas Press.

———. 1984. *Problems of Dostoevsky's Poetics.* Minneapolis: University of Minnesota Press.

Barth, Fredrik. 1975. *Ritual and Knowledge among the Baktaman of New Guinea.* New Haven, CT: Yale University Press.

Barthes, Roland. 1958. *Mythologies.* Paris: Seuil.

Bateson, Gregory. 1958. *Naven: A Survey of the Problems Suggested by a Composite Picture of the Culture of a New Guinea Tribe Drawn from Three Points of View.* Stanford, CA: Stanford University Press.

———. 1972. *Steps to an Ecology of Mind.* New York: Ballantine.

Bauman, Richard. 1986. *Story, Performance, and Event: Contextual Studies of Oral Narrative.* New York: Cambridge University Press.

Bauman, Richard, and Charles L. Briggs. 1990. "Poetics and Performances as Critical Perspectives on Language and Social Life." *Annual Review of Anthropology* 19: 59–88.

Becker, Howard S. 1982. *Art Worlds.* Berkeley: University of California Press.

———. 1991. *Outsiders: Studies in the Sociology of Deviance.* New York: Free Press.

Beckman, Karen. 2003. *Vanishing Women: Magic, Film, and Feminism.* Durham, NC: Duke University Press.

Beeching, Kate. 2004. "Pragmatic Particles—Polite but Powerless? Tone-Group Terminal *Hein* and *Quoi* in Contemporary Spoken French." *Multilingua* 23: 61–84.

Beeman, William O. 2000. "Humor." *Journal of Linguistic Anthropology* 9(1–2): 103–106.

Beidelman, T. O. 1993. "Secrecy and Society: The Paradox of Knowing and the Knowing of Paradox." In Mary H. Nooter, ed. *Secrecy: African Art That Conceals and Reveals.* New York: Museum for African Art, 41–47.

Belamy, Zakary. 2004. *Double faces: Portraits de magiciens.* Chasseneuil du Poitou, France: C. C. Éditions.

Bell, Allan. 2001. "Back in Style: Reworking Audience Design." In Penelope Eckert and John R. Rickford, eds. *Style and Sociolinguistic Variation.* New York: Cambridge University Press, 139–169.

Bellman, Beryl L. 1984. *The Language of Secrecy: Symbols and Metaphors in Poro Ritual.* New Brunswick, NJ: Rutgers University Press.

Benhamou, Françoise. 2004. "L'exception culturelle: Exploration d'une impasse." *Esprit,* May: 85–113.

Benjamin, Walter. 1969. "Paris: Capital of the Nineteenth Century." *Perspecta* 12: 163–172.

Beretta, Laurent. 2005. "Joseph véchicle une image positive de la magie." *Magicus* 137: 15.

Berger, Peter L., and Thomas Luckmann. 1967. *The Social Construction of Reality: A Treatise in the Sociology of Knowledge*. New York: Anchor Books.

Berry, P. 1902. "Les vandales." *L'Illusionniste* 7: 5–6.

Bilis, Bernard. 2005. "Il restera dans l'histoire de notre art le maître incontesté." *Revue de la Prestidigitation* 549: 4.

Binet, Alfred. 1894. "La psychologie de la prestidigitation." *Revue des Deux Mondes* 125: 903–922.

Blanche, Abel. 1934. *Notes et souvenirs d'un illusionniste*. Paris: Author.

Blon, Philippe. 1993. *La belle magie: Artifices, illusion, raison, XVIe–XVIIIe siècles*. Exhibition catalog. Paris: Ministère de la culture, Direction du livre et de la lecture.

Blum, Susan D. 2007. *Lies That Bind: Chinese Truth, Other Truths*. New York: Rowman & Littlefield.

Boas, Franz. 1930. *The Religion of the Kwakiutl Indians*. Part 2. New York: Columbia University Press.

Boisseau, Rosita. 2010. "La 'magie nouvelle' sort du chapeau." *Le Monde*, December 30.

Born, Georgina. 1995. *Rationalizing Culture: IRCAM, Boulez, and the Institutionalization of the Musical Avant-Garde*. Berkeley: University of California Press.

Bourdieu, Pierre. 1977. *Outline of a Theory of Practice*. New York: Cambridge University Press.

———. 1984. *Distinction: A Social Critique of the Judgment of Taste*. Cambridge, MA: Harvard University Press.

Boyer, Dominic. 2008. "Thinking through the Anthropology of Experts." *Anthropology in Action* 15(2): 38–46.

Boyer, Henri. 1997. "Le statut de la suffixation en -os." *Langue Française* 114(1): 35–40.

Brahma, Pierre. 1979. "Les 'bons' magiques." *Lui* 191: 122–124, 198–214.

———. 1998. *La Malle des Indes: Les nuits d'un magicien*. Paris: Fallois.

———. 2000. "Allez Bébel." *Magicus* 106: 28–32.

Briard, Clotilde. 2003. "Quand les marques se dopent à la potion magique." *Les Echos*, April 23.

Briggs, Charles L. 1986. *Learning How to Ask: A Sociolinguistic Appraisal of the Role of the Interview in Social Science Research*. New York: Cambridge University Press.

Briggs, Charles L., and Richard Bauman. 1995. "Genre, Intertextuality, and Social Power." In Ben G. Blount, ed. *Language, Culture and Society: A Book of Readings*. Long Grove, IL: Waveland Press, 567–608.

Bromberger, Christian and Denis Chevallier. 1999. *Carrières d'objets: Innovations et relances*. Paris: Éditions de la Maison des sciences de l'homme.

Brown, Penelope, and Stephen C. Levinson. 1987. *Politeness: Some Universals in Language Usage*. Cambridge: Cambridge University Press.

Brown, Roger, and Albert Gilman. 1960. "The Pronouns of Power and Solidarity." In Thomas A. Sebeok, ed. *Style in Language*. Cambridge, MA: MIT Press, 253–276.

Bryant, Rebecca. 2005. "The Soul Danced into the Body: Nation and Improvisation in Istanbul." *American Ethnologist* 32(2): 222–238.

Bugier, Jacques. 1998. "La ville de Blois tente un coup de baguette magique." *Le Monde*, August 5.

Burger, Eugene. 2009. "Stories of the Origin of Magic." In Eugene Burger and Robert E. Neale, eds. *Magic and Meaning*. Seattle, WA: Hermetic Press, 57–82.

Bürger, Peter. 1984. *Theory of the Avant-Garde*. Minneapolis: University of Minnesota Press.

Buscatto, Marie. 2007. *Femmes du jazz: Musicalités, feminité, marginalisations*. Paris: CNRS Éditions.

Butler, Judith. 1993. "Critically Queer." *GLQ* 1(1): 17–32.

Caillois, Roger. 2001. *Man, Play and Games*. Chicago: University of Illinois Press.

Caldès, A. 1909. Untitled article. *Journal de la Prestidigitation* 16: 7.

Caroly, Jean. 1907. "Ferraris (Folletto)." *L'Illusionniste* 64: 257–258.

Carr, E. Summerson. 2010. "Enactments of Expertise." *Annual Review of Anthropology* 39: 17–32.

Cassell, Joan. 1998. *The Woman in the Surgeon's Body*. Cambridge, MA: Harvard University Press.

Castiglione, Baldesar. 2003. *The Book of the Courtier*. New York: Penguin Classics.

Cavanaugh, Jillian R. 2007. "Making Salami, Producing Bergamo: The Transformation of Value." *Ethnos* 72(2): 149–172.

Centre National des Arts de la Magie et de l'Illusion. N.d. Prospectus. Author's collection.

Clark, Herbert H., and Richard J. Gerrig. 1990. "Quotations as Demonstrations." *Language* 66(4): 764–805.

Club des Magiciens Collectionneurs. 2005. 1er Congrès Européen: Magie, histoire & collections, à l'occasion du bicentenaire de Robert-Houdin. Conference Program. Paris: Club des Magiciens Collectionneurs. Author's collection.

Cocteau, Jean. 2003. Untitled poem [1953]. In Association Française des Artistes Prestidigitateurs. *100 ans d'histoire, 100 ans de magie*. Paris: Association Française des Artistes Prestidigitateurs, 102.

Cohn, Carol. 1987. "Sex and Death in the Rational World of Defense Intellectuals." *Signs* 12(4): 687–718.

Coleman, Gabriella. 2009. "Code Is Speech: Legal Tinkering, Expertise, and Protest among Free and Open Source Software Developers." *Cultural Anthropology* 24(3): 420–454.

Cook, James W. 2001. *The Arts of Deception: Playing with Fraud in the Age of Barnum*. Cambridge, MA: Harvard University Press.

Coppa, Francesca. 2008. "The Body Immaterial: Magicians' Assistants and the Performance of Labor." In Francesca Coppa, Lawrence Hass, and James Peck, eds. *Performing Magic on the Western Stage from the Eighteenth Century to the Present*. New York: Palgrave Macmillan, 85–106.

Corcos, Christine A., ed. 2010. *Law and Magic: A Collection of Essays*. Durham, NC: Carolina Academic Press.

Cordier, Marine. 2007. "Le cirque contemporain entre rationalisation et quête d'autonomie." *Sociétés Contemporaines* 66: 37–59.

Coulangeon, Philippe. 1999a. "French Jazz Musicians: From Subculture to Subsidy and Social Insurance." In Karlijn Ernst, Marlite Halbertsma, Susanne Janssen, and Teunis Ijdens, eds. *Taking Stock: Trends and Strategies in the Arts and Cultural Industries*. Rotterdam: Barjesteh, 173–181.

———. 1999b. *Les musiciens de jazz en France à l'heure de la rehabilitation culturelle: Sociologie des carrières et du travail musical*. Paris: L'Harmattan.

Coulmas, Florian, ed. 1986. *Direct and Indirect Speech*. New York: Mouton de Gruyter.

Coy, Michael W. 1989. "Being What We Pretend to Be: The Usefulness of Apprenticeship as a Field Method." In Michael W. Coy, ed. *Apprenticeship: From Theory to Method and Back Again*. Albany: State University of New York Press, 115–135.

Curry, Paul. 1965. *Magician's Magic*. New York: Franklin Watts.

d'Alcy, Léo. 1905. "Causerie." *Journal de la Prestidigitation* 1: 4.

Darnton, Robert. 1984. *The Great Cat Massacre and Other Episodes in French Cultural History*. New York: Vintage.

Daugereilh, Isabelle, and Philippe Martin. 2000. "Les intermittents du spectacle: Une figure du salariat entre droit commun et droit spécial." *Revue Française des Affaires Sociales* 3–4: 77–91.

Deafenbaugh, Linda. 1989. "Hausa Weaving: Surviving amid the Paradoxes." In Michael W. Coy, ed. *Apprenticeship: From Theory to Method and Back Again*. Albany: State University of New York Press, 163–179.

Dearborn, Karen. 2008. "Intersecting Illusions: Performing Magic, Disability, and Gender." In Francesca Coppa, Lawrence Hass, and James Peck, eds. *Performing Magic on the Western Stage from the Eighteenth Century to the Present*. New York: Palgrave Macmillan, 177–196.

Debailleul, Clément. 2011. Interview with Aude Lavigne. *La Vignette.* Radio France, January 5.

Delord, Jacques. 1991. *Enseignement de la magie et de l'illusion comme poétique du geste et du mot.* Report presented to Maison de Robert-Houdin. Author's collection.

Detienne, Marcel, and Jean-Pierre Vernant. 1978. *Cunning Intelligence in Greek Culture and Society.* Atlantic Highlands, NJ: Humanities Press.

Dhotel, Jules. 1929. "Non! Pas tout le monde." *Journal de la Prestidigitation* 48: 1–2.

———. 1930. Editorial. *Journal de la Prestidigitation* 53: 1–2.

———. 1935. "Débinage ou propagande." *Journal de la Prestidigitation* 85: 1–3.

———. 1987. *La prestidigitation sans bagages, ou, Mille tours dans une valise* [1936–1944]. Paris: Champion-Slatkine.

Dilley, R. M. 1989. "Secrets and Skills: Apprenticeship among Tukolor Weavers." In Michael W. Coy, ed. *Apprenticeship: From Theory to Method and Back Again.* Albany: State University of New York Press, 181–198.

Din, Peter. 2004. *La grande magie des tout petits.* Plaisir, France: Alternance-Théâtre.

Dore, John, and R. P. McDermott. 1982. "Linguistic Indeterminacy and Social Context in Utterance Interpretation." *Language* 58(2): 374–398.

Dougherty, F. Jay. 2010. "Now You Own It, Now You Don't: Copyright and Related Rights in Magic Productions and Performances." In, Christine A. Corcos, ed. *Law and Magic: A Collection of Essays.* Durham, NC: Carolina Academic Press, 101–122.

Downey, Greg. 2005. *Learning Capoeira: Lessons in Cunning from an Afro-Brazilian Art.* New York: Oxford University Press.

Dumont, Nicholas. 2006. "Le travail de l'illusion pour des enfants à l'hôpital." *Imaginaire & Inconscient* 17: 147–160.

Dunbar-Hester, Christina. 2008. "Geeks, Meta-Geeks, and Gender Trouble: Activism, Identity, and Low-Power FM Radio." *Social Studies of Science* 38(2): 201–232.

Duranti, Alessandro. 2003a. "Language as Culture in U.S. Anthropology." *Current Anthropology* 44(3): 323–347.

———. 2003b. "The Voice of the Audience in Contemporary American Political Discourse." In Deborah Tannen and James E. Alatis, eds. *Linguistics, Language, and the Real World: Discourse and Beyond.* Washington, DC: Georgetown University Press, 114–134.

———. 2006. "Transcripts, Like Shadows on a Wall." *Mind, Culture, and Activity* 13(4): 301–310.

———. 2008. "Further Reflections on Reading Other Minds." *Anthropological Quarterly* 81(2): 483–494.

Durbach, Nadja. 2010. *Spectacle of Deformity: Freak Shows and Modern British Culture.* Berkeley: University of California Press.

During, Simon. 2002. *Modern Enchantments: The Cultural Power of Secular Magic.* Cambridge, MA: Harvard University Press.

Durkheim, Emile. 1995. *Elementary Forms of the Religious Life.* New York: Free Press.

Eamon, William. 1994. *Science and the Secrets of Nature: Books of Secrets in Medieval and Early Modern Culture.* Princeton, NJ: Princeton University Press.

Erikson, Kai T. 1966. *Wayward Puritans: A Study in the Sociology of Deviance.* New York: John Wiley & Sons.

Fahy, Thomas. 2006. *Freak Shows and the Modern American Imagination: Constructing the Damaged Body from Willa Cather to Truman Capote.* New York: Palgrave Macmillan.

Fauchart, Emmanuelle, and Eric von Hippel. 2006. "Norms-Based Intellectual Property Systems: The Case of French Chefs." MIT Sloan School of Management Working Paper 4576-06. Cambridge, MA: MIT Sloan School of Management.

Fechner, Christian. 2002. *La magie de Robert-Houdin: Une vie d'artiste.* Paris: Éditions FCF.

———. 2005a. *La magie de Robert-Houdin: Secrets et souvenirs des Soirées fantastiques.* Paris: Éditions FCF.

———. 2005b. "La pensée magique de Robert-Houdin." *Revue de la Prestidigitation* 549: 14–16.

FFAP (Fédération Française des Artistes Prestidigitateurs). 2005. "Célébration du bi centenaire de la naissance de Robert-Houdin." Paris: Fédération Française des Artistes Prestidigitateurs. Author's collection.

Fine, Gary Alan. 1998. *Morel Tales: The Culture of Mushrooming.* Cambridge, MA: Harvard University Press.

———. 2002. *Shared Fantasy: Role-Playing Games as Social Worlds.* Chicago: University of Chicago Press.

Fischer, Lucy. 1979. "The Lady Vanishes: Women, Magic and the Movies." *Film Quarterly* 33(1): 30–40.

Fleischman, A. S. 1949. "Words in Modern Magic." *American Speech* 24(1): 38–42.

Folletto, Ferraris. 1907. "Eloges à l'art sublime de la prestidigitation." *L'Illusionniste* 64: 265–266.

Foucault, Michel. 1984. "What Is an Author?" In Paul Rabinow, ed. *The Foucault Reader.* New York: Pantheon Books, 101–120.

Fourmaux, Francine. 2006. "Le nouveau cirque ou l'esthétisation du frisson." *Ethnologie Française* 36(4): 659–668.

Freud, Sigmund. 1959. "Family Romances." In James Strachey, ed. *The Standard Edition of the Complete Works of Sigmund Freud*. Volume 9. London: Hogarth, 237–241.

Garfinkel, Harold. 1984. *Studies in Ethnomethodology*. New York: Basil Blackwell.

Gauthron, Maurice. 1955. "Réflexions sur le débinage." *Journal de la Prestidigitation* 185: 1–2.

———. 1968. "Une association démocratique." *Journal de la Prestidigitation* 263: 446.

Gell, Alfred. 1998. *Art and Agency: An Anthropological Theory*. Oxford: Clarendon.

Goffman, Erving. 1959. *The Presentation of Self in Everyday Life*. New York: Anchor.

———. 1961. *Encounters: Two Studies in the Sociology of Interaction*. Indianapolis, IN: Bobbs-Merrill.

———. 1967. *Interaction Ritual: Essays on Face-to-Face Behavior*. New York: Pantheon.

———. 1969. *Strategic Interaction*. Philadelphia: University of Pennsylvania Press.

———. 1974. *Frame Analysis: An Essay on the Organization of Experience*. New York: Harper Colophon.

———. 1976. "Gender Commercials." *Studies in the Anthropology of Visual Communication* 3(2): 92–154.

———. 1981. *Forms of Talk*. Philadelphia: University of Pennsylvania Press.

Goldenweiser, Alexander. 1942. *Anthropology: An Introduction to Primitive Culture*. New York: F. S. Crofts.

Goodwin, Charles. 2000. "Action and Embodiment within Situated Human Interaction." *Journal of Pragmatics* 32(10): 1489–1522.

Goodwin, Marjorie Harness, and Charles Goodwin. 2000. "Emotion within Situated Activity." In Alessandro Duranti, ed. *Linguistic Anthropology: A Reader*. Malden, MA: Blackwell, 239–257.

Gourarier, Zeev, ed. 2002. *Jours de cirque*. Exhibition catalog. Arles: Actes Sud.

Grac, Florise. 1999. "La magie et le droit d'auteur." DEA thesis, Université Panthéon-Assas.

Grasseni, Cristina. 2007. "Good Looking: Learning to be a Cattle Breeder." In Cristina Grasseni, ed. *Skilled Visions: Between Apprenticeship and Standards*. New York: Berghahn, 47–66.

Guillemin, Fanch. 2002. "L'inconturnable Robert-Houdin." *Revue de la Prestidigitation* 528: 22–23.

Gumperz, John. 1962. "Types of Linguistic Communities." *Anthropological Linguistics* 4(1): 28–40.

Guy, Jean-Michel, ed. 2001. *Avant-garde, cirque! Les arts de la piste en révolution.* Paris: Autrement.

Hahn, Tomie. 2007. *Sensational Knowledge: Embodying Culture through Japanese Dance.* Middletown, CT: Wesleyan University Press.

Hallowell, Alfred Irving. 1971. *The Role of Conjuring in Saulteaux Society.* New York: Octagon.

Hamburger, Jeffrey. 1984. "Bosch's 'Conjuror': An Attack on Magic and Sacramental Heresy." *Simiolus: Netherlands Quarterly for the History of Art* 14(1): 5–23.

Hansen, George P. 2001. *The Trickster and the Paranormal.* Philadelphia: Xlibris.

Haring, Kristen. 2007. *Ham Radio's Technical Culture.* Cambridge, MA: MIT Press.

Hass, Lawrence. 2008. "Life Magic and Staged Magic: A Hidden Intertwining." In Francesca Coppa, Lawrence Hass, and James Peck, eds. *Performing Magic on the Western Stage from the Eighteenth Century to the Present.* New York: Palgrave Macmillan, 13–31.

Hay, Henry. 1975. *Learn Magic.* New York: Dover.

Haydn, Whit. 2000. *The Chicago Surprise: A Card Routine.* Alta Loma, CA: School for Scoundrels.

Hegel, G. W. F. 1975. *Aesthetics: Lectures on Fine Art.* Volume 1. Oxford: Clarendon.

Herzfeld, Michael. 2004. *The Body Impolitic: Artisans and Artifice in the Global Hierarchy of Value.* Chicago: University of Chicago Press.

Holmes, Janet. 1990. "Hedges and Boosters in Women's and Men's Speech." *Language & Communication* 10(3): 185–205.

Holt, Elizabeth. 1996. "Reporting on Talk: The Use of Direct Reported Speech in Conversation." *Research on Language and Social Interaction* 29(3): 219–245.

Holt, Elizabeth, and Rebecca Clift, eds. 2007. *Reporting Talk: Reported Speech in Interaction.* New York: Cambridge University Press.

Homer. 1996. *The Odyssey.* New York: Penguin.

Houdini, Harry. 1908. *The Unmasking of Robert-Houdin.* New York: Publishers Printing Co.

Howe, Leo. 2000. "Risk, Ritual and Performance." *Journal of the Royal Anthropological Institute* 6(1): 63–79.

Hyde, Lewis. 1999. *Trickster Makes This World: Mischief, Myth and Art.* New York: North Point Press.

Ingram, Mark. 2011. *Rites of the Republic: Citizens' Theatre and the Politics of Culture in Southern France.* Toronto: University of Toronto Press.

Jacobs-Huey, Lanita. 2006. *From the Kitchen to the Parlor: Language and Becoming in African American Women's Hair Care.* New York: Oxford University Press.

Jacoby, Sally, and Elinor Ochs. 1995. "Co-construction: An Introduction." *Research on Language and Social Interaction* 28(3): 171–183.

Johnson, Karl. 2005. *The Magician and the Cardsharp: The Search for America's Greatest Sleight-of-Hand Artist.* New York: Henry Holt.

Johnson, Paul Christopher. 2002. *Secrets, Gossip, and Gods: The Transformation of Brazilian Candomblé.* New York: Oxford University Press.

Jones, Graham M. 2008. "The Family Romance of Modern Magic: Contesting Robert-Houdin's Cultural Legacy in Contemporary France." In Francesca Coppa, Lawrence Hass, and James Peck, eds. *Performing Magic on the Western Stage from the Eighteenth Century to the Present.* New York: Palgrave Macmillan, 33–60.

————. 2010. "Modern Magic and the War on Miracles in French Colonial Culture." *Comparative Studies in Society and History* 52(1): 66–99.

Jones, Graham M., and Bambi B. Schieffelin. 2009a. "Enquoting Voices, Accomplishing Talk: Uses of *Be + Like* in Instant Messaging." *Language & Communication* 29(1): 77–113.

————. 2009b. "Talking Text and Talking Back: 'My BFF Jill' from Boob Tube to YouTube." *Journal of Computer Mediated Communication* 14(4): 1050–1079.

Jones, Graham, and Lauren Shweder. 2003. "The Performance of Illusion and Illusionary Performatives: Learning the Language of Theatrical Magic." *Journal of Linguistic Anthropology* 13(1): 51–70.

Julia, Guilhem. 2009. "La protection du secret du magicien par la chorégraphie de l'invisible." *Gazette du Palais* 205–206: 3–10.

Kapchan, Deborah. 1996. *Gender on the Market: Moroccan Women and the Revoicing of Tradition.* Philadelphia: University of Pennsylvania Press.

Keane, Webb. 1997. *Signs of Recognition: Powers and Hazards of Representation in an Indonesian Society.* Berkeley: University of California Press.

Kelley, Harold H. 1980. "Magic Tricks: The Management of Causal Attributions." In Dietmar Görlitz, ed. *Perspectives on Attribution Research and Theory.* Cambridge, MA: Ballinger, 19–35.

Kelty, Christopher. 2008. *Two Bits: The Cultural Significance of Free Software.* Durham, NC: Duke University Press.

Kenneybrew, Tony A. 2006. "Employing the Performing Artist in France." *Tulsa Journal of Comparative and International Law* 13(2): 249–277.

Kondo, Dorinne K. 1990. *Crafting Selves: Power, Gender, and Discourses of Identity in a Japanese Workplace.* Chicago: University of Chicago Press.

Kotthoff, Helga. 2006. "Gender and Humor: The State of the Art." *Journal of Pragmatics* 38(1): 4–25.

Kristeller, Paul Oskar. 1990. "The Modern System of the Arts." In *Renaissance Thought and the Arts: Collected Essays.* Princeton, NJ: Princeton University Press, 163–227.

Kuhn, Gustav, Alym A. Amlani, and Ronald A. Rensink. 2008. "Towards a Science of Magic." *Trends in Cognitive Science* 12(9): 349–354.

Kulick, Don, and Bambi B. Schieffelin. 2004. "Language Socialization." In Alessandro Duranti, ed. *A Companion to Linguistic Anthropology*. Malden, MA: Blackwell, 349–368.

Lachapelle, Sophie. 2008. "From the Stage to the Laboratory: Magicians, Psychologists, and the Science of Illusion." *Journal of the History of the Behavioral Sciences* 44(4): 319–334.

Lakoff, Robin Tolmach. 2004. *Language and Woman's Place*. New York: Oxford University Press.

Lamont, Peter. 2005. *The Rise of the Indian Rope Trick: How a Spectacular Hoax Became History*. New York: Thunder's Mouth Press.

Lamont, Peter, John M. Henderson, and Tim J. Smith. 2010. "Where Science and Magic Meet: The Illusion of a 'Science of Magic.'" *Review of General Psychology* 14(1): 16–21.

Lamont, Peter, and Richard Wiseman. 1999. *Magic in Theory: An Introduction to the Theoretical and Psychological Elements of Conjuring*. Hertfordshire, UK: University of Hertfordshire Press.

Lang, Jack. 2002. "Culture and the Economy" [1982]. In Jeremy Ahearne, ed. *French Cultural Policy Debates: A Reader*. New York: Routledge, 111–120.

Latarjet, Bernard. 2004. *Pour un débat national sur l'avenir du spectacle vivant*. Report presented to the Ministère de la Culture et de la Communication. Paris: Ministère de la Culture et de la Communication.

Latour, Bruno. 1987. *Science in Action*. Cambridge, MA: Harvard University Press.

———. 1993. *The Pasteurization of France*. Cambridge, MA: Harvard University Press.

Lavabre, Sylvie. 2003. "Magie: Une carte maîtresse pour stimuler les ventes." *LSA* 1808: 76–77.

Lave, Jean, and Etienne Wenger. 1991. *Situated Learning: Legitimate Peripheral Participation*. New York: Cambridge University Press.

Le Bel, Edith. 1991. "Le statut remarquable d'un pronom inaperçu." *La Linguistique* 27(2): 91–109.

Lebovics, Herman. 1999. *Mona Lisa's Escort: André Malraux and the Reinvention of French Culture*. Ithaca, NY: Cornell University Press.

Levelt, Willem J. M. 1989. *Speaking: From Intention to Articulation*. Cambridge, MA: MIT Press.

Levi, Heather. 2008. *The World of Lucha Libre: Secrets, Revelations, and Mexican National Identity*. Durham, NC: Duke University Press.

Lévi-Strauss, Claude. 1963. *Structural Anthropology*. New York: Basic Books.

Lewis, Gilbert. 2002. "Between Public Assertion and Private Doubts: A Sepik Ritual of Healing and Reflexivity." *Social Anthropology* 10: 11–21.

Lewis, J. Lowell. 1992. *Ring of Liberation: Deceptive Discourse in Brazilian Copoeira.* Chicago: University of Chicago Press.

Looseley, David. 1995. *The Politics of Fun: Cultural Policy and Debate in Contemporary France.* New York: Berg.

———. 1999. "Cultural Policy in the Twenty-First Century: Issues, Debates and Discourse." *French Cultural Studies* 10(1): 5–20.

Loshin, Jacob. 2010. "Secrets Revealed: Protecting Magicians' Intellectual Property without Law." In Christine A. Corcos, ed. *Law and Magic: A Collection of Essays.* Durham, NC: Carolina Academic Press, 123–141.

Lucy, John A. 1993. "Reflexive Language and the Human Disciplines." In John A. Lucy, ed. *Reflexive Language: Reported Speech and Metapragmatics.* New York: Cambridge University Press, 9–32.

Luhrmann, Tanya M. 1989a. "The Magic of Secrecy." *Ethos* 17(2): 131–165.

———. 1989b. *Persuasions of the Witch's Craft: Ritual Magic in Contemporary England.* Cambridge, MA: Harvard University Press.

———. 1997. "Magic." In Thomas Barfield, ed. *The Dictionary of Anthropology.* Malden, MA: Blackwell, 298–299.

Macknik, Stephen L., Mac King, James Randi, Apollo Robbins, Teller, John Thompson, and Susana Martinez-Conde. 2008. "Attention and Awareness in Stage Magic: Turning Tricks into Research." *Neuroscience* 9: 871–879.

Macknik, Stephen L., Susana Martinez-Conde, and Sandra Blakeslee. 2010. *Sleights of Mind: What the Neuroscience of Magic Reveals about Our Everyday Deceptions.* New York: Henry Holt.

Magicus. 2004. "Quand la magie se conjugue au feminine." *Magicus* 135: 11–21.

———. 2007. "Magie et polique." 148–149: 10–14.

———. 2009. "Magicothérapie: Le bonheur de la corde réparée . . ." *Magicus* 159: 12–17.

———. 2011. "La magie nouvelle lave-t-elle plus blanc?" *Magicus* 171: 24–28.

Malinowski, Bronislaw. 1984. *Argonauts of the Western Pacific.* Prospect Heights, IL: Waveland.

Mangan, Michael. 2007. *Performing Dark Arts: A Cultural History of Conjuring.* Chicago: Intellect.

Mann, Thomas. 1989. "Mario and the Magician." In *Death in Venice.* New York: Vintage, 133–178.

Marchand, Trevor H. J. 2009. *Masons of Djenné.* Bloomington: Indiana University Press.

Marnette, Sophie. 2005. *Speech and Thought Presentation in French: Concepts and Strategies.* New York: John Benjamins.

Marsh, James, dir. 2008. *Man on Wire.* New York: Magnolia Home Entertainment, DVD.

Maskelyne, Nevil. 1946. "The Theory of Magic." In Nevil Maskelyne and David Devant. *Our Magic.* Berkeley Heights, NJ: Fleming Book Company, 105–168.

Mattingly, Cheryl. 1998. *Healing Dramas and Clinical Plots: The Narrative Structure of Experience.* New York: Cambridge University Press.

Mauss, Marcel. 1990. *The Gift: The Form and Reason for Exchange in Archaic Societies.* New York: W. W. Norton.

———. 2001. *A General Theory of Magic.* New York: Routledge.

———. 2006. *Techniques, Technology, and Civilization.* New York: Berghahn Books.

McAllister, James W. 1996. *Beauty and Revolution in Science.* Ithaca, NY: Cornell University Press.

McArthur, J. A. 2009. "Digital Subculture: A Geek Meaning of Style." *Journal of Communication Inquiry* 33(1): 58–70.

Mead, George Herbert. 1967. *Mind, Self, and Society from the Standpoint of a Social Behaviorist.* Chicago: University of Chicago Press.

Mel'čuk, Igor. 1994. "Suppletion: Toward a Logical Analysis of the Concept." *Studies in Language* 18(2): 339–410.

Melton, H. Keith, and Robert Wallace. 2009. *The Official CIA Manual of Trickery and Deception.* New York: William Morrow.

Menger, Pierre-Michel. 1997. *La profession de comédien.* Paris: Ministère de la Culture et de la Communication.

———. 1999. "Artistic Labor Markets and Careers." *Annual Review of Sociology* 25: 541–574.

———. 2002. *Portait de l'artiste en travailleur: Métamorphoses du capitalisme.* Paris: Seuil.

———. 2005. *Les intermittents du spectacle: Sociologie d'une exception.* Paris: Éditions de l'École des hautes etudes en sciences sociales.

Merkur, Daniel. 1985. *Becoming Half Hidden: Shamanism and Initiation among the Inuit.* Stockholm: Almqvist & Wiksell International.

Merlin, Jean. 1982. "Le débinage . . . Ça n'éxiste pas . . ." *L'Illusionniste* 266: 128–130.

Mertz, Elizabeth. 2007. *The Language of Law School: Learning to "Think Like a Lawyer."* New York: Oxford University Press.

Metayer, Jean. 1962. "Mauvais goût et débinage." *Journal de la Prestidigitation* 228: 109–110.

———. 1976a."Débinage ou vulgarisation?" *L'Illusionniste* 209: 129.

———. 1976b. "Paradoxe d'une époque." *L'Illusionniste* 211: 161.

Meyerhoff, Barbara. 1978. *Number Our Days: A Triumph of Continuity and Culture among Jewish Old People in an Urban Ghetto.* New York: Simon and Schuster.

Mimosa. 1992. "Le mollard dans la gamelle." *Revue de la Prestidigitation* 445: 30–33.

———. 2005. *Magie sans artifices.* Paris: Magic Dream.

Monson, Ingrid. 1996. *Saying Something: Jazz Improvisation and Interaction.* Chicago: University of Chicago Press.

Morris, Rosalind C. 2000. "Modernity's Media and the End of Mediumship? On the Aesthetic Economy of Transparency in Thailand." *Public Culture* 12(2): 457–475.

Munn, Nancy D. 1986. *The Fame of Gawa: A Symbolic Study of Value Transformation in a Massim (Papua New Guinea) Society.* New York: Cambridge University Press.

Musée de la Magie. 2009. *Guide du Musée de la Magie.* Paris: Éditions Georges Proust.

Myers, Fred R. 1994. "Beyond the Intentional Fallacy: Art Criticism and the Ethnography of Aboriginal Acrylic Painting." *Visual Anthropology Review* 10(1): 10–43.

———. 1998. "Uncertain Regard: An Exhibition of Aboriginal Art in France." *Ethnos* 63(1): 7–47.

———. 2006. "The Complicity of Cultural Production: The Contingencies of Performance in Globalizing Museum Practices." In Ivan Karp, Corinne A. Kratz, Lynn Szwaja, and Tomás Ybarra-Frausto, eds. *Museum Frictions: Public Cultures/Global Transformation.* Durham, NC: Duke University Press, 504–535.

Myers, Greg. 1999. "Unspoken Speech: Hypothetical Reported Discourse and the Rhetoric of Everyday Talk." *Text* 19(4): 571–590.

Nadis, Fred. 2005. *Wonder Shows: Performing Science, Magic, and Religion in America.* New Brunswick, NJ: Rutgers University Press.

Nardi, Peter M. 1984. "Toward a Social Psychology of Entertainment Magic (Conjuring)." *Symbolic Interaction* 7(1): 25–42.

———. 1988. "The Social World of Magicians: Gender and Conjuring." *Sex Roles* 19(11–12): 759–770.

———. 2010. "Why Have Women Magicians Vanished?" *Miller-McCune,* February 25. http://www.miller-mccune.com/culture-society/why-have-women-magicians-vanished-8369/.

Navarro, Raphaël. 2011a. Interview with Aude Lavigne. *La Vignette.* Radio France, January 3.

———. 2011b. Interview with Aude Lavigne. *La Vignette.* Radio France, January 4.

Nelms, Henning. 1969. *Magic and Showmanship: A Handbook for Conjurors.* New York: Dover.

Nichols, Sallie. 1980. *Jung and Tarot: An Archetypal Journey.* York Beach, ME: Samuel Weiser.

Nieman, Damian, dir. 2005. *Shade: Les maîtres du jeu*. Paris: Metropolitan Filmexport, DVD.

Ochs, Elinor. 1979. "Transcription as Theory." In Elinor Ochs and Bambi B. Schieffelin, eds. *Developmental Pragmatics*. New York: Academic Press, 43–72.

———. 2004. "Narrative Lessons." In Alessandro Duranti, ed. *A Companion to Linguistic Anthropology*. Malden, MA: Blackwell, 269–289.

Ochs, Elinor, and Lisa Capps. 2001. *Living Narrative: Creating Lives in Everyday Storytelling*. Cambridge, MA: Harvard University Press.

Ochs, Elinor, and Bambi B. Schieffelin. 1984. "Language Acquisition and Socialization: Three Developmental Stories and Their Implications." In Richard A. Shweder and Robert A. LeVine, eds. *Culture Theory: Essays on Mind, Self, and Emotion*. New York: Cambridge University Press, 276–320.

———. 1989. "Language Has a Heart." *Text* 9(1): 7–25.

Oliar, Dotan, and Christopher Sprigman. 2008. "There's No Free Laugh (Anymore): The Emergence of Intellectual Property Norms and the Transformation of Stand-Up Comedy." *Virginia Law Review* 94(8): 1787–1867.

Padis, Marc-Olivier. 2004. "De la polémique sur les intermittents aux choix fondamentaux de la politique culturelle." *Esprit*, May: 52–54.

Pang, Laikwan. 2004. "Magic and Modernity in China." *positions* 12(2): 299–327.

Paxson, Heather. 2006. "Artisanal Cheese and Economies of Sentiment in New England." In Richard R. Wilk, ed. *Fast Food/Slow Food: The Cultural Economy of the Global Food System*. Lanham, MD: Altamira, 201–217.

———. 2010. "Locating Value in Artisan Cheese: Reverse Engineering *Terroir* for New-World Landscapes." *American Anthropologist* 112(3): 444–457.

Perrenoud, Marc. 2007a. *Les musicos: Enqûete sur des musiciens ordinaires*. Paris: La Découverte.

———. 2007b. "Note sur les 'abus' dans le régime des intermittents du spectacle en France: Le cas des musiciens ordinaries." *Carnets de Bord* 13: 106–110.

Price, Sally. 2007. *Paris Primitive: Jacques Chirac's Museum on the Quai Branly*. Chicago: University of Chicago Press.

Proust, Georges. 1997. Interview with Steve Gotson. *Revue de la Prestidigitation* 497: 10–13.

Prus, Robert C., and C. R. D. Sharper. 1991. *Road Hustler: Grifting, Magic, and the Thief Subculture*. New York: Richard Kaufman and Alan Greenberg.

Puech, Didier. 1997. "Ambigus et ambidextres." *Magicus* 92: 25.

———. 2005. "Le monde de la magie, est-il mysogine, sectaire et raciste?" *Magicus* 141: 8–9.

———. 2011. "Choux blanc." *Magicus* 171: 3.

Raynaly, Édouard. 1904. "Causerie." *L'Illusionniste* 31: 254–256.

———. 1905a. "Economie professionnelle." *L'Illusionniste* 38: 10–11.

———. 1905b. "Le numéro de Music-Hall." *L'Illusionniste* 39: 18–19.

———. 1905c. "La Postiche—Marco." *L'Illusionniste* 41: 42–43.

———. 1906a. "Les 'Débineurs.'" *L'Illusionniste* 49: 114–115.

———. 1906b. "Les Débineurs (suite)." *L'Illusionniste* 50: 122–124.

———. 1909. "Dictionnaire Philosophico-Magique." *L'Illusionniste* 96: 247–249.

Reed-Danahay, Deborah. 1996. "Champagne and Chocolate: 'Taste' and Inversion in a French Wedding Ritual." *American Anthropologist* 98(4): 750–761.

Régil, Jean. 2002. "Les cabarets." *Revue de la Prestidigitation* 532: 32–33.

Rhod, Daniel. 1998. *Magie virtuelle: Sa magie "d'avant-garde."* Cergy-Pontoise, France: Joker Deluxe.

———. 2000. *Techno pièces: Les techniques essentielles pour générer des miracles.* Cergy-Pontoise: Joker Deluxe.

Robert-Houdin, Jean-Eugène. 1878. *Comment on devient sorcier; les secrets de la prestidigitation et de la magie.* Paris: Calmann Lévy.

———. 1995. *Confidences d'un prestidigitateur* [1858]. Paris: Stock.

Rogers, Susan Carol. 2001. "Anthropology in France." *Annual Review of Anthropology* 30: 481–504.

———. 2002. "Which Heritage? Nature, Culture, and Identity in French Rural Tourism." *French Historical Studies* 25(3): 475–503.

Roigt, Jean, and René Klein. 2002. *Contribution à la réflexion des partenaires sociaux sur les origines des écarts entre les différentes sources statistiques sur les artistes et techniciens intermittents du spectacle, et les aménagements à apporter au fonctionnement des annexes 8 et 10 du régime d'assurance-chômage.* Report presented to the Inspection Générale des Affaires Sociales. Paris: Inspection Générale des Affaires Sociales.

Rollat, Alain. 1998. "Tour de passe-passe." *Le Monde,* September 10.

Romaine, Suzanne. 1999. *Communicating Gender.* Mahwah, NJ: L. Erlbaum.

Rosemberg, Julien. 2004. *Arts du cirque: Esthétiques et évaluation.* Paris: L'Harmattan.

Roux, Emmanuel de. 1993. "A Blois une maison de l'illusion pour M. Jack Lang." *Le Monde,* March 12.

Sacks, Harvey. 1980. "Button Button Who's Got the Button?" *Sociological Inquiry* 50(3–4): 318–327.

———. 1984. "On Doing 'Being Ordinary.'" In J. Maxwell Atkinson and John Heritage, eds. *Structures of Social Action: Studies in Conversation Analysis.* New York: Cambridge University Press, 413–429.

Sardina, Maurice. 1950. *Where Houdini Was Wrong.* London: George Armstrong.

Schegloff, Emanuel A. 2007. *Sequence Organization in Interaction: A Primer in Conversation Analysis.* Volume 1. New York: Cambridge University Press.

Schieffelin, Bambi B. 1990. *The Give and Take of Everyday Life: Language Socialization of Kaluli Children*. New York: Cambridge University Press.

———. 2008. "Speaking Only Your Own Mind: Reflections on Talk, Gossip, and Intentionality in Bosavi (PNG)." *Anthropological Quarterly* 81(2): 431–441.

Schieffelin, Edward. 1996. "On Failure and Performance: Throwing the Medium Out of the Seance." In Carol Laderman and Marina Roseman, eds. *The Performance of Healing*. New York: Routledge, 59–89.

Schmidt, Leigh Eric. 1998. "From Demon Possession to Magic Show: Ventriloquism, Religion, and the Enlightenment." *Church History* 67(2): 274–304.

Scot, Reginald. 1972. *The Discoverie of Witchcraft* [1584]. New York: Dover.

Seldow, Michel. 1959. *Les illusionnistes et leurs secrets*. Paris: A. Fayard.

Sennett, Richard. 2008. *The Craftsman*. New Haven, CT: Yale University Press.

SFP (Société Française de Prestidigitation). 2004. Product Catalog 20–21. Peymeinade, France: Société Française de Prestidigitation.

Sherzer, Joel. 2002. *Speech Play and Verbal Art*. Austin: University of Texas Press.

Shiner, Larry. 2001. *The Invention of Art: A Cultural History*. Chicago: University of Chicago Press.

Shklovsky, Victor. 1965. "Art as Technique." In Lee T. Lemon and Marion J. Reis, eds. *Russian Formalist Criticism*. Lincoln: University of Nebraska Press, 3–24.

Siegel, Lee. 1991. *Net of Magic: Wonders and Deceptions in India*. Chicago: University of Chicago Press.

Sifianou, Maria. 1992. *Politeness Phenomena in England and Greece: A Cross-Cultural Perspective*. Oxford: Clarendon Press.

Silverman, Kenneth. 1996. *HOUDINI!!! The Career of Ehrich Weiss*. New York: Harper Collins.

Simmel, Georg. 1950. *The Sociology of Georg Simmel*. New York: Free Press.

Singer, Isaac Bashevis. 1968. *The Magician of Lublin*. New York: Bantam.

Singer, Philip. 1990. " 'Psychic Surgery': Close Observation of a Popular Healing Practice." *Medical Anthropology Quarterly* 4(4): 443–451.

Singleton, John. 1998. "Situated Learning in Japan: Our Educational Analysis." In John Singleton, ed. *Learning in Likely Places: Varieties of Apprenticeship in Japan*. New York: Cambridge University Press, 3–19.

Sinigaglia, Jérémy. 2009. "The Mobilization of Intermittents in the Entertainment Sector in France." *French Politics* 7(3–4): 294–315.

Sizorn, Magali. 2008. "Une ethnologue en 'Trapézie': Sport, art, ou spectacle?" *Ethnologie Française* 38(1): 79–88.

Solomon, Matthew. 2010. *Disappearing Tricks: Silent Film, Houdini, and the New Magic of the Twentieth Century*. Chicago: University of Illinois Press.

Stafford, Barbara Maria. 1994. *Artful Science: Enlightenment, Entertainment, and the Eclipse of Visual Education*. Cambridge, MA: MIT Press.

Stahl, Christopher. 2008. "Outdoing Ching Ling Foo." In Francesca Coppa, Lawrence Hass, and James Peck, eds. *Performing Magic on the Western Stage from the Eighteenth Century to the Present*. New York: Palgrave Macmillan, 151–176.

Stebbins, Robert A. 1984. *The Magician: Career, Culture, and Social Psychology in a Variety Art*. Toronto: Clarke Irwin.

Steinmeyer, Jim. 2003. *Hiding the Elephant: How Magicians Invented the Impossible and Learned to Disappear*. New York: Carroll & Graf.

——. 2005. *The Glorious Deception: The Double Life of William Robinson, aka Chung Ling Soo, the "Marvelous Chinese Conjurer."* New York: Carroll & Graf.

Stoichita, Victor Alexandre. 2008. *Fabricants d'émotion: Musique et malice dans un village tsigane de Roumanie*. Nanterre, France: Société d'ethnologie.

Stone, David. 2005a. *Close up: Les vrais secrets de la magie*. Paris: Pamadana Editions.

——. 2005b. "Damien, fils de pub . . ." *Magicus* 137: 16–17.

——. 2006. *The Real Secrets of Magic*. Volume 1. Directed by Jean-Luc Bertrand. Paris: Close Up Magic and MagicZooM, DVD.

——. 2007. *The Real Secrets of Magic*. Volume 2. Directed by Jean-Luc Bertrand. Paris: Close Up Magic and MagicZooM, DVD.

——. 2008. *Close Up: The Real Secrets of Magic*. Paris: Pamadana Editions.

Stradda. 2010. "Magie nouvelle: Les apparitions d'un art contemporain." 16: 6–20.

Strathern, Marilyn. 2001. "The Patent and the Malanggan." *Theory, Culture & Society* 18(4): 1–26.

Sudnow, David. 2001. *Ways of the Hand: A Rewritten Account*. Cambridge, MA: MIT Press.

Swiss, Jamy Ian. 2002. *Shattering Illusions: Essays on the Ethics, History, and Presentation of Magic*. Seattle, WA: Hermetic Press.

Tamariz, Juan. 1987. *La via mágica: El méthodo de las pistas falsas y la vía mágica*. Madrid: Editorial Frakson.

——. 1988. *The Magic Way: The Theory of False Solutions and the Magic Way*. Madrid: Editorial Frakson.

Tannen, Deborah. 1986. "Introducing Constructed Dialogue in Greek and American Conversational and Literary Narrative." In Florian Coulmas, ed. *Direct and Indirect Speech*. New York: Mouton de Gruyter, 311–332.

Taussig, Michael. 1997. *The Magic of the State*. New York: Routledge.

——. 2003. "Viscerality, Faith, and Skepticism: Another Theory of Magic." In Birgit Meyer and Peter Pels, eds. *Magic and Modernity: Interfaces of Revelation and Concealment*. Stanford, CA: Stanford University Press, 272–306.

Terrio, Susan J. 2000. *Crafting the Culture and History of French Chocolate*. Berkeley: University of California Press.

Thiels, Norbert. 1905. Editorial. *Journal de la Prestidigitation* 3: 1–2.

Thompson, E. P. 1971. "The Moral Economy of the English Crowd in the Eighteenth Century." *Past & Present* 50(1): 76–136.

Tigner, Steven S. 1989. "Magic and Magicians." In Thomas Inge, ed. *Handbook of American Popular Culture*. 2nd edition. New York: Greenwood Press, 671–720.

Tomasello, Michael. 2009. *Why We Cooperate*. Cambridge, MA: MIT Press.

Topas. N.d. *Presentation Secrets*. Stuttgart: Author.

Trubek, Amy B. 2008. *The Taste of Place: A Cultural Journey into Terroir*. Berkeley: University of California Press.

Truffaut, François, dir. 2001. *Baisers volés* [1968]. Paris: mk2 éditions, DVD.

Tufte, Edward, and Jamy Ian Swiss. 1997. "Explaining Magic: Pictorial Instructions and Disinformation Design." In Edward Tufte. *Visual Explanations*. Cheshire, CT: Graphics Press, 54–71.

Vaillant, Gaston. 1998. "Débinage et débineurs" [1905]. *Revue de la Prestidigitation* 500: 9.

Vasek, Marie E. 1986. "Lying as a Skill: The Development of Deception in Children." In Robert W. Mitchell and Nicholas S. Thompson, eds. *Deception: Perspectives on Human and Nonhuman Deceit*. Albany: State University of New York Press, 271–292.

Voignier, Jacques. 1994. *Les laboratoires de legerdemain: Fabricants et marchands d'appareils de magie en France (1769–1992)*. San Francisco: Albo Classic Magic with Apparatus.

———. 1998. "Historique du 'Journal de la Prestidigitation.'" *Revue de la Prestidigitation* 500: 2–7.

———. 2003. "Cent ans de collection." In Association Française des Artistes Prestidigitateurs, ed. *100 ans d'histoire, 100 ans de magie*. Paris: Association Française des Artistes Prestidigitateurs, 253–285.

Volkmann, Kurt. 1956. *The Oldest Deception: Cups and Balls in the 15th and 16th Centuries*. Minneapolis, MN: C. W. Jones.

Voloshinov, V. N. 1986. *Marxism and the Philosophy of Language*. Cambridge, MA: Harvard University Press.

Vygotsky, L. S. 1981. *Mind in Society: The Development of Higher Psychological Processes*. Cambridge, MA: Harvard University Press.

Wacquant, Loïc. 2004. *Body and Soul: Notebooks of an Apprentice Boxer*. New York: Oxford University Press.

Wallon, Emmanuel, ed. 2002. *Le cirque au risque de l'art*. Arles, France: Actes sud.

Warner, Michael. 2002. *Publics and Counterpublics*. New York: Zone Books.

Weiner, Annette B. 1985. "Inalienable Wealth." *American Ethnologist* 12(2): 210–227.

Wessely, Otto. 2010. "Wake-Up!" http://www.otto-wessely.com/magicus gaypride.htm.

————. 2011. *Je suis une star comme tout le monde (Mes débuts: 1945–2010)*. Paris: Fédération Française des Artistes Prestidigitateurs.

Whaley, Bart. 2007. *Encyclopedic Dictionary of Magic*. 3rd edition. Published electronically by Lybrary.com.

Wood, David, Jerome S. Brunner, and Gail Ross. 1976. "The Role of Tutoring in Problem Solving." *Journal of Child Psychology and Psychiatry* 17(2): 89–100.

Yankah, Kwesi. 1985. "Risks in Verbal Art Performance." *Journal of Folklore Research* 22(2–3): 133–153.

Zempléni, Andras. 1976. "La chaîne du secret." *Nouvelle Revue de Psychanalyse* 14: 313–324.

Index

Text:	10/14 Palatino
Display:	Univers Condensed Light 47 and Bauer Bodoni
Compositor:	Westchester Book Group
Indexer:	Julie Grady
Printer and binder:	IBT Global

CPSIA information can be obtained
at www.ICGtesting.com
Printed in the USA
FSOW02n2124241016
26541FS

9 780520 270473